FLINT

by the same author
THE LIVING LANDSCAPE OF BRITAIN

Top: Black flint beach-pebbles cut and polished to show (*left*) differential staining, and (*right*) a fossil sponge. *Below:* A fossil sponge preserved in chalcedonized flint.

FLINT

Its Origin, Properties and Uses

WALTER SHEPHERD

FABER AND FABER
3 Queen Square
London

*First published in 1972
by Faber and Faber Limited
3 Queen Square London WC1
Printed in Great Britain at
The Pitman Press, Bath
All rights reserved*

ISBN 0 571 09926 2

London Borough
of Enfield
Public Libraries

L80617

553.65

L.V. 14102

© *1972 by Walter Shepherd*

Preface

IF YOU were asked to name the most remarkable kind of stone in the world you could say 'flint' without the slightest hesitation. Flint is remarkable for its intrinsic qualities, its mysterious origin, its natural journeyings and transformations, and its age-old utility to man. This book has something to say on all these aspects of flint, and one of its objects is to give at least some sort of an answer to all the odd questions people are liable to ask about flint. It has therefore to make occasional excursions into folklore and popular fancy, and even dip into linguistics, but its main theme is the study of flint as a mineral.

The history of serious research on flint is given in some detail and the reader is brought right up to date in this field. Technical terms are avoided or carefully defined and the text should present no difficulties to the interested layman. More specialized information is given in ten short Appendices, and it should be mentioned that all the specimens illustrated have been preserved. Some are in the author's own collection, others in the museum at Silcoates School, Wakefield, and a few in the national museums. None of the photographs has been retouched, but the two large 'banded' flints in Plate XVII are drawings adapted from engravings in S. P. Woodward's classic paper on the subject. They are quite typical and much clearer than available photographs.

The story of the numerous researches into the nature of flint is fully supported by references to the original works and often with quotations. A raised number in the text refers the reader to the numbered list of References beginning at page 235, but the books listed are by no means all 'sources'. Many of them are suggestions for further reading on subjects only incidentally involved in the story of flint. The reader will have no difficulty in judging the purpose of each reference from its context.

Some of the references are of purely historical interest, so that a few of the books listed date back to the 18th century and some to the 19th. There are many references to the very productive period between the two World Wars and it would be a great mistake to treat these old papers as if they were out of date. Good observations, accurately reported, are never out of date, and some may become of unique importance if the original phenomena are destroyed or obliterated.

Even some of the old theories of the origin of flint are liable to be re-discovered and offered in slightly different form as if they were new. To say of any type of theory that it is out of date generally means no more than that it is out of fashion. There will always be those who hail every new announcement as if it automatically cancelled everything that went before, but the wise will never believe this of any theory about flint. The old theories are too prone to bob up again.

For example, the sea-floor precipitation theories went out of favour for a long time, and first Richardson's and later Wroost's percolating rain-water theories were generally accepted. Serious doubts were then raised and sea-floor genesis was revived by a number of eminent geologists. This was everywhere hailed as a major breakthrough, but in 1960 came Millot's discovery that sea-floor precipitation can only rarely happen, and this led to a new kind of chemical exchange theory. This was 'the last word' for a short time only, for in June, 1971, scarcely disputable evidence was discovered that sea-floor precipitation of an 'improbable' type (originally suggested at about the time of the First World War) has actually occurred more than once on quite a big scale. The fact is, no single theory has ever succeeded in covering all the possible contingencies that may arise in nature, and there is probably no such theory to be found.

The amount of published argument on such matters is prodigious and it would be quite impossible to recount all the opinions expressed. Fortunately, the various theories of the origin of flint fall into five groups, and these have been represented by characteristic examples

PREFACE

with occasional excursions into interesting side-paths. The author also describes some of his own researches and the conclusions he draws from them, but wishes to make it quite clear that his suggestions would not necessarily be accepted by others. In fact, the reader is everywhere made aware that nothing can yet be accepted as final in such matters as the origin of flint, its growth, its patination, and many other aspects of its study.

Other subjects dealt with include the manipulation of flint as a raw material, and its uses by early man and in manufacture. However, the subject of this book is strictly 'flint', the mineral, and the fields of social history and industry are visited only because they are littered with flints and provoke their own sets of questions about flint.

To cover such a wide ground specialists in various subjects have been consulted, and the author is especially indebted to the following for both information and advice: Dr. Derek Ager, Dr. Raymond Casey, Mr. C. P. Chatwin, Mr. Herbert Edwards, Mr. Geoffrey Fowler, Dr. P. J. Goodhew, Mr. David Green, Dr. J. N. Jennings, Dr. L. H. P. Jones, Mr. W. F. Rankine, Mr. H. S. Robertson, the late Dr. H. Dighton Thomas and Mr. Christopher Wood. Acknowledgements are also due to H.M. Geological Survey for permission to reproduce Plates I (*top*) and X (*foot*), and to the British Museum (Natural History) for Plates XVIII (*foot*) and XXVIII.

W.S.

London
1972

Contents

Preface   *page* 5

1. THE NATURE OF FLINT   17
   Appearance of flint—Fossils in flint—Composition
   and structure of flint—Physical properties of flint

2. THE STORY OF CHALK   40
   The nature of chalk—The Chalk sponges—The
   Chalk formation—The English Chalk

3. THE SEGREGATION OF FLINT   68
   Syngenetic theories—Penecontemporaneous
   theories—Epigenetic theories—Physical theories—
   Chemical theories—Secondary silica

4. DERIVED FLINTS   108
   Residual deposits—Patination, gloss and staining—
   Banded, furrowed and spiral flints—Gravels—
   Shingles

5. PREHISTORIC USES OF FLINT   145
   Artificial fracture—Pebble and core tools—Flakes,
   blades and microliths—Celts and hafted tools—
   Mining and trade—Reconstructions and frauds

CONTENTS

6. FLINT IN THE HISTORICAL PERIOD   179
    Fire and firearms—Flint knapping—Odd uses of flint—Building and road-work—Pottery and glass

Appendices   211
    I. The Solubility of Silica
   II. Silica in Natural Water
  III. The Fossils in Fig. 18
  IV. Effects of Folding on the Water-Table
   V. Silica and Vegetation
  VI. Silicates in the Chalk
 VII. Water on a Molecular Scale
VIII. Stone Age Cultures and Industries
  IX. Later English Flint Workings
   X. 'Flint' in Many Tongues

References   235

Index   245

Illustrations

PLATES

	Flint pebbles cut and polished	*frontispiece*
I.	Bands of flint in the Chalk and a sectioned nodule	*facing page* 24
II.	Accidental flints	*after page* 24
III.	Fossil sea-urchins in flint	24
IV.	Flint nodules bearing fossils	*facing page* 25
V.	Small fossils in flint	32
VI.	Cast in flint of crustacean burrows; a mollusc shell with bryozoan	33
VII.	Photomicrographs of bryozoa preserved in flint	48
VIII.	Photomicrographs of sponge spicules	49
IX.	Fossil sponges in flint	80
X.	Desilicified flint and flint moulds of burrows	81
XI.	Nodules suggesting the recent formation and growth of some flint	96
XII.	The deposition of crystalline substances in blocks of chalk	97
XIII.	Silica and fine chalk deposited on flint surfaces by percolating water	112
XIV.	Secondary minerals deposited inside hollow flint nodules	113
XV.	Derived flints damaged by frost	128
XVI.	Bleached, stained and patinated flints	129
XVII.	Furrowed, banded and calcined flints	136

ILLUSTRATIONS

XVIII. Flint pebbles and Hertfordshire 'puddingstone' *after page* 136
XIX. Beach-pebbles showing differential staining and erosion 136
XX. Beach-pebbles bearing marks resembling inscriptions *facing page* 137
XXI. Beach-pebbles showing borings by marine organisms 144
XXII. Palæolithic hand-axe and scraper 145
XXIII. A 'disc-core', possibly used as a throwing-stone 160
XXIV. Neolithic blade implements *after page* 160
XXV. Mesolithic and Neolithic implements 160
XXVI. Flint arrow-heads *facing page* 161
XXVII. Palæolithic pick and Neolithic celt 176
XXVIII. A flint nodule reconstructed from a core and the flakes struck off it by Palæolithic man 177
XXIX. Gun-flints made in 1851 at Northfleet, Kent 200
XXX. Walls built of unarranged rough flints 200
XXXI. Walls in patterned and knapped flints 200
XXXII. Flint rubble-work; 'diaper-work' in flint and stone *facing page* 201

TEXT FIGURES

1. Nodular and tabular flint *page* 20
2. A paramoudra and flint rings 21
3. Flint nodules and Crustacean burrows 28
4. Crystallites of quartz in flint, $\times 100{,}000$ 34
5. Violent fracture of flint 38
6. Fracture of flint by frost 39
7. Map of the world showing areas once covered by the Chalk Sea 41
8. Flints embedded in timber 43
9. Examples of Foraminifera, $\times 20$ 47
10. A nodule and twinned crystal of marcasite 49

ILLUSTRATIONS

11. Coccoliths from the Chalk, ×3,750 — page 51
12. Interior of a hollow flint showing 'honeycomb' structure — 53
13. Anatomy of a simple sponge — 54
14. Types of sponge spicules and skeletal arrangements — 56
15. Map of the world in late Cretaceous times showing maximum transgression of the Chalk Sea — 61
16. Distribution of land and sea over the British area in Middle Chalk times — 62
17. A geological section across the London Basin and the Weald — 63
18. A generalized section through the English Chalk formation — 65
19. The relation between the percentage of flint and soluble silica in the English Chalk — 81
20. The water-table in a hill compared with the levels at which bands of flint occur in the English Chalk — 85
21. The general appearance of Liesegang's rings — 89
22. The distribution of bands of silver dichromate in gelatin — 90
23. The distribution of bands of flint in the English Chalk, and of precipitated salts in blocks of chalk — 91
24. The rhythmic distribution of nodules of copper sulphate in blocks of chalk — 95
25. Solution-holes or 'pipes' in the top of a chalk-pit — 98
26. Diagrams typifying the history of the Chalk since its formation — 113
27. White tabular flint, broken to show the distinction between cortication and patination — 115
28. The distribution of zones of water-concentration in zeolite crystals and banded flints — 126
29. Section through an agate, showing zones — 127
30. Spiral flints, parallel and tapered — 128
31. The area of gravel deposited by a meandering river — 131
32. A river terrace and present flood-plain — 132
33. Water from a breaking wave falling on beach-pebbles — 137

ILLUSTRATIONS

34.	A Polychaete worm and its U-shaped burrow	*page* 140
35.	Small rock-boring molluscs	141
36.	How groynes prevent the pebbles of a beach from travelling along the coast	143
37.	The cultural periods during which flint has been used by man	147
38.	Dreikanters, or pebbles faceted by blown sand	148
39.	The natural flaking of flint	149
40.	The artificial fracture of flint	151
41.	Shaping flint by percussion	153
42.	Shaping flint by pressure	154
43.	Pebble-tools and other 'core' implements	156
44.	Palæolithic core and flake implements	157
45.	Implement-making by the Tachenghit technique	160
46.	Types of flint 'scrapers'	161
47.	Blade implements, Helwan arrow-heads, and other typical forms	163
48.	Flint saws, sickle-blades and microliths	164
49.	Gravers, ripple-flaking, and 'points'	165
50.	Methods of hafting implements	168
51.	Prehistoric uses of bone and antler	170
52.	Section through the shaft of a Neolithic flint-mine	171
53.	How sparks are struck from steel by a piece of flint	181
54.	A household tinder-box of about 1800, with accessories	183
55.	The coal-miners' 'steel-mill'	184
56.	The mechanisms of the wheel-lock and snaphaunce flintlock firearms	186
57.	Flint-knappers' and flint-miners' tools	189
58.	A flint-knapper using a large flaking hammer	190
59.	How flakes are struck for making gun-flints	191
60.	The parts of a typical gun-flint	192
61.	Ornamental uses of flint in walls	199
62.	Section across a typical Roman road	201
63.	The loss in weight of flint at different temperatures during calcination	206

ILLUSTRATIONS

64. Common types of flint crushing and grinding machinery *page* 207
65. The stresses in folded strata at different levels 217
66. The expected form of the water-table in an anticline 218
67. The chief Stone Age cultures or main styles of workmanship 230
68. Localities in the English Chalk country notable for their associations with Neolithic and later flint 233

1
The Nature of Flint

THE OLD ENGLISH word *flint*, a hard stone, is often successfully used in simile or metaphor without deliberate reference to any clearly defined species of stone, yet it somehow conveys the salient qualities of the mineral now specifically called 'flint' almost as well as the sight of an actual specimen. It has assonances with 'clink', 'sling', 'fling', 'splinter' and 'scintillation'—all good descriptive words of the nature and age-old uses of flint, and though a vast number of people have never seen a piece of flint, none needs to be told what is meant by a 'skinflint', a 'flinty eye' or a 'heart of flint', or to have Captain Flint's character elaborated upon.

One may 'set one's face like a flint', or say of another that he is 'as true as flint', but one might as well try to 'skin a flint' or 'wring water from a flint' as understand why the name of some other hard stone would not have done as well. Even when some other stone is clearly meant it may still be more satisfying to call it 'flint', as in Dyer's *Ruins of Rome* (written in 1740, when strike-a-light flints were familiar to everybody):

> Those ancient roads, o'er whose broad flints
> Such crowds have roll'd.

The paving stones of ancient Rome were not of flint, yet the word is undeniably used with effect—as it has been in much more unlikely contexts. Moses, for example, flourishing his staff, brought forth 'water out of a rock of flint'—according to the writer of Deuteronomy 8, 15. Probably another writer, at Deuteronomy 32, 13, reports that Jacob was made 'to suck . . . oil out of the flinty rock',

THE NATURE OF FLINT

and in Psalm 114, 8, we read that the God of Jacob 'turned . . . the flint into a fountain of waters'. The rendering of the Hebrew *challamish* as 'flint' or 'flinty' by the translators of the Authorized Version is not in question. It is repeated in modern translations, such as Dr. Moffatt's[84], and is so given in *Young's Analytical Concordance*.

Again, if one wished to convey the idea of an immense army of cavalry, one might do worse than the writer of Isaiah 5, 28, who proclaimed of the avenging hosts that 'their horses' hoofs shall be counted like flint'. Not, observe, like the pebbles on a beach, but specifically like *flint*—on which you can hear the clink of hoofs and see the sparks fly. Such are the qualities of this stone, and so well known are they, that we find haunting allusions to it in the literature of many peoples and the idioms of many languages*. The local sound of its name (see Appendix X) is not, after all, important in itself, and the peculiar ring of the English word 'flint' is merely one of the felicities of our language. That the power of the word is not dependent on its phonic quality, even in English, seems evident in this description by Ruskin of an angry sea:

'. . . not in any wise limiting itself to a state of liquidity, but now striking like a steel gauntlet, and now becoming a cloud, and vanishing, no eye could tell whither; one moment a flint cave, the next a marble pillar, the next a mere white fleece thickening the thundery rain.'†

A *flint cave*? Remarkable image, indeed, and conveying something about the implacable sea that no rational description could ever give, yet there is no such thing as a flint cave in all the annals of geology —nor can one be imagined!

There is surely something archetypal about flint, for all mankind was once familiar with every aspect of it, spent leisure and daily labour fashioning implements from it, and prized it so highly that

---

* The Hebrew examples were ready to hand, but while this passage was being written another turned up by chance in Chatto & Windus's *The Slang Dictionary*, dated 1873. It is odd enough to quote, but 'without prejudice' (as the lawyers say), for it states under the headword 'Skinflint' that 'Abdul-Malek, one of the Ommeyade Khaliphs, noted for his extreme avarice, was surnamed Raschal-Hegiarah, literally, "the SKINNER of a FLINT"'. (Abdal Malik—to use a modern spelling—was the Omayyad caliph from 685 to 705.)

[84] See References at end of book wherever these numerals occur in the text.

† *The Harbours of England*, 1856.

it was often imported from distant countries in preference to local 'hard stones' of inferior quality. There was 'nothing like flint', and man relied chiefly upon it for his very livelihood through twenty-five thousand generations. His food varied from day to day, but not his preoccupation with flint; the very evolution of his intelligence was guided by the contemplation and manipulation of flint—never a day could have passed through a hundred times the span of recorded history but the thought of flint crossed his mind or its image lay before his eyes.

That this is no exaggeration we shall presently see, yet today there are many parts of Britain, and much vaster areas outside it, where flint is little more than a legend, and where—alas!—the name refers primarily to that pyrophoric preparation of rare earths used in cigarette lighters. This, of course, bears no resemblance to flint other than that sparks may be struck from it. That flint is virtually unknown in some regions may seem strange to those who live south of Tees and east of Trent and Avon, for many of whom the common stones in the garden, the shingle of the beach, and the gravels in the river-beds and quarries, are almost exclusively of flint. In southern England there must be some few millions of the population who have never seen any *other* kind of stone, except in a building, a cemetery or an ornament. Yet it is true that dealers in mineralogical specimens are able to sell pieces of common flint to students and collectors in many parts of the world as an interesting exotic curiosity.

Flint is, however, very common in most parts of Europe, in large parts of Asia, and some parts of Africa and America. A variety of flint is also found in a few localities in Australia. It was probably first discovered by Stone Age man in Africa, after long experimentation with pebbles of quartz and eruptive igneous rocks (lavas), and is the oldest industrial mineral in the world. It was predominant in Europe from Palæolithic times and has been utilized for various purposes ever since. It may claim to have been of continuous economic importance for at least half a million years, and yet it is still something of a mystery. In modern times its nature and mode of occurrence have been intensively studied, but its formation is still not certainly understood. The origin of flint, so far as it is known, makes one of the most challenging stories in mineralogy, and it is all the more intriguing in that *finis* has not yet been put to it.

Appearance of flint

In its native state flint occurs in the form of nodules or concretions embedded in the soft white limestone known as chalk; it is also found less abundantly in a few other limestones. At some levels the nodules seem to be scattered sporadically through the rock, but at others they form well-marked layers associated with the bedding-planes of the chalk or, more rarely, cutting across the bedding-planes and even forming vertical trains. (See Plate I.) At other levels, it assumes a tile-like habit, forming flat slabs measuring from a quarter of an inch

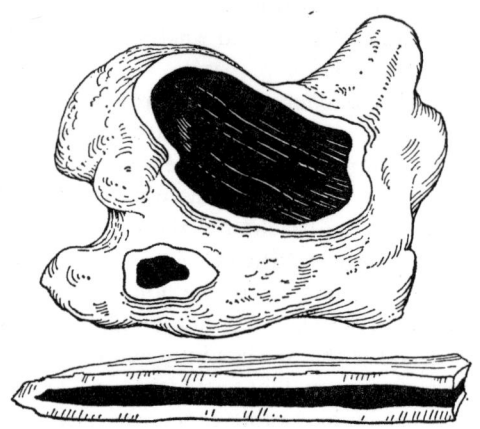

FIG. 1. A typical flint nodule (*above*) and a broken section of tabular flint.

to six inches thick. Such a slab may extend with varying width for several yards. Known as 'tabular' flint, small specimens often look like fossil sandwiches, a thin layer of black 'meat' being enclosed between equally thin parallel layers of white 'bread' (Fig. 1).

Flint nodules come in all sizes. Some are smaller than a grain of sand; others form blocks two or more feet across. They may be of almost any shape, from a perfectly round ball or a slender rod like a long finger, to an irregular agglomeration of assorted lumps, hollows and protuberances. They may be perforated with holes of any kind and form misshapen pipes, nozzles, funnels or doughnuts. Small specimens with holes were once threaded on a string and hung on the key of an outer door, on a bed-post, or round the neck, to guard against witches and the 'evil eye'. When so used they were known as 'hag-stones', but they might also be attached to a horse's collar as a charm against disease and children still call them 'lucky stones', even today.

Other flint nodules are as hollow as a rubber ball and may contain smaller nodules loosely inside them, thus becoming 'rattle-stones'.

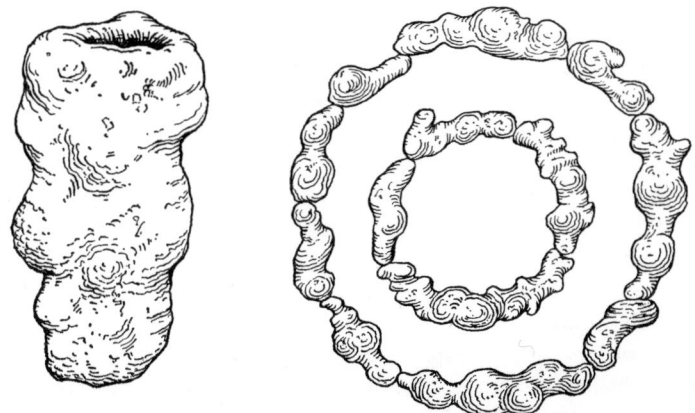

FIG. 2. *Left:* A paramoudra measuring about 4 feet high. *Right:* Flint rings; the outer circle has a diameter of about 9 feet. (*After* Clement Reid[3].)

Or the hollow may be lined with other minerals and sparkle with minute crystals when broken open (Plate XIV). Often, a hollow flint is filled with a powdery chalk 'meal', usually called 'flint meal', which may contain sponge spicules and other micro-fossils, to be described in the next chapter. The 'remarkable flints' found on Riddlesdown by Caleb Evans, in 1870, are described in his classic paper* (pp. 14–15) as 'nearly all cylindrical in shape, and on being split show a tubular cavity containing a cylindrical core of flint, which is covered and the cavity in the outer flint is lined with the white powder frequently met with in the interior of flints'.

In Norfolk, and a few other districts, the nodules sometimes take the form of a large hollow cylinder one or two feet in diameter and

* *On Some Sections of Chalk Between Croydon and Oxted, with Observations on the Classification of the Chalk*, read to the Geologists' Association on January 7, 1870. (Now a rarity.)

up to four feet long, set upright like a drain-pipe stood on end. (See Fig. 2.) These are called 'potstones' or 'paramoudras', a name introduced from Ireland and said to be derived from the Erse for 'sea-pears'[1]. Whole sets of paramoudras have been found side by side, so that their exposed upper surfaces form a sort of pavement, and an exceptional specimen measured five feet across its upper end. C. B. Rose[2] found a 'series of six or more in a vertical position, placed one upon another, and in contact'.

In other places large flints are found disposed in shallow rings (Fig. 2) measuring up to nine feet in diameter, each flint joining or touching its neighbours, and there may be two or more concentric rings with a paramoudra in the centre. An oval ring with a long diameter of fifteen feet has also been recorded[3]. These remarkable appearances are all natural formations. They occur in the body of the undisturbed chalk and show only where the covering rock has been removed by weathering or the waves of the sea-shore, yet they are so regular that, were this not known, they might well have been mistaken for artificial arrangements.

The colours of flint form a study in themselves, but native flint is usually jet black, with a somewhat horny appearance, though grey flints are common and black flints often have grey patches in them. Egyptian flints are often pinkish, while yellow, dark blue, pale violet, brown, and even red varieties are also known, but the colour of a flint is seldom seen until a nodule has been broken, because it is usually entirely covered with a white crust or 'cortex'. This may be as thin as paper or a few inches thick, and sometimes it forms the greater part—or even the whole—of a nodule. A flint which has lost its cortex (by attrition, frost-splitting, violent fracture or artificial trimming) is said to be 'decorticated', while one that still retains it is 'undecorticated'—such is the jargon used by geologists. In defence of the double negative it may be pointed out that it is reasonable to use this term of exceptional specimens found where decorticated flints are to be expected.

The white cortex is an altered part of the black (or grey) flint, for its colour has nothing to do with the surrounding chalk. It may, nevertheless, be a pure, unblemished, dead white, and its junction with the black 'core' is nearly always quite sudden. (See Fig. 2 and Plate I.) The colour of even the blackest core is deceptive, however, because a thin splinter chipped off it is seen to be translucent and of a pale straw yellow or nearly colourless. The black appearance is thus an optical effect, and arises from the fact that light readily penetrates to the interior of the flint where it is lost by scattering, and practically none is reflected out again. (The trapped light doubtless results in a rise in the temperature of the flint, though the effect must be far too small to measure.)

The scattering is caused by the microscopic structure of the flint, but some light may be absorbed by coloured impurities, which may include traces of carbonaceous matter and sometimes iron. The colour of a thin flake may be attributed to these, but it is not in the least true—as is sometimes stated—that the blackness of flint is black of carbon.

Although the colour and texture of a flint nodule often appear to be quite uniform throughout the core, microscopic examination will show that it is far from homogeneous in even the smallest splinter. Moderate magnification of a thin section reveals shadowy lines and patches suggesting minute particles fused or cemented together, and though much higher magnification presents a somewhat different picture (as we shall see) the irregularities are certainly present. Moderate magnification with crossed nicols* shows a multitude of bluish specks, separate but very close together, the overall effect being greyish-blue. This indicates a cryptocrystalline structure (page 31), but in many specimens stronger patches of light map out the positions of former sponge spicules, microscopic shells and other inclusions[4]. These have all been transformed into flint and cannot be distinguished under high magnification. It is evident that they are now present only as repeated small variations in density, and that the apparent homogeneity of flint is a remarkably uniform average.

The alteration which produces the white cortex of a flint nodule and causes the light there to be completely reflected nearly always starts on the outer surface and creeps slowly inwards, but at a rate which evidently varies enormously with circumstance. When it is still so extremely thin as to form but a transparent film over the black core, the flint appears blue, but as it thickens the blue fades rapidly, becoming white when it measures about a hundredth of an inch.

* Or crossed polaroid filters; the technique is familiar to microscope users but cannot be elaborated here.

In some grey flints the same sort of change may be incipient throughout the nodule, but the greyness of others is known to be caused by a difference in the microstructure and this is probably the usual explanation. The opaqueness of grey flint has also been attributed to the inclusion of chalk, but this is just a naive guess and quite unsupported by evidence. Analyses that have been made show no chalk, though there may be rare exceptions and isolated microscopic crystals of calcite are occasionally reported[132]. However, mixtures of chalk and more or less loosely-compacted flint grains do occur, both as whole nodules and as a soft gritty outer rind to normal flints. These anomalies will be more fully described in Chapter 3.

Flints which have been washed out of their native chalk, or have otherwise become exposed to weather, soil-water, the roots of vegetation, contact with other minerals, or the mechanical action of running water or breaking waves, are subject to many kinds of staining and other changes. White, yellow, black, brown, pink and red flints are commonly seen in gravels and shingles, where they are called 'derived' flints (Chapter 4), but secondary staining of this kind is not to be confused with the originally coloured flint mentioned above.

Fossils in flint

A fossil is, etymologically speaking, anything of interest which is dug up (Latin *fossilis*), but in its more restricted meaning it refers only to the mineralized remains of living organisms, such as bones, shells, plants and such impressions of these as may be preserved. Before the collection and study of fossils became a scientific discipline little distinction was made between curious or suggestively-shaped stones and genuine organic remains, and even today the uninformed often confuse them. This is not surprising, especially in the case of flint nodules, which frequently assume forms more fantastic than any sculptor's dream. They are, indeed, often as effective as sculpture and have been displayed as *objets trouvés* in exhibitions of art*. In addition to those collected for their aesthetic appeal there are others, called 'accidental flints', which chance to resemble the heads of animals and other such objects. These are sometimes very striking, like the examples in Plate

---

* Henry Moore has expressed his unending interest in 'flintstones' and pebbles as sources of inspiration for sculptures. He might well have been intrigued by the example illustrated (for another purpose) in Plate VI, had he found it.

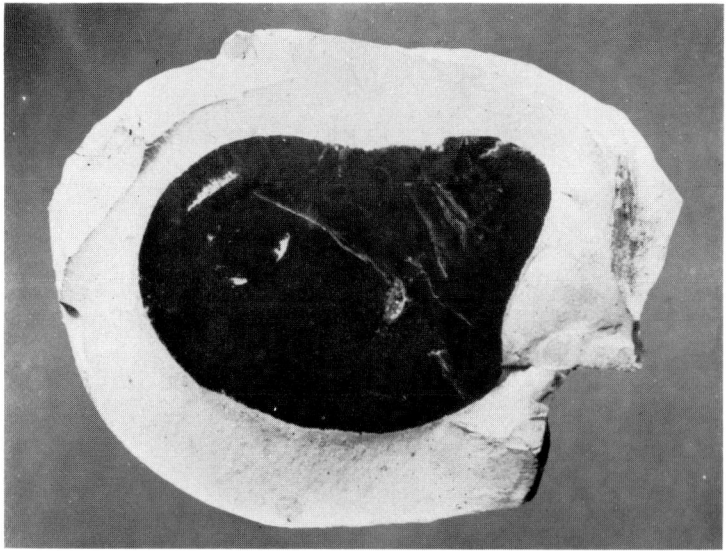

PLATE I. *Above:* A pit in the Upper Chalk at High Salvington, Sussex, showing bands of flint nodules. Note the small fault towards the left. *Below:* Section through a typical flint nodule, showing black core and white cortex.

PLATE II. Untrimmed accidental flints, exactly as found, the 'dog's-head' from coarse gravels at Southampton and the 'lion's-head' from Bostal Hill, Alciston, Sussex.

PLATE III. Fossil sea-urchins in flint. *Top: (left)* Brown soil-pebble, *Phymosoma*; *(right) Conulus albogalerus* in black flint (1 in. high). *Centre: (left)* Brown pebble from gravels near Croydon, *Echinocorys scutatus*; *(right)* under-surface of *C. albogalerus* (above). *Foot: (left) E. scutatus* in grey flint (2 in. long); *(right)* heart-urchin, *Micraster cor-anguinum*, in black flint.

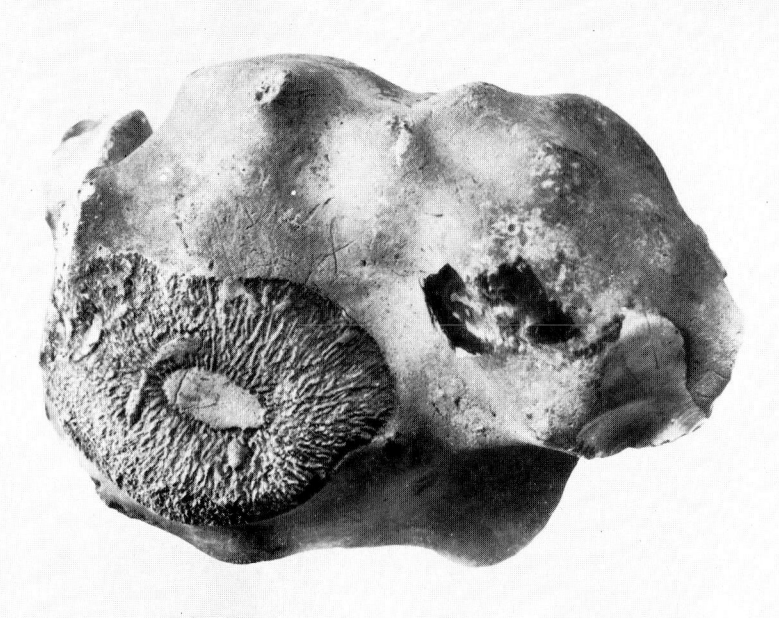

PLATE IV. Fossils in flint nodules. *Above:* A sea-urchin, *Cidaris*, with a spine $1\frac{1}{4}$ in. long, preserved in calcite. *Below:* The lithistid sponge *Siphonia koenigi*, in flint.

II, but they are of little interest except as curiosities. They have, however, given rise to local legends of 'fossilized dragons' in Kent and elsewhere, and whole 'zoos' of them have been collected*.

The grave reader may be surprised to find these objects mentioned here at all, but any information relating to flint, including the few small items of folklore, is surely proper in a book intended to provide at least a comment on all the common queries about flint. Geological museums are frequently required to explain accidental flints sent in by members of the public, and some museums even exhibit them to show how deceptive appearances may be. For example, the Natural History Museum, London, has a large flint nodul resembling a human skull (partly reproduced in Plate X), and the Tudor House Museum, Southampton, exhibits a flint 'dolphin' for the amazement of visitors. The Sloane Collection in the British Museum contains 'a black flint in the form of a duck rising out of the water', while spiral flints (Fig. 30), of which the British Museum possesses three, have been described as 'fossil snakes'. These spirals are remarkably regular, rather like the turned spiral legs of a small table, and have never been explained (but see page 128).

Somewhat similar oddities are sometimes found in the shapes of grey or other-coloured 'inclusions' seen on the broken surfaces of black flints, or as black patches on grey flints. The Sloane Collection includes one picturing 'a papall crown', another 'wherein appears a woman praying', and yet another depicting a tree-covered hill with a figure on top. Sir Hans Sloane (1660–1753) listed them as 'Mocha stones'† or 'Pretious stones', and if he thought them significant this would not have been surprising, for the 'plastic virtue' theory then in vogue accounted for them very nicely. Though this theory was not specifically concerned with flint, it explained accidental stones and fossils of all kinds and is interesting enough to warrant a short digression.

* Some have even been referred to in print as the remains of *Ichthyosaurus* and in the 1920's a humorous guide to the Chislehurst Caves used to quote a string of such names and then, with a fearful glance over his shoulder, whisper, 'And there is always the *Idonthinkysaurus* [I-don't-think-he-saw-us] which still lives here!'

† 'Mocha stone' is an old name for 'moss-agate', a form of chalcedony exhibiting accidental deposits of iron or manganese oxides resembling sprigs of moss, and similar mineral freaks. It is derived from Mocha, in Arabia, whence many marvels came into Europe during the Dark Ages.

THE NATURE OF FLINT

It appears to have been first formulated about 300 B.C. by Aristotle's pupil and successor at the Lyceum, Theophrastus, who made a special study of minerals, though it was implicit in the 'pluralist' theory of Anaxagoras (*c.* 450 B.C.)*. Although remarkably correct explanations of fossils had been given very much earlier†, Theophrastus taught that all mineral forms resembling animals or plants (or recognizable parts of them) are the products of a *vis plastica* or 'formative virtue' at work in the earth. There was no ground for distinguishing between such remarkable resemblances as the 'dog's head' in Plate II and the fossil sea-urchins in Plate III; both were regarded simply as partial failures of the plastic virtue, live dogs and real sea-urchins being the successes.

Correct accounts of fossils were given again by Strabo (*c.* 10 B.C.) and Avicenna (*c.* A.D. 950), but in the 13th century the universal veneration of Aristotle and his school led Albertus Magnus and others to assume that 'spontaneous generation' must somehow be implied in Avicenna's account of petrifying springs, and they therefore revived the plastic virtue theory. Maintained by Robert Plot (1676) and others, it continued to have adherents right through to the 19th century. The traditional belief that flints are stones that *grow*, still widely held, is doubtless a surviving relic of it, kept alive by the coincidence of some curious evidence of mineralogical growth to be noted in Chapter 3‡.

---

* The 'pluralist' theory maintained that the earth and all things in it are made of an infinite variety of 'seeds', possessing all the qualities of all the things we are capable of knowing. In bread, for example, the bread-like qualities come uppermost and show, but when we eat and digest the bread, these are suppressed and the flesh-like qualities come to the fore, and so on. Everything contains the essence of everything else, and things differ from one another only in the way in which their constituent seeds are arranged.

† For example, by Anaximander (*c.* 570 B.C.), Xenophanes (*c.* 520 B.C.), and Herodotus (*c.* 450 B.C.).

‡ Another way of accounting for this belief was suggested by T. W. Shore[85] in 1900. Referring to some Hampshire soils, he says that flints 'are so numerous that it is difficult to realize any crops can be grown on such land. . . . The removal of the surface flints by hand makes very little difference to their apparent number, for others a little below the surface are turned up by the plough, or come to the surface assisted by the action of rain. It is this re-appearance of other flints after successive collections of them from the surface have been made, which has led to the former widespread belief among the country people that these flints "grow"'.

It is by no means always easy to decide whether a particular specimen is a fossil or not. The author has a small flint nodule (Fig. 30) so closely resembling a Gastropod shell that it provoked lively discussion among palæontologists when it was found. There is, of course, no question of the impossibility of the preservation in flint of such things as dogs' heads and human limbs, even as impressions, because the Chalk was laid down tens of millions of years before dogs' heads and human limbs had evolved. Of the more probable subjects it may be said that true fossils are seldom known only by a single individual, whereas accidental forms are almost invariably unique, are completely lacking in diagnostic details, and often show inconsistent features.

The genuine fossils found preserved in flint include numerous species of sea-shells, sponges, sea-urchins and other marine organisms. The preservation is sometimes very nearly perfect; it may show astonishing detail even on a microscopic scale. Sometimes the fossils occur as part of an irregular nodule, as illustrated in Plate IV, but often they are complete stony replicas of their originals. Some of the micro-fossils and fossil sponges, which have particular relevance to the story of flint, are discussed further in the following chapter.

The mode of fossilization varies considerably. Some fossils are the internal casts of shells which have somehow become filled with flint before being dissolved away, as in the Brachiopod (lamp-shell) in Plate V. In other cases, the flint casts are covered by a mineralized copy of the shell itself in crystalline calcite, so that both the inside and the outside of the shell are preserved. This is so in the fossil sea-urchin shown in Plate IV. Belemnites are usually preserved as solid calcite but, like calcite shell-fragments, may be enclosed or embedded in flint (Plate X). Very often, and particularly with sponges and Bryozoa, the form and structure of the animal is revealed as a slight change in the mineral constitution and colour of the flint. This may be very beautifully shown when the flint is cut and polished, as in the specimens shown in the frontispiece.

Some flint fossils are locally common enough to have acquired folk-names, such as 'shepherd's crown', 'fairy loaf', 'Queen Mab's button', 'pixy helmet' and 'fairy heart' (all sea-urchins). They were once prized as amulets, the loaf ensuring provision of food, the helmet protection from enemies, the heart requited love, and so on.

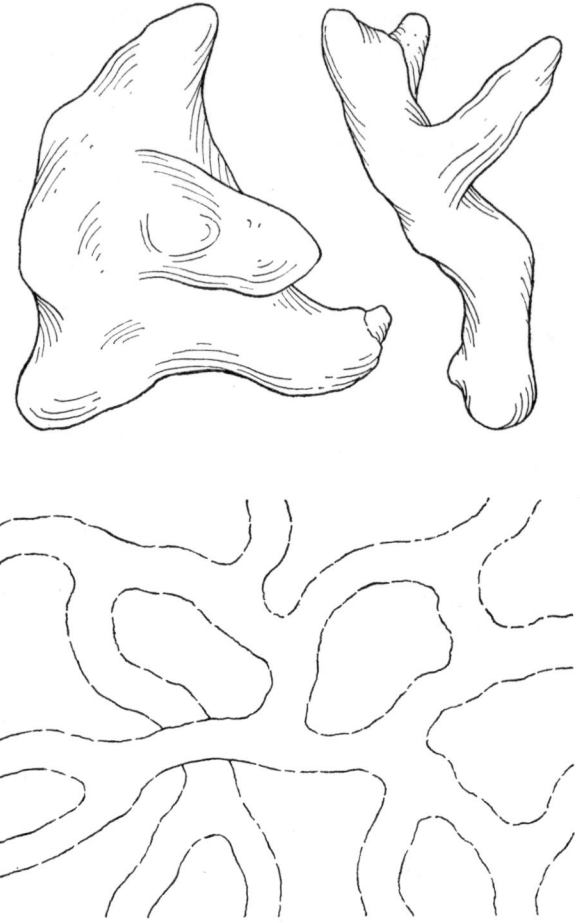

FIG. 3. *Above:* Flint nodules probably formed in Crustacean burrows. *Below:* Plan of a typical system of Crustacean burrows in the Chalk. The burrows measure from ½ in. to 2 ins. in diameter. (*Adapted from* R. G. Bromley[6].)

Those shown in Plate IV are all internal casts of the tests. A magnifying-glass will often show the skeletons of protozoans, bryozoans and other minute creatures apparently engraved, embossed or painted on the surface of another fossil, as in Plates V, VI and VII. Entire

COMPOSITION AND STRUCTURE OF FLINT

sponges are not infrequently found (Plate IX), and the delicate sponge-structure may be beautifully preserved inside a hollow specimen, as in Plates V and VIII.

Many of the grotesque forms of flint nodules, and particularly those which are elongated like fingers, limbs or branching stag-horns, usually with tapering ends, are undoubtedly the casts of burrows made by small crustaceans, probably resembling the living *Callianassa* (Thalassinidea). Examples are shown in Fig. 3 and Plate VI. The soft, loosely-built bodies of these creatures have not been preserved as fossils, unless the rare Chalk lobster *Enoploclytia leachi* (Mantell) is one, but their burrows in the chalk sometimes contain grooves and fine parallel scratches showing how they were excavated.

The burrows form extensive branching systems at many levels in the Chalk, and when not occupied by flint may be hollow or filled with softer chalk which can often be shaken out. Sometimes the flint has formed around a burrow, leaving it as a tubular hollow in the nodule, as in Plate X. The interpretation of these burrows as of crustacean origin was first suggested by L. Cayeux[5] in 1950, and they have since been thoroughly investigated, particularly by R. G. Bromley[6] (1967).

Composition and structure of flint

The Latin name for flint is *silex*, and the mineral substance of flint is called 'silica'. There are, however, several other mineral forms of silica and at least two of them are traditionally involved in the formation of flint. It will therefore be as well to describe some of these other forms before tackling the complexities of flint.

Silica is the dioxide of silicon, a non-metallic element used in transistors and current rectifiers, and for converting sunlight into electricity in the solar cells carried by artificial satellites. After oxygen, silicon is the most abundant element in the earth's crust and nearly all rocks contain it, either as silica (SiO_2) or combined with metals in the form of silicates. Silica is most familiar as sand-grains, for nearly all common sands consist almost entirely of it. The sand-grains were derived originally by processes of erosion from the quartz in some igneous rocks (e.g. granite, granophyre, pegmatite, quartz-porphyry, rhyolite, aplite, greisen, quartz-diorite, tonalite, etc.), but they are often 'second-hand' in the sense that they come from sandstones made from older sands. In the form of quartz silica is, as a rule, absolutely transparent and colourless, and until the late 17th century was thought to be petrified ice, but in most quartz sands it is stained yellow or red by iron. Unstained sands appear white and are called 'silver' sands.

Quartz. In the igneous rocks, the quartz crystallized on cooling from the molten state in the form of irregular glassy-looking granules, or as a continuous glassy matrix filling the interstices between other minerals, and its crystal form is seldom seen. It is, however, often deposited as perfect crystals from water which has drained over or permeated siliceous rocks and carried away some of the silica in solution.

The characteristic crystals are hexagonal prisms with pyramidal ends, and are known as 'rock-crystal' (particularly when found in large clear blocks from which flawless pieces may be cut). Clusters of crystals are very frequently found lining cracks and hollows in rocks of all kinds, where they have been growing by almost inconceivably slow deposition through tens of thousands—or even many millions—of years, sometimes attaining an enormous size. Small quartz crystals are often found lining hollow flints, as shown in Plate XI. When tinted by traces of other minerals good crystals may be cut as semi-precious stones, amethyst being purple quartz, cairngorm brown quartz, citrine yellow quartz, and so on. Quartz is also found in large shapeless masses which are white and opaque but have a glassy lustre. All forms of quartz are extremely hard and will readily scratch glass.

Opal. Amorphous and apparently amorphous (i.e. non-crystalline) forms of silica are also known, the chief being opal, chalcedony, flint and chert. Opal appears to be completely amorphous, and is composed of silica with about 10 per cent of water in the form of a colloid; it is a 'hydrogel' and may be pictured as a sort of solidified jelly. It is translucent and is not as hard as quartz, though it ranks among the hard minerals. Also deposited from aqueous solution, it is the most soluble of the mineral forms of silica, though the solubility of

COMPOSITION AND STRUCTURE OF FLINT

all of them is so slight that they are often classed as 'insoluble' in published lists of their properties. (See Appendix I.)

Opal is found in rock cavities in regions of hot springs, as in Czechoslovakia, where it occurs in cracks in igneous rocks (andesites). In sedimentary rocks, it sometimes replaces the original material of fossils, particularly fossil wood ('wood-opal'). The richest deposits occur in Australian sandstones, on the boundary between Queensland and New South Wales. The iridescent and fiery colours of precious opal are caused by the overlapping of extremely thin films which cause interference in the light reflected from them. The silica found in living organisms, such as the skeletons of some sponges, the tests of diatoms, and the tissues of many plants, is invariably opaline in character.

Chalcedony. This form of silica is familiar in such semi-precious stones as agate, onyx, carnelian and plasma. It is frequently found lining the cavities in hollow flints, encrusting other minerals, and lining crevices in sandstones and igneous rocks. Deposited from solution in water, it is translucent and has a waxy appearance. It often presents a mammillary surface, resembling numerous small overlapping blisters, as illustrated in Plate XIV. It may be milky white, pink, lavender, yellowish-green, brown, or even black, and frequently occurs in parallel zones of different colours (as in agate). These may indicate that it has been deposited intermittently, traces of colouring minerals in the water varying after long periods. On the other hand, in many cases it seems more likely that the zones were produced by the diffusion of coloured solutions inwards from the surface, a method used in the jewellery trade to enhance the zones (see page 88*n*).

Chalcedony appears to be amorphous, but the miscroscope shows it to consist of a matted tangle of very minute needle-like or fibrous crystals of silica so that it is more properly described as 'cryptocrystalline'. The micro-crystals or 'crystallites' are sometimes referred to as 'chalcedonic quartz', for they were discovered early in the present century to have peculiar features. H. A. Miers[7] emphasized that 'they are therefore quite distinct from true quartz, and chalcedony is not, as was formerly supposed, merely massive or micro-crystalline quartz'. More recent descriptions, based on X-ray analysis and electron microscope techniques, refer to the crystallites as of common quartz without noting any distinguishing characters, but Miers' description is quoted below for readers familiar with crystallographic terms*. It is difficult to believe that Miers would make such a positive statement of a doubtful observation, but the peculiarities he cites may have been anomalous, or the term 'true' quartz too strictly used.

No matter how wide we make the definition of 'true' quartz, the distinctive appearance of typical chalcedony may not be due solely to its micro-crystalline nature. It was for long attributed to the presence of other forms of silica, and in 1936 J. D. H. Donnay[133] proposed that chalcedony consists of 90 per cent quartz and 10 per cent opal. This view was generally held for several years and confirmed work done by C. W. Correns and G. Nagelschmidt[134] in 1933, but critical analyses made in 1950 (and since) have failed to detect the presence of any opal. X-ray powder photography seems to identify both chalcedony and flint as composed of nothing but quartz and a trace of water held in microscopic pores. These have been found to measure about 1/100,000 millimetre in diameter, in chalcedony, by means of an electron microscope.

Chalcedonic silica has a slightly lower refractive index than common quartz, but in 1952 this was shown by R. L. Folk and C. E. Weaver[8] to be due to the water-pores. Working with chert, they found that the crystallites have the same refractive index as quartz. The water-pores are also held to account for the lower hardness of chalcedony, which is intermediate between that of quartz and opal.

Flint. We now come at last to flint, and since it commonly consists of about 98 per cent pure silica we shall not consider here the minute balance of impurities which sometimes colour it. Like chalcedony, flint has a compact cryptocrystalline structure and was until quite recently thought to be an intimate mixture of opal and micro-crystalline silica[4], but containing more opal than chalcedony. The removal of the more soluble opaline silica by percolating water was

---

* Miers distinguishes the crystallites in chalcedony as 'minute fibres, which are biaxial and positive, with straight extinction, and elongated along the obtuse bisectrix, *i.e.* in a negative direction'. Common quartz exhibits holoaxial symmetry.

PLATE V. Small fossils in flint. *Top (left):* Internal cast of a brachiopod shell, *Gibbithyris semiglobosa* (×1½); *(right)* fragment of a lamellibranch shell, *Neithea sexcostata*. *Centre (left):* Rough unpolished back of the small fossil sponge in the frontispiece; *(right)* black beach-pebble bearing a bryozoan in white silica (see Plate VII). *Foot (left):* A delicate sponge skeleton, *Ventriculites,* filling a hollow dark-grey soil-pebble from Epsom; *(right)* cast of canals of the sponge *Callopegma* in a brown soil-pebble from Sussex (×3).

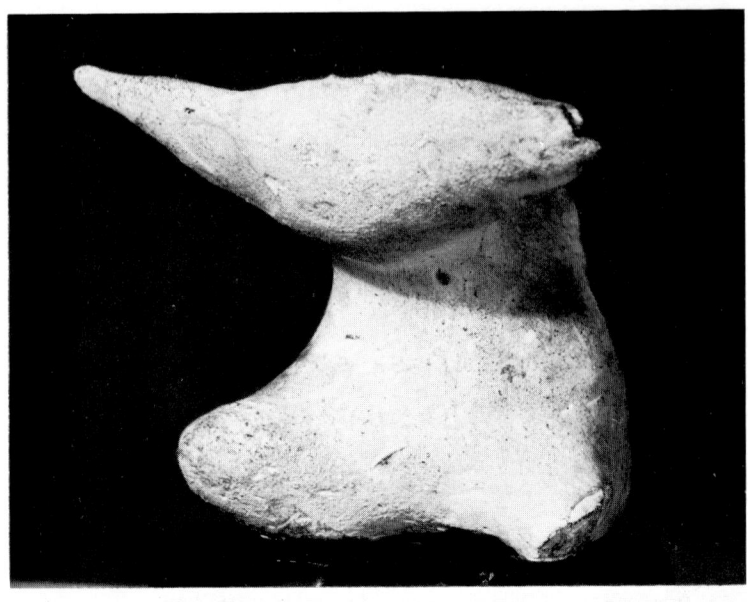

PLATE VI. *Above:* A flint nodule possibly formed in a crustacean burrow—*not* a piece of sculpture by Henry Moore! *Below:* A brown gravel-flint with a cast of a lamellibranch shell, *Inoceramus*. In the dark central shadow the fine network of a bryozoan can be seen in a paler tone (see Plate VII).

assumed to account for the white cortex, since it would leave the faces of the crystallites separated and able to reflect light.

The cortex is not, however, visibly porous (except when weathered or 'rotted'), but this was consistent with the view that the spaces left by the opaline silica are ultra-small—in fact, from ten to a hundred times molecular dimensions. They would permit the passage of very small numbers of molecules of water and the rate of transfusion would be almost incredibly slow, but it could nevertheless take place. In both core and cortex, therefore, flint was distinguished from chalcedony by containing a different proportion of opaline silica, but it was still held to be basically chalcedonic. Moreover, it occasionally seems to have become transformed into typical chalcedony, as in the large specimen in the frontispiece, and this has been explained as the simple conversion of some of the opaline silica into a crystalline form.

This theory appeared to be highly satisfactory, at least in principle, and it is still frequently cited, but it can no longer be regarded as true. The unique appearance of flint led to the suggestion that it might contain varieties of crystalline silica other than quartz, such as cristobalite (a cubic form) of tridymite (an orthorhombic form), and in 1951 J. H. Weymouth and W. O. Williamson[9] examined typical flint for the presence of both opal and cristobalite but found no trace of either. They describe the flint as consisting entirely of minute crystallites of quartz, often arranged fanwise, the spaces between them being filled with water, air, or both.

Since the crystallites in chalcedony were shown to be also arranged fanwise by J. F. White and J. F. Corwin[10] in 1961, when they succeeded in synthesizing the mineral, the only demonstrated difference between typical flint and chalcedony is the size of the water-pores, those in flint having been found in 1950 to measure about 1/7,140 of a millimetre in diameter, which is fourteen times larger than the pores in chalcedony (about 1/100,000 millimetre*). This difference did, in fact, lead H. G. Midgley[11] to propose, in 1951, that the only distinction between flint and chalcedony is that flint contains more than 1 per cent of water and chalcedony less. It is, however, likely that the pores in chalcedony are separated while those in flint are interconnected. This seems to be required to account for the formation

* The diameter of a molecule of water is about 1/3,000,000 of a millimetre, which is 30 times smaller still.

of the cortex, which may now be conceived as the result of the simple removal of water from the interstices between the crystallites. Independent evidence that this is all that is necessary to turn a flint white is afforded by the black flints of Brandon, which may turn 'milky' quite soon after removal from the chalk [101] (see page 189).

Black flint will also turn white if put into a fire, when the heat drives out all the moisture. This change has been known since prehistoric times, and flints so treated are said to be 'calcined', because they

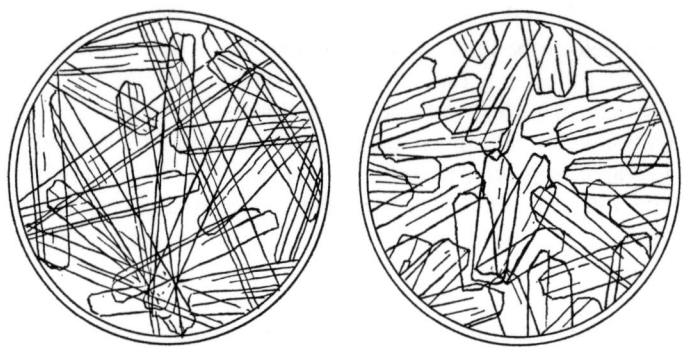

FIG. 4. Crystallites of quartz in flint, magnified ×100,000. *Left:* As observed and measured by A. T. Jensen *et al*[12]. *Right:* As observed and measured by Meldau and Robertson[13]. (*Adapted from electron photomicrographs and descriptions.*)

appear superficially to have been changed into chalk or lime (Latin *calx*). However, very thin sections of calcined flint appear brown by transmitted light[9], a phenomenon not yet explained.

Typical black flint would appear, then, to consist of a compact mass of microscopic needle-like crystals of silica, identifiable in their general atomic structure with quartz, and of nothing else except the trace of water in the fine pores of the core. It also seems likely that in grey flint the crystals are less fibrous. In Fig. 4 the needle-like crystals measured by A. T. Jensen and others[12] in black flint are compared with the stouter but much shorter crystals measured by R. Meldau and R. H. S. Robertson[13] in Irish grey flint.

However, the question can by no means be considered as settled, for in 1957 other forms of silica were found in Danish flint, superficially indistinguishable from common British flint, by A. T. Jensen and co-workers[12]. Using X-ray diffractometry, they found the proportion of common quartz ranged from nearly 100 per cent to only 4 per cent, the balance in some specimens consisting of granules of glassy quartz and in others of platy cristobalite, or of mixtures of these*. The width of the granules was found to average about 1/25,000 of a millimetre, and they are thought to have been most likely deposited from a solution of opaline silica.

It is evidently wrong to assume that all flints, or even all parts of the same flint, have exactly the same composition, in spite of their apparent homogeneity. Since the polished surfaces of some flints reveal the structure of siliceous sponges as forming part of the very stuff of the flint, as in the smaller specimen in the frontispiece, there must be at least some differentiation in the micro-structure even if other forms of silica are not present. There is, therefore, no single definitive description of flint based on its composition or structure, unless in very general terms.

To sum up, although opal, chalcedony, cristobalite and tridymite may all occur adventitiously in flint, none of them is essential, and dense aggregates of pure quartz crystallites of appropriate size, suitably arranged and spaced, may possess all the characteristic properties which distinguish flint from other natural deposits of silica. But there is one other factor which may turn out to be of considerable importance, and this is the quantity and state of the water held in the pores. The astonishing tensile strength of water in pores or tubes of microscopic size is a recent discovery and is discussed further in Appendix VII.

Chert and *hornstone*. Chert is a form of nodular silica which is sometimes so like flint that it is difficult to distinguish between them. In many cases, chert appears to be the mineral which corresponds to flint in limestones other than chalk. It is also found in sandstones, where it may form thick continuous sheets of hard rock, showing a splintery fracture and a resinous lustre on freshly-broken surfaces. It is usually grey, yellow or brown, but is often black. It may be full of fossil sponge spicules, or riddled with fine holes showing where

* Buurman and Plas[132] have also found traces of tridymite in two specimens, using the same method of analysis.

the opaline spicules have been dissolved out. Some cherts are composed largely of the siliceous tests of diatoms (single-celled plants) or *Radiolaria* (single-celled animals), and many owe their existence to inorganic agencies such as thermal springs.

Both chert and flint may be found as pebbles in the same gravel bed, where they look very much alike, and the word 'chert' has been associated with the Irish *ceart*, a pebble (though the derivation is doubtful). Chert is sometimes regarded simply as an impure kind of flint, and this is the traditional English view as expressed, for example, by John Martyn in the *Philosophical Transactions* of the Royal Society for 1729 (Vol. 36, p. 30). The reverse view that flint is merely a kind of chert is usual today in America and Australia. It hardly matters which way round we put it in speech, but foreign reports of discoveries of 'flint' often turn out to refer to what we should call 'chert', and *vice versa*, so caution is sometimes needed in reading*.

From the chemical point of view, there is little—if any—difference between typical flint and typical chert, but the great variety of cherts indicates a considerable range of structural differences. Buurman and Plas[132] suggest that the only real difference between flint and chert is that flint loses water when exposed to the air but chert does not. Now, it is true that chert does not form a well-marked cortex through loss of water, but some translucent cherts lose enough to become opaque towards the surface, and some Lower Greensand cherts dry out to become quite friable. Other Greensand cherts weather to reveal tangled masses of sponge spicules visible in their thousands to the naked eye, while the *Rhaxella* chert is riddled with microscopic holes where sponge spicules have been dissolved out. Probably much depends upon word-usage. We call all these different deposits of silica 'chert' for want of other names, and then wonder at the range of forms assumed by this remarkable mineral 'chert'! Flint was, perhaps, just the lucky one to get a name of its own. Very poor quality flints are often described as 'cherty', but this term refers only to the way they fracture when struck with a hammer, as described below.

* For example, the American JOIDES Deep Sea Drilling Project announced in December, 1971, that they had found 'chalk' containing layers of 'hard flint' 1,237 feet below the sea-floor south-east of Japan, where the ocean is more than 20,000 feet deep. But the calcareous rock here is not chalk but a consolidated Foraminiferal ooze (page 47), while the 'flint' turns out to be Radiolarian chert!

PHYSICAL PROPERTIES OF FLINT

Hornstone (not to be confused with *hornfels* or *hornblende*, two quite unrelated minerals) is a grey or black aqueous deposit of silica, generally described as 'chalcedonic'. It has a horny appearance, is opaque, and breaks with a more or less flat fracture quite distinct from the typical conchoidal fracture of flint. It occurs in nodules and continuous beds in limestones of many geological periods but, unlike flint and most cherts, shows no evidence of an organic origin. It is occasionally confused with flint and often with chert, though its peculiar texture is usually quite unmistakable.

Physical properties of flint

Flint is much too hard to be scratched with a steel knife, and readily scratches glass. A point or splinter of flint makes an excellent substitute for a steel-wheel glass-cutter, but it scores the glass like a diamond instead of crushing it. It can be used on very thin glass, such as a microscope coverslip, which will not stand the pressure necessary with a wheel-cutter, though it is, of course, inferior to diamond. The specific gravity of flint varies from about 2·55 to 2·65.

When shattered, flint breaks in the manner of glass, producing a splintery conchoidal fracture with curved or wavy surfaces. (See Fig. 5.) If the fracture is nearly parallel with a surface, a flake with a razor-sharp edge is produced. When struck by iron or a piece of iron pyrites or marcasite*, a flint may appear to emit sparks, but these usually consist of fragments of the iron or pyrites struck off by the much harder flint. The sharpness of the hard edge of the flint ensures that the whole force of the blow is concentrated in a very small area, and it thus raises the detached particles to white heat. All these properties were exploited by Stone Age man and will be more thoroughly discussed in Chapters 5 and 6, but here we may note some old names for flint as the producer of fire.

In the Latin of the Epinal Glossary (c. A.D. 700) we find *petra-focaria*, the 'fire-stone', defined as flint, and in another glossary (dated 1050) *petra-focaria* is translated as 'frystan' or 'flynte'. 'Frystan' is obviously a metathesis of 'fyr-stan', and in German *feuerstein* (fire-stone) is still the word for flint. The Greeks also called flint the fire-stone, *pyrites lithos*, but this was used of any stone which would

* Iron pyrites and marcasite are described in the following chapter.

produce fire and has long since been transferred to the other partner in spark-production.

Once flint has been removed from its native chalk, its mechanical properties are liable to change. Old exposed flints, impure flint, and the flints of gravels often show a 'hackly' fracture. The surfaces are broken by steps or ledges and appear 'blocky', while the edges are

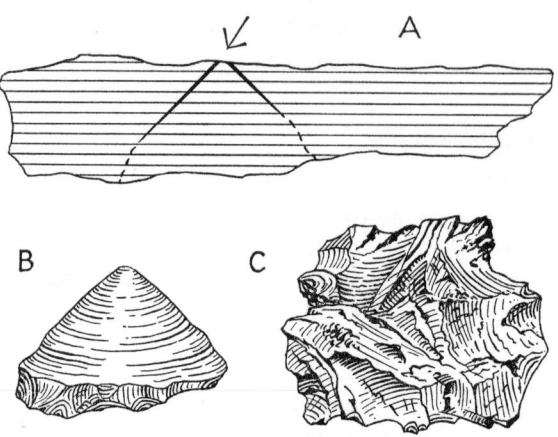

FIG. 5. Fracture in flint. A, Section showing the lines of a typical conchoidal fracture when fresh flint is struck at the point marked by an arrow. B, The cone detached resembles that produced when a bullet strikes plate glass. C, Hackly fracture of cherty or weathered flint.

jagged rather than sharp. (See Fig. 5, C.) These are also the characteristics of fracture in chert, and they make it difficult to chip stones to a desired shape.

Flint is readily shattered by heating it in a fire and then plunging it into cold water, for it is a poor conductor of heat and the sudden quenching shrinks only the surface layers, which instantly become covered with a network of fine cracks like the crazing of 'crackleware' glass or pottery glazes. (See Plate XVII.) If cold water is continually applied the cracks spread rapidly right through the flint. Calcined flint, whether visibly cracked or not, crushes more easily than raw flint, a property which is exploited in the pottery and other industries[9].

PHYSICAL PROPERTIES OF FLINT

Flint is also split by frost if it contains a deep hollow or a crack into which water can penetrate. Such cracks may be far too small to be seen, but they are liable to occur when, for example, a nodule falls from a cliff-face on to a hard surface. When the absorbed water freezes it expands with a force equal to perhaps a ton per square inch and causes a 'spall' to spring off. This usually takes the form of a circular disc with a convex inner surface (representing a shallow cone), and when large it is called a 'pot-lid'.

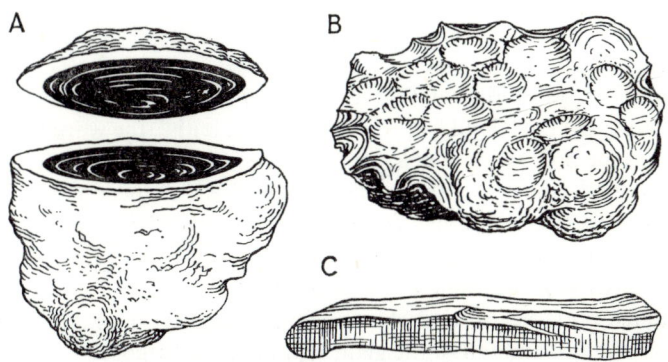

FIG. 6. Fracture of flint by frost. A, Pot-lid fracture. B, Frost-pitting. C, Columnar or starch fracture.

A large nodule may be covered with numerous small pot-lid fractures and is then said to be 'frost-pitted'. Flints chipped naturally in this way are often mistaken for artefacts. (See Fig. 6 and Plate IV.) The white cortex, when thick, fractures in yet another manner. It breaks into rods of remarkably square or rectangular section, a type of breakage called a 'columnar' or 'starch' fracture, because the pieces suggest giant starch grains (Fig. 6).

Flint is immensely durable and is not attacked by acids, though it is by strong alkalis. It has been widely used in building for at least two thousand years, and it outlasts granite and perhaps all other stones. The flints in walls many centuries old are still are good as new, though the mortar may have decayed. Flint knives ten thousand or more years old are often still razor-sharp, and equally old axe-heads have been used experimentally, and without difficulty, for felling trees.

2

The Story of Chalk

WHEN IT IS said that flint nodules in their native state occur embedded in the 'Chalk', spelt with a capital initial, the word is being used as the proper name of a distinct and continuous series of characteristic soft white limestones. They comprise the upper part of the Cretaceous system (named from the Latin *creta*, chalk) and are the last sedimentary rocks to have been laid down in the Mesozoic era. This was the great 'middle' or 'Secondary' era of the fossil record, in which both animal and plant evolution made remarkable strides. It saw the rise and fall of the giant reptiles, and witnessed the emergence of mammals, birds and flowering plants. The period during which the Chalk was deposited (and in which the Dinosaurs became extinct) lasted from about 100 million to 65 million years ago—an unbroken stretch of about 35 million years.

This period was ushered in by a steady invasion of the land by the sea, an advance which had already begun before the first chalk made its appearance. It now continued on an unprecedented scale, relentlessly but without violence, drowning the greater part of Europe and the British Isles, a large part of Asia, Saharan Africa, and nearly half America. Australia had been largely submerged in lower Cretaceous times, and the land had begun slowly to rise again when the 'Cenomanian transgression', as it is called, crept over the other continents and smothered them in chalk. It culminated in the maximum extension of the sea and minimum exposure of dry land in the known history of the world, and at its peak about 80 per cent of the earth's surface was probably covered by water. (See Fig. 7.)

The story of flint begins in these vast oceans, and the three great problems which have exercised geologists for more than a century

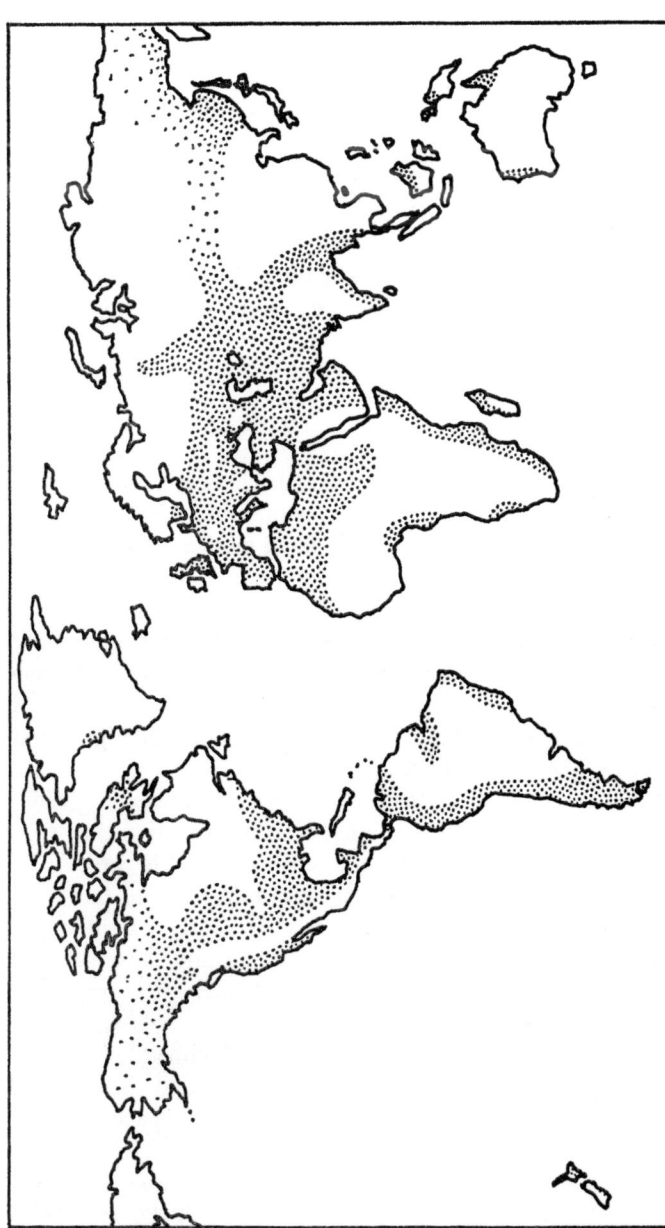

Fig. 7. Areas (dotted) of the present land-surfaces of the world which were once covered by the Chalk Sea—and very largely by chalk. Most of the chalk has since disappeared, but the flints from it have often survived in pebble-beds and more recent conglomerates, and are found over an even wider area.

are: 1. What is the nature of the chalk in which the flints are found? 2. Whence came the silica of which the flints are composed? and 3. How came the silica to be concentrated in hard nodules? The answer to the first question has now been found and that to the second provided in the form of a few alternatives, but even the most plausible so far suggested for the third can be only partly true and should still be called a hypothesis. The three problems are not wholly separable, so that though we shall take them in order, reserving the third for the following chapter, a certain amount of overlapping will be unavoidable.

The nature of chalk

It was known in the early 19th century that chalk is a consolidated oceanic ooze*, for it is fairly uniform in composition, has a very fine amorphous structure, and contains scattered marine fossils of many kinds, including fishes, ammonites, belemnites, sea-urchins, sea-lilies, sponges and corals. There are also several species of brachiopods (lamp-shells) and bivalve molluscs, but univalves (Gastropoda) are rare. The bivalves sometimes attain a very large size, the giant *Inoceramus platinus* of the Kansas chalk, U.S.A., attaining a yard in diameter. Some typical Chalk fossils are illustrated in Fig.18 and others will be found in the plates.

The majority of shells consist of calcium carbonate, originally secreted in layers by the animals inhabiting them so that they split readily into leaves parallel with their surfaces. But the process of fossilization re-arranges (or replaces) their molecules so that they form solid sheets of calcite crystals which break nearly at right-angles to their surfaces along the cleavage-planes. Many have been so broken, and odd crystals or groups of crystals having this origin are often found scattered in the Chalk.

Both the fauna and the occurrence of the green mineral glauconite indicate that the climate was everywhere warm, and the bottom-dwelling species show that the water in which the ooze accumulated

---

* Chalk has nothing to do with 'blackboard chalk' or 'French chalk', which are artificial products prepared chiefly from steatite (talc or soapstone), a hydrated silicate of magnesium. Chalk is, however, used for making whitewash or 'whiting'.

THE NATURE OF CHALK

was of moderate depth and even shallow at times. It probably seldom exceeded 150 fathoms (900 feet), and since the total thickness of the Chalk may have approached a mile, the deposition of the ooze must have kept pace with a much deeper subsidence of the sea-floor. The

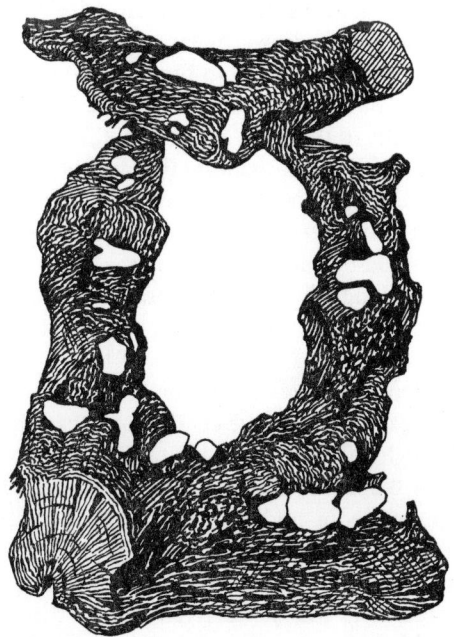

FIG. 8. White flints embedded in timber. See note at foot of page 44.

warm climate probably contributed by the melting of polar ice, which could have raised the sea-level by several hundred feet.

Pieces of fossil wood are occasionally found in the Chalk, sometimes encased in flint[14], and it is evident that this has never been subjected to the pressures of the abyss. It is undoubtedly driftwood and lends plausibility to the theory that boulders of completely foreign and much older rock which are occasionally found in the Chalk, especially in the bottom layers, were carried out to sea entangled or embedded in the roots of fallen trees and there dropped*.

The land which was invaded had evidently been worn down to a peneplain over vast areas, for though the lower layers of the Chalk contain a considerable proportion of clay (forming 'marls'), derived from the land, there are no extensive deposits of terrigenous materials such as would be brought down by large rivers, and this implies the absence of high mountain ranges to bring down rain and melt-water from snows. The Chalk appears to have accumulated in a fairly pure condition quite close to the land, and it sometimes contains a scattering of very small spherical sand-grains of the 'millet-seed' type characteristic of deserts. These must have been dropped over the sea by the wind and may later have been distributed by currents.

The presence of desert sands suggests that an arid climate prevailed over much of the land, though elsewhere slow rivers are presumed to have kept the oceans supplied with a solution of the minerals of which chalk is composed. In some parts of the world, however, the contemporary deposits were marine or lacustrine sands and clays, and there is, for example, no true chalk in Australia† and very little, if any, flint, though chert is found. However, a chalky limestone was deposited in the Nullarbor Plain in Eocene times and this contains some interesting siliceous nodules which have been studied particularly at Wilson's Bluff. According to Dr. J. N. Jennings, these closely resemble flints but often fail to fracture in a truly conchoidal manner. He has compared them with the derived flints of the Chalky Boulder Clay of Cambridgeshire and considers that, on the whole, 'flint' is

* That the wood of trees can completely enclose pieces of stone is known from numerous instances, and Fig. 8 shows a drawing of part of the root of an oak enclosing several large flints. This is taken from a photograph exhibited by C. Carus-Wilson at the Linnean Society of London in 1909, the description stating: 'The stones are actually embedded in the solid oak, and not merely included within forked portions which may have grown together subsequently. The tissue of the wood appears to have grown around the stones and enveloped them.' This specimen originally contained 67 stones, some weighing 'several pounds'. The same author also reports flints embedded in yews and raised to 12 feet above the ground by the growth of the trees[15].

† The so-called 'Gingin chalk' of Western Australia is described[16] as containing up to 25 per cent of aluminium, iron and magnesium silicates, including garnet, ruttle, zircon, tourmaline and many other minerals. It is therefore not a true chalk though it contains typical Chalk fossils and bears cherty nodules towards the top.

THE NATURE OF CHALK

a better name for them than 'chert'*. Again, borings in the Great Artesian Basin are reported to have passed through beds of flint, but this has been queried by Australian geologists[17].

Elsewhere the chalk ooze was deposited over enormous areas through several millions of years as almost pure calcium carbonate ($CaCO_3$). It is astonishingly pure through great thicknesses in its upper levels, that at Newhaven, Sussex, for example, having the following composition:

Calcium carbonate	97·89
Magnesium carbonate	0·75
Silica	0·65
Calcium phosphate	0·22
Iron and aluminium oxides	0·14
Water (combined)	0·35
	100·00

In this region there are about 1 ton of flints to every 130 tons of chalk, the flints being almost wholly black with a very thin cortex[18]. This ton of flints consists of perhaps 98 per cent silica, so that we have the remarkable (but by no means exceptional) phenomenon of one pure mineral embedded in another without any sort of mixture or gradation between them†. If we regard the silica of the flint as part of the overall composition of the rock, the total percentage of silica is about 1·4, so that it is nearly twice as abundant as any other ingredient after the calcium carbonate (which now comprises 97·1 per cent). This must represent the composition of a very large part of the original ooze, for since it is impossible to regard the flints as having been introduced 'ready-made' from some external source, they must have obtained the bulk of their silica from the ooze itself by some process of segregation.

The first attempts to account for the ooze were made in the 19th century, and were based on comparisons with calcareous oozes which are accumulating on many parts of the ocean floor today. When crushed chalk, or the loose chalk 'meal' found in hollow flints, is

---

* In a private communication to the author.
† This is the general rule, but at some levels in some localities fairly sudden gradations of a peculiar kind are found. These are discussed in Chapter 3.

examined under the microscope it is seen to consist of somewhat rounded but usually irregular and apparently structureless grains, some almost spherical (called 'coccospheres'). Among them, the calcareous tests of various species of lime-secreting micro-organisms can sometimes be recognized.

The most easily identified of these belong to the Foraminifera, a class of unicellular animals (Protozoa) well-known today as inhabitants of the surface-waters of warm oceans, and included in the plankton on which the baleen whales subsist. There are also bottom-dwelling Foraminifera. In 1861 the presence of coccoliths ('berry-stones') in the chalk was noticed for the first time, though they were not thought to be common. Coccoliths are the limy secretions of unicellular Algae, minute relatives of the seaweeds and comparable in size with the microscopic *Chlorella* which turns pond-water green. There were also scatterings of siliceous sponge spicules (page 54) and minute crystals of calcite (the commonest crystalline form of calcium carbonate) regarded as derived from broken sea-shells. The general view, put beyond reasonable doubt by H. C. Sorby[19], one of the founders of modern petrology, was that the Chalk consists almost wholly of cominuted organic remains of these kinds, and Sorby expressed the opinion in 1879 that the dominant organisms were coccoliths.

Very few of the fragments could, however, be definitely associated with specific organisms, and of those that could, Foraminifera of the genera *Globigerina* and *Textularia* were the most common. Their tests consist of a few irregular globular chambers, usually arranged in a rough spiral in the *Globigerina* but in a sort of zig-zag in the *Textularia*, though fragments are more often found than complete specimens. (See Fig. 9.) Their living representatives have been studied in detail, and in one large group the walls of the chambers are perforated, the cell-protoplasm extending through the holes to form pseudopods and also enclosing the test. There is another group without perforations, though the class-name Foraminifera is Latin for 'hole-bearers'. The tests commonly measure about 1/20th inch in diameter, but there is a considerable range of sizes.

When a 'Foram' (the common abbreviation for a member of the Foraminifera) dies, its protoplasm decays and the test sinks slowly to the bottom of the ocean. In the open sea, a constant rain of these

THE NATURE OF CHALK

minute particles of calcium carbonate must always be falling to the ocean floor, and where the water is free from land-derived sediments the ooze consists of little else. A *Globigerina* ooze of this kind is found today on the bottom of the greater part of the Atlantic and Indian Oceans, and in the south-east quadrant of the Pacific, and is in general several hundred feet thick. Its present rate of accumulation is estimated at about half an inch per 1,000 years. Washed and dried specimens of *Globigerina* ooze bear a close superficial and chemical

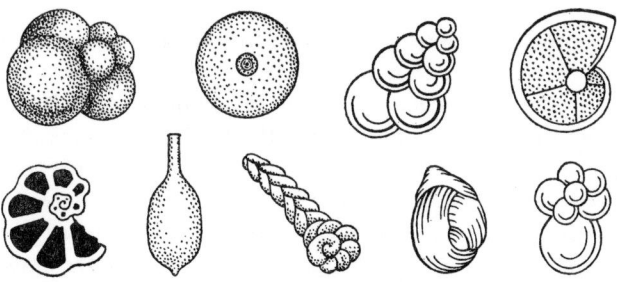

FIG. 9. Examples of Foraminifera, unequally magnified but averaging about ×20. Each is about as big as a pin's-head. (Giant Forams measuring an inch or more in diameter are found in more recent rocks.)

resemblance to chalk, and in 1858 T. H. Huxley called it 'modern chalk', repeating this description with emphasis in 1870. Chalk was thus commonly described as a *Globigerina* or Foraminiferal ooze from Huxley's time through the first quarter of the present century*.

The Foraminiferal ooze theory came under suspicion when analyses showed that, on the average, only about 5 per cent of the Chalk can be definitely associated with Foraminifera, and the theory had virtually been abandoned by 1935, when the Geological Survey (in the first edition of its 'Regional Guides'[20]) expressed uncertainty whether the structureless 95 per cent consists of broken-down seashells or chemical precipitates.

* This description was still being given, without qualification, in a text-book for university students published in 1965, and it is frequently taught in schools even today.

THE STORY OF CHALK

It was, however, very difficult to explain the chalk as broken-down sea-shells, even allowing for profound mineralogical changes. They could hardly have been reduced to a nearly uniform powder through 3,000 feet over something like 40 million square miles, even if there were enough of them, and if they were, how did the individuals now found here and there as fossils escape the surrounding destruction? The reduction to powder was attributed partly to mechanical pressure and partly to physical or chemical changes resulting in the rearrangement of the molecules, but no *modus operandi* for such a process was established.

Attempts to account for the Chalk by inorganic chemical precipitation were also doomed to failure. At present the sea contains about 0·123 per cent of calcium carbonate in solution, which is sufficient to supply the material required for the shells of sea-creatures, and it must all originally have been brought to the sea by rivers flowing over limestones, weathered basic igneous rocks, and igneous rocks containing calcite*. In solution, it is combined with hydrogen as the bicarbonate, $Ca(HCO_3)_2$, and processes by which the much less soluble normal carbonate, $CaCO_3$, could have been precipitated chemically from this off the mouths of large rivers were mooted, but they demanded improbable conditions and implied only local results.

However, in 1939 A. Earland[21] put forward a plausible theory of organic precipitation founded on a discovery made by G. H. Drew[22] in the Bahamas in 1911 and 1912. Drew had found that the white calcareous ooze off Andros Island (and between there and the Florida coast) was being precipitated by a species of marine bacterium which he named *Bacterium calcis*. He estimated from a study of cultures that the ooze (now known as 'drewite') contained some 160 million bacteria per cubic centimetre, and noted that it smelt of sulphuretted hydrogen†. Chemically and in appearance it closely resembled chalk, even in the spherical character of some of its grains, and from Drew's information Earland developed the promising 'bacterial ooze' theory of the origin of chalk, which was widely held until 1953.

---

* Large crystals of calcite are found in cavities in the dolerites of Iceland as 'Iceland spar', and it also occurs in recent eruptive rocks and in some tuffs and schists.

† Sulphuretted hydrogen, H_2S, is the gas responsible for the smell of bad eggs, in which it is produced by decay bacteria.

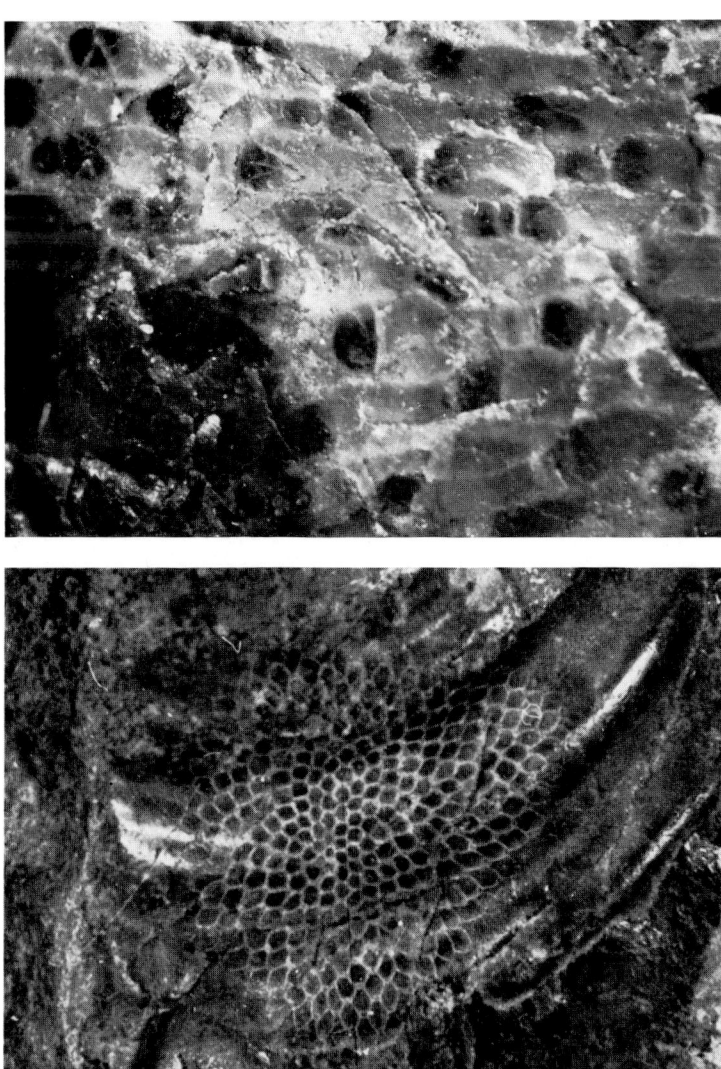

PLATE VII. Photomicrographs of the bryozoa shown in natural size in Plates V and VI. *Above: Onychocella inelegans,* ×35. *Below: Lateroflustrellaria robusta,* ×4.

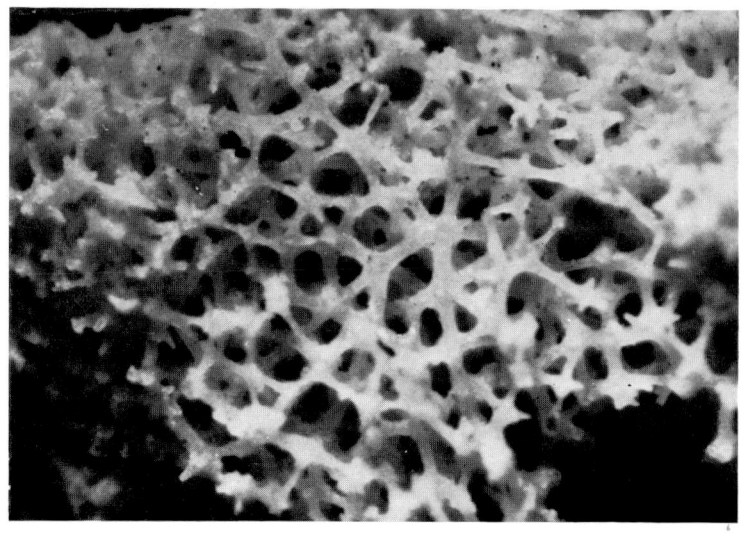

PLATE VIII. Photomicrographs of sponge spicules. *Above:* The skeletal network of a haxactinellid sponge from the interior of a hollow flint, ×30. *Below:* Modern loose sponge spicules, ×20.

THE NATURE OF CHALK

According to Earland, the coccospheres are not themselves organic structures but were formed round bubbles of sulphuretted hydrogen produced by the bacteria as they secreted the calcium carbonate. This, of course, would require the presence of sulphur, but there is always sulphur where there are living organisms and the sea contains about 0·09 per cent of it in one form or another. It also occurs in the Chalk at some levels in the form of nodules of iron sulphide (FeS_2), though they are by no means as common as the flints. Before showing how the bacterial ooze theory was superseded, it will be convenient to describe these sulphide nodules here, as part of the

FIG. 10. A nodule of marcasite and (*right*) twinned crystals of marcasite forming an 'arrow-head'.

story of chalk, for they will be referred to again in another context (in Chapter 6).

They occur in the mineral form of marcasite, though they are sometimes incorrectly referred to as iron pyrites*. They are most common in the lower part of the Chalk, and are found as yellow or brown, rounded, cauliflower-like, solid lumps of all shapes and sizes, showing radiating, brassy-looking crystals when broken. (See Fig. 10.) They are more than half as heavy as iron and countryfolk, who often call them 'thunderbolts' or 'meteorites', use them for paper-weights or door-stops (though they are rarely large enough for this). If kept

---

* Both minerals have the same chemical composition, but marcasite crystallizes in the orthorhombic system, and pyrites in the cubic. Marcasite (pronounced to rhyme with *bite*) should not be confused with the jewellers' 'marcasite' (pronounced to rhyme with *beet*), which is simply highly polished steel used as a semi-precious stone.

exposed to moist air they are liable to decay, and this is incipient in the dark-brown nodules whose colour is caused by a coating of limonite (hydroxide of iron). As a nodule decays it produces white fibrous growths of ferrous sulphate crystals ('green vitriol') on its surface, while surrounding moisture is found to contain sulphuric acid. The limonite is finally transformed into a crumbly mass of hydrated oxides of iron (rust), sometimes forming 'rust balls'.

In Kent, twinned crystals of marcasite resembling brass arrowheads, but sometimes called 'spear-pyrites', are found in the chalk at Folkestone, and the local tradition is that they are relics of the weapons used by the Romans in the invasion of 55 B.C.! These occurrences of marcasite indicate that the sulphur in the Chalk Sea eventually became concentrated or 'segregated' in a somewhat similar manner to the silica of flint. There appears to have been little research on the subject, though R. G. Bromley[6] has associated them with the burrows of crustaceans, in which he thinks they may be especially liable to form.

The sulphur utilized by the various forms of life in the Chalk Sea may very well have re-appeared as sulphuretted hydrogen during processes of decomposition, or by microbic action of the kind postulated in the bacterial ooze theory. And if it was present it could certainly have diffused through the chalk and eventually combined with iron atoms, where it found them, to produce ferrous sulphide in the form of marcasite. However, the bacterial ooze theory has been rejected as an explanation of the chalk on evidence of a different kind. This is that the calcium carbonate in drewite is deposited as microscopic crystals of aragonite, whereas in chalk the crystals are invariably of calcite. It is true that aragonite sometimes changes slowly into calcite, but that no aragonite at all should have survived is extremely improbable.

Moreover, in drewite there are practically no Forams, coccoliths or shell-debris, such as are found in chalk, and the bacterial ooze theory was still undergoing criticism of this kind when, in 1953, Maurice Black[23] examined the minute structure of chalk with an electron microscope, using a special technique. Employing magnifications up to $\times 25{,}000$, he observed structures not visible in an optical microscope and was able to show that the characteristic constituent grains of chalk are undoubtedly the remains of coccoliths.

THE NATURE OF CHALK

These form the matrix in which the other organic debris, chiefly of Foraminifera, shells and sponge spicules, are embedded in comparatively small proportions. With Barbara Barnes[24] he published a detailed description illustrated by electron photomicrographs in 1959, and the drawings in Fig. 11 are based on these pictures.

Coccoliths flourish today in the warm surface-water of the oceans, where they form part of the plankton and, like the Foraminifera, sink to the bottom when they die. Thus, the 'coccolith ooze' theory, now

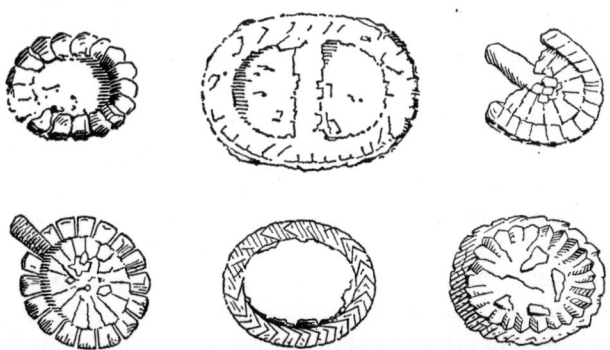

FIG. 11. Coccoliths from the Chalk, magnified about ×3,750. These six would lie side by side on a circle 1/1,000 inch in diameter. A dot just visible to the naked eye could contain about twenty. (*Adapted from electron photomicrographs by* Maurice Black *and* Barbara Barnes[24].)

generally accepted, is similar to that of the Foraminiferal ooze except that the lowly unicellular animals are replaced by lowly unicellular plants. The coccolith remains were found to be dominant throughout the Chalk, of which they constitute more than 60 per cent, and they must have been remarkably abundant in the Chalk Sea. We may reasonably assume that 900 metres (3,000 feet) of the Chalk accumulated in 30 million years, and that about 550 metres of it (60 per cent) consisted of coccoliths. The coccoliths were thus being deposited at about 18 mm. per 1,000 years, which is 18 times as fast as they are at present accumulating on the floor of the N. Atlantic.

While the Chalk ooze was being laid down, countless generations of brachiopods, molluscs, sea-urchins, fishes and other marine animals must have lived and died in the waters from which it settled. What happened to *them*? Had the ooze settled more quickly it might have entombed vast numbers of them, but for generation after generation there was scarcely any change in the sea-floor and the dead bodies would have laid exposed to scavengers, chemical changes and general solution without a chance of burial.

Shrimps and other crustaceans, larvae of various kinds, worms and micro-organisms got to work on their flesh almost as soon as they arrived, and their bones and shells were bored away by sponges and worms or filed and scraped by molluscs, leaving, eventually, only a trace of calcium phosphate and a few molecules of sulphur compounds to mingle with the ooze. The skeletons of siliceous sponges, the calcareous shells and tests, and the teeth and scales of fishes were the most durable, and sometimes these lasted long enough to become completely buried—but more likely by accident than by the slow sedimentation. The fortuitous swirl of a current, the flick of a fish's tail, or the scoop of a crab's claw might have accomplished the necessary interment, and some may have become buried at once by falling into the hole of a burrowing echinoderm or crustacean, or into a natural hollow in the sea-floor in process of being gradually filled by gravity with the surrounding ooze. Once covered, they stood a chance of being preserved as fossils, but such occasions were not common for they are nowhere very plentiful in the Chalk and are widely scattered. Moreover, any two found only four feet apart may also be 50,000 years apart!

The Chalk sponges

Most common and most important to the story of the flint are the sponge spicules, for these lay scattered through the Chalk at all depths and, though some silica may have been deposited independently of the sponges, their significance is attested by the comparatively abundant occurrence of fossil sponges in flint. The living sponges, of course, extracted their silica from the sea-water, which at present contains a mean of about 0·00015 per cent (see Appendix II). This supplies enough for all living siliceous sponges and, like the calcium carbonate, is maintained by the contributions of rivers flowing over suitable rocks and by submarine vulcanism. A great many of the

THE CHALK SPONGES

Chalk sponges have left identifiable traces in the flint nodules and are frequently responsible for their curious shapes. Sometimes a hollow flint, when broken open, shows a lining of honeycomb pitting marking where a former sponge has been dissolved out, as in Fig. 12.

The part played by sponges in the formation of flint warrants a brief description of these primitive animals. They are composed of differentiated cells forming a few distinct types of tissue, and living harmoniously together as a single organized body by division of

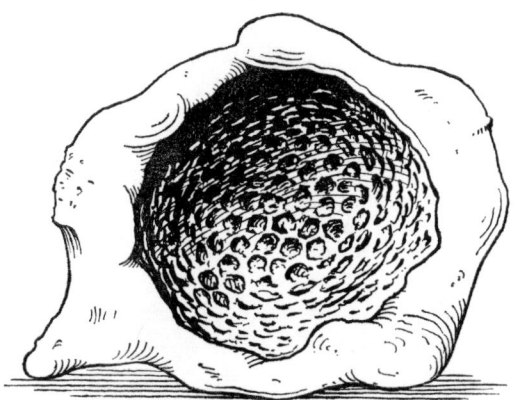

FIG. 12. Interior of a hollow flint showing 'honeycomb' evidence of sponge-structure, the sponge having long since vanished.

labour. The body in each species conforms to the same general pattern, but the individuals may associate in connected colonies with no particular plan. Reproduction is usually sexual and practically all sponges are hermaphrodite, but some sponges reproduce by budding, the buds usually remaining joined to the parent body as part of the colony.

The 'flesh' of a sponge is a jelly-like cellular substance enclosed between two membranes, one forming the outer skin and the other lining cavities within the body. These cavities are connected to form a series of canals, which break through the surface of the sponge at intervals to form raised openings called 'oscules'. The outer skin is also pierced by numerous small pores, and the living sponge draws

THE STORY OF CHALK

in water carrying food-particles through these, extracts dissolved oxygen and nourishment from it, and expels it through the oscules. There is no mouth, and the water is kept in circulation by whip-like 'flagella' born by some of the lining cells. (See Fig. 13.)

The body, which is sessile and cemented to a rock, shell or seaweed stem by a sort of foot, or 'holdfast', may be of almost any shape. It is often globular or cake-shaped (any cake!), but in other species may

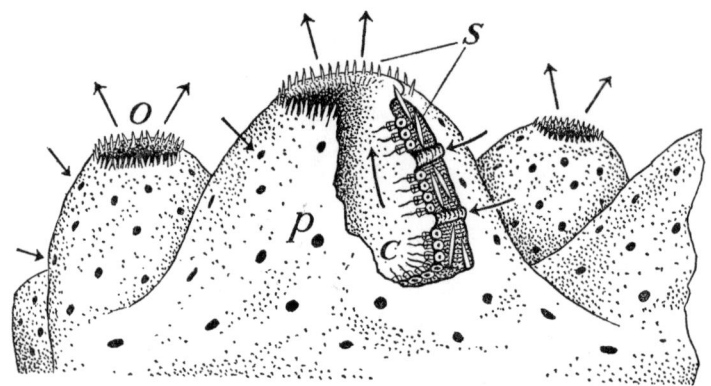

FIG. 13. Part of a colony of simple sponges, with cut-out section to show details. *o*, Oscule. *p*, Pore. *s*, Spicules. *c*, Collar-cells with flagella, which waft the water so that it flows in the direction of the arrows.

resemble a blown-up glove, a cucumber, an inverted pear, a large cup or basin, a tall slender vase, a tulip on a long stalk, or a bunch of roughly folded and re-folded cabbage-leaves. It may be of almost microscopic size* or measure several feet across.

The skin may be tough and leathery, but its shape is usually maintained by a sort of skeleton, the minute thorn-like elements of which are called 'spicules'. These may be unconnected and scattered in great numbers through the flesh, where they behave like collar stiffeners or corset 'bones', or joined together in bundles or star-shaped groups resembling miniature lanterns or caltrops. They vary considerably in size but are nearly always very small, a common

* The smallest known sponge, *Leucosolenia blanca*, is as thin as a hair and about one-tenth of an inch long.

length being about 1/20 inch, though spicules more than half an inch long may be met with. In one genus of living glass-sponges (*Monoraphis*) the single spicule which anchors it to the bottom is nearly half an inch thick and two or three feet long[25]. In many species the skeletal spicules unite to form a lattice of slender girders, or a continuous network like fine lace. In the horny or 'bath' sponges they are replaced by a mesh of flexible fibres, reminiscent of a 'loofah' but on a very much finer scale.

The skeletal material may give a sponge a rubbery texture, provide it with a thick rind, or protect it with rigid plates as hard as stone. Often the skin contains special 'dermal' spicules, quite unlike the structural units of the skeleton and often granular, and a single species may contain spicules of two or three different kinds. There is one group of sponges which does without any skeletal material at all, but neither these 'slime sponges', as they are called, nor the horny sponges concern us, for they are not preserved as fossils.

We are interested only in the 'stony' sponges, and though most of these have spicules of silica, there are some with spicules of calcium carbonate (calcite). The fossil sponges are therefore usually considered by geologists[26] as falling into two classes: the Calcispongiae or Calcarea, which have skeletons of calcium carbonate, and the Silicispongiae or Silicea, which have skeletons of silica and are often called 'glass-sponges'. The Silicea are further divided into the three orders: Monaxonida, in which the spicules consist of a single 'ray' pointed at each end; the Tetraxonida, in which each spicule has four rays; and the Hexactinellida, which have six-rayed spicules. (See Fig. 14.) The Tetraxonida are again divided into the sub-orders Choristida in which the spicules are loose, and the Lithistida in which they are united into a continuous skeleton.

Purely morphological classifications of this sort are arbitrary and matters of convenience. They are limited in referring to the structural spicules only, for the dermal spicules are often of indeterminate and variable shapes. Some palæontologists prefer rather different schemes, and zoologists yet others. So little is known of the phylogeny of the sponges that at least half a dozen different classifications may be found in contemporary text-books (1970). The zoological classifications are based largely on soft anatomical details not preserved in fossils, but the purely skeletal classifications do enable species to be

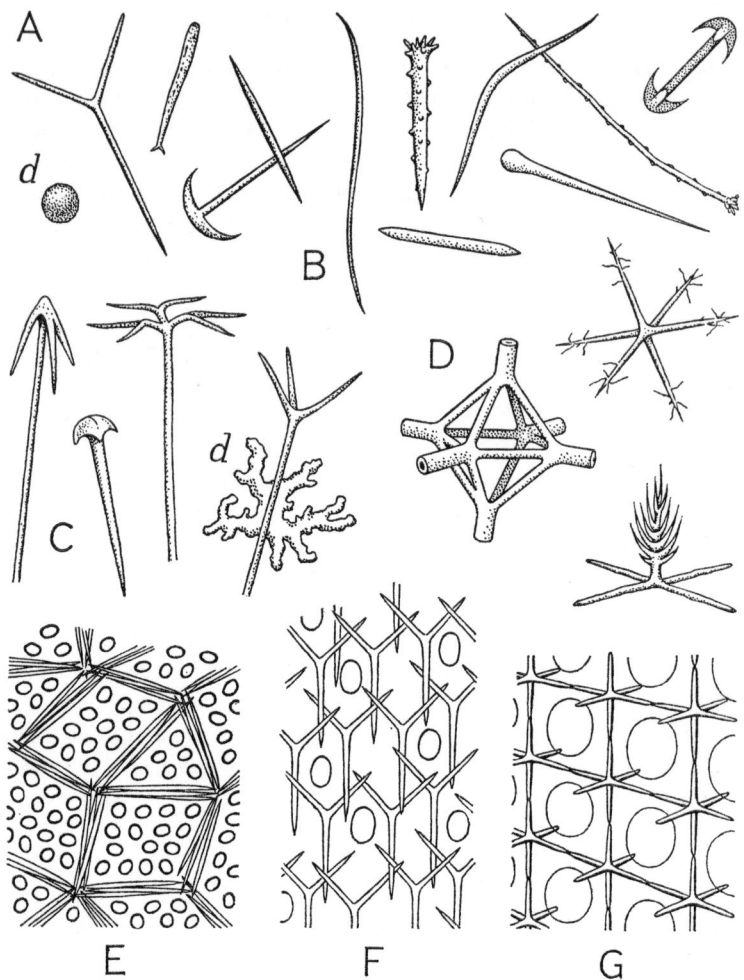

FIG. 14. Typical sponge spicules, all greatly magnified. A, five calcareous sponges. Siliceous sponges: B, seven monaxonids; C, five tetraxonids; D, three hexactinellids. *d*, Dermal spicules. The arrangements of the spicules in monaxonid, calcareous and hexactinellid sponges are exemplified at E, F and G, respectively. The circles or ovals represent the pores. When preserved in flint the individual spicules are rarely visible, but the pattern made by their network, or by the infilled pores and canals, is often characteristic. Loose spicules are sometimes found in hollow flints, while some cherts appear to be composed entirely of recognizable spicules matted together.

distinguished and to be sufficiently described for comparison with living species.

The calcareous sponges which flourished in the Chalk Sea added nothing to the calcium carbonate of the chalk except to return what they had borrowed, yet they are often preserved in deposited flint, as are many other calcareous structures*. Each spicule of a calcareous sponge consists of a single crystal of calcite, but they are usually arranged to form some sort of network the pattern of which may be faithfully preserved. The general shape of the sponge, too, may be evident in the form of a flint nodule, though sometimes it is revealed only by a reddish or yellowish stain of iron oxide in the chalk. The common calcareous Chalk sponge *Raphidonema* (Plate IX) is cup-shaped or funnel-shaped, and the equally common *Porosphaera* is often almost perfectly round and may be mistaken for a marble, a stone shot—or even a petrified golf-ball!

The most important group in connection with flint is the Silicea, though of these the Monaxonida are known solely by their loose spicules except for the single genus *Cliona*, a group of small boring sponges of which flint casts of their bore-holes in shells are sometimes found. Of the Tetraxonida, the lithistid sponges are often beautifully preserved in flint, the positions of the pores, canals and oscules being perfectly outlined. Very common among these are sponges of the genera *Siphonia*, a pear-shaped type with a stalk (illustrated in the frontispiece and Plate IV); *Doryderma*, which are branching cylindrical or finger-like sponges; and *Verruculina*, which form cups or irregular bowls on short stalks.

The Hexactinellida of the Cretaceous period have their six-rayed spicules firmly joined in a network, the junctions between the rays forming right-angles. A very complex lattice often results, but even the finest details may be preserved in a flint nodule. (See Plate VIII.) The most important genera are *Ventriculites*, in which most species form a narrow cone or trumpet with folded walls, and have a root-like holdfast; and *Plocoscyphia*, in which a coarse network takes the form of a gathering of frilled, folded and overlapping sheets or 'laminae'.

These sponges, some of which are shown in Fig. 18, form some of the most characteristic flint fossils, and often constitute the nuclei of

* *Per contra*, some siliceous sponges are preserved in calcite.

large nodules. There are also many other common genera, but a sufficient picture has been drawn to provide a backcloth for the theoretical and experimental adventures to be described in the next chapter. This section has been concerned chiefly to answer the second of the three problems on page 42, for some theories rely on the spicules of the siliceous sponges as the main source of the silica in flint. Before we tackle the third problem yet another scene—or set of scenes—must be provided, for it has not yet been shown how the series of rocks known as the Chalk came to be formed from the coccolith ooze on the bottom of the Chalk Sea.

The Chalk formation

At a depth of 150 fathoms, the Chalk ooze was subject to a pressure of about 4 hundredweight per square inch, or nearly 30 tons per square foot. A hundred feet farther down the weight of the covering ooze, added to that of the water, would have produced a pressure of nearly 40 tons per square foot. At 500 feet below the sea-floor it would approach 70 tons, and at 2,000 feet more than 200 tons per square foot, or $1\frac{1}{2}$ tons per square inch. A much lower pressure than this would have sufficed to squeeze the ooze into a comparatively dry rock. Moreover, during the extremely slow process of accumulation the slight solubility of calcium carbonate would result in a sort of cementation by the fusion of crystals, much as damp salt or sugar sets into lumps.

At times when the water was sufficiently shallow for currents to sweep the sediment away before it could settle, thus exposing already consolidated ooze, cementation took place comparatively rapidly in the surface layers. The proximity of land often ensured a continuous supply of calcium carbonate in solution and the ooze was considerably hardened. That this sometimes occurred within the top few feet is evident from the fact that some of the burrows of the Crustaceans described on page 29 were clearly occupied after the sea-floor had begun to harden[6]. Again in very shallow water, the bottom was often swept by strong currents which so disturbed the ooze that the resulting hardened rock has a 'blocky' character and is called 'nodular' chalk. The nodules are frequently coated with green glauconite and often contain a significant proportion of calcium phosphate.

THE CHALK FORMATION

Sometimes vast continuous layers were hardened by a general influx of calcium phosphate (in very weak solution), with the production of 'phosphatic hardgrounds'. R. Casey has studied the periodic influxes of phosphates from late Jurassic times through the Cretaceous, and associates them with submarine vulcanicity accompanying the opening up of the North Atlantic Ocean*. The separation of the American continent from Europe provided enormous new magmatic sources of minerals, notably silica and phosphates, which were carried away in solution by currents. Dr. Casey states (in a private communication to the author) that 'the distribution of the phosphates shows conclusively that N. W. Europe . . . lay on the eastern margin of a typical ocean circulatory system'†.

The greater part of the Chalk ooze would already have become rock long before its 35 million years of sedimentation had been run through. Except for the slow widening of the Atlantic floor and some violent activity in India, the crust of the earth seems to have been fairly stable through most of this period, though gradual changes of level had noticeable effects at wide intervals. The occurrence of bands of harder rock has been mentioned, but there are also zones of exceptionally soft rock sometimes 100 feet or more thick. These often contain clay introduced by rivers or coastal erosion and are called 'marls', but the proportion, though sufficient to interfere with the normal cementation, was usually very small.

Towards the end of the period the great earth-movements began which eventually raised the Rocky Mountains high above the sea, and elsewhere brought the drowned continents back into the light of day. They came up so slowly, however, that the living creatures of the time would have noticed no difference through many generations. Nevertheless, they came up—covered with perhaps 5,000 feet or more of solid chalk in some regions and at least 3,000 feet over several million square miles.

* The theory of continental drift explains the widening of the gap between N. America and Europe as the result of an upwelling of deep-seated magma along the mid-Atlantic Ridge and its spreading eastwards and westwards from that line. This 'sea-floor spreading', as it is called, takes place at normal crustal temperatures in the solid rocks, which are able to flow very slowly under the enormous pressures imposed by the convection-currents in the earth's mantle.

† Dr. Casey's paper on this subject, *Facies, Faunas and Tectonics in Late Jurassic-Early Cretaceous Britain*, in the press at the time of writing this note, is to appear in a symposium to be published by Queen Mary College, London.

THE STORY OF CHALK

But except on the shores, where the waves would have cut superficial cliffs, no white chalk was ever visible. Sands and muds would have covered it as it rose through the shore-zone, and vegetation would have clothed the surface as fast as it became land. The land rose in gentle folds, coming up a little faster than the exposed surface was removed by denudation, for this also began the instant it appeared and the top layers survived only in the few regions where they were substantially covered by other deposits.

The period of the uplift is scarcely definable, but the major operation must have occupied some few million years. This would suggest a possible rate of about one-sixteenth of an inch per year, or six inches per century. The islands which had projected above the shallow Chalk Sea imperceptibly grew larger, just as England, at the present day, is imperceptible growing smaller*. To the north-west of the British area lay the mainland known to geologists as the North Atlantic Continent or 'Atlantis'† but, in reality—according to the theory of continental drift—eastern Canada. The south and west of Ireland appear to have been part of it but may have formed islands which, like the peaks of Snowdonia and perhaps some of the Scottish Highlands, had never been submerged. There were other such islands, some much larger, in France, Spain, Germany and the Balkans, while Scandinavia formed part of another small continent called Scandis, which was possibly connected with Atlantis in the far north. (See Fig. 15.)

Rivers from these lands brought down sand and mud to settle over the top of the still-submerged chalk. These deposits later formed the first land surface (as described above), but they must all have been destroyed before the agents of erosion could have begun their attack on the chalk. Over very large areas, including the greater part of the British Isles, the whole of the Chalk itself was eventually lost, and where later deposits cover the surviving Chalk they rest on already denuded surfaces.

---

* South-east England is sinking at a rate of about a quarter of an inch per year, so that the City of London should become a sort of second Venice in 5,000 years' time, with the North Sea washing round the Bank of England.

† Not, of course, Plato's *Atlantis*, which would have to be placed scores of millions of years later. However, it now seems likely that Plato himself misinterpreted the Egyptian legend, and that his fabled ancient civilization was a daughter of Minoan Crete situated on the site of Santorin in the Aegean Sea.

THE CHALK FORMATION

Chalk covered most of England and Europe, however, for a very long period, and in some places the elevation of the land raised even the bottom layers far above sea-level. Over the Pennine Chain, for example, before the top layers had been substantially removed, the surface of the land must have stood a mile or two above sea-level. (See Fig. 16.)

FIG. 15. The map of the world in late Cretaceous times according to the theory of continental drift, showing the maximum encroachment of the Chalk Sea over the land. Shaded areas: land remaining above sea-level. At, Atlantis. I, Peninsular India. A, Australia, still attached to Antarctica.

The eventual removal of nearly all the chalk must have required several million years, during which gentle but extensive earth-movements folded or buckled up the strata, raising it in some places but lowering it in others. This resulted in uneven denudation, so that the top of the surviving Chalk is of different ages in different regions. In many places only the oldest or bottom layers remain, but in others the Chalk is more than 1,500 feet thick though its surface is still several hundred feet below the original surface of the ooze. In some parts of Denmark the actual top of the Chalk formation survives, the beds passing insensibly into the overlying clays and limestones

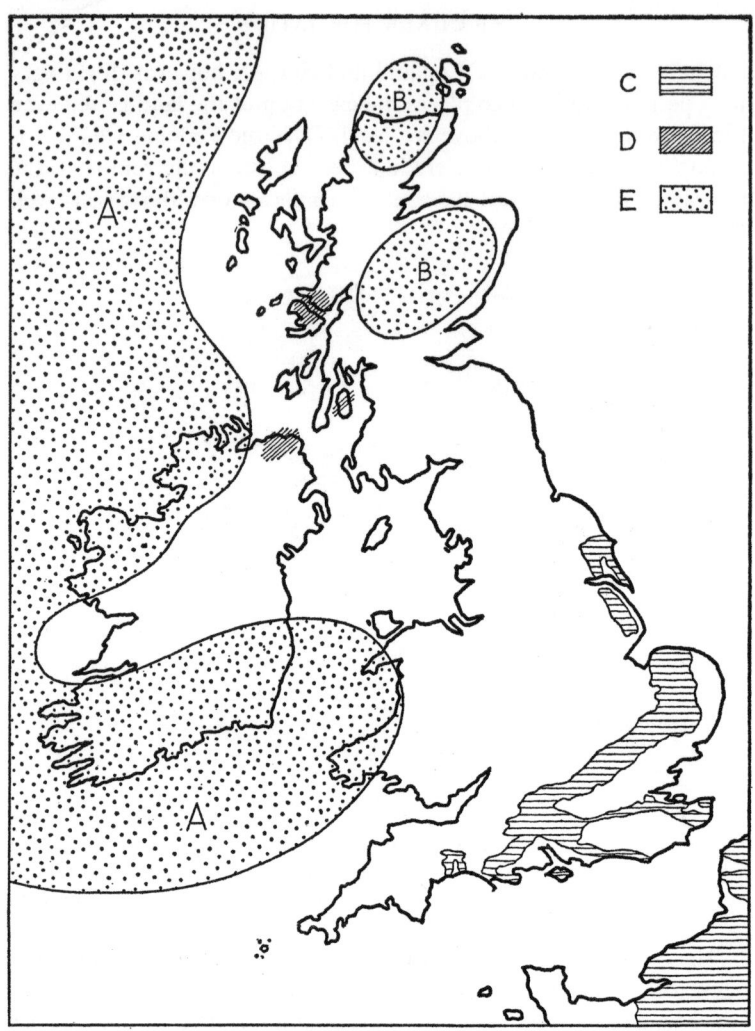

Fig. 16. The British Isles, showing the area covered by the Chalk Sea at the end of the Middle Chalk period, and the present exposure of the Chalk. A, Atlantis (virtually eastern Canada). B, Probable islands. C, Present-day outcrops of the Chalk. D, Areas with deposits of chalk too small to map in detail. E, Possibly desert sands, at least near the coast (see page 44). The coast of Atlantis steadily retreated until the whole of Wales was submerged in middle Upper Chalk times, when the Scottish islands probably also disappeared temporarily.

THE CHALK FORMATION

of the Tertiary period[41]. In other parts of Denmark, and in Belgium and France, there appear to have been small regressions of the sea during which only a few feet of the top of the Chalk were removed, followed by renewed transgressions.

In south-east England the land rose to form a sort of oval dome, the chalk covering of which united the present North and South Downs. (See Fig. 17.) This uprising was compensated by downfoldings over the areas now occupied by the London, Hampshire and Paris Basins. The sea occupied and connected these areas, reaching as far west as Berkshire and as far east as the Netherlands. The

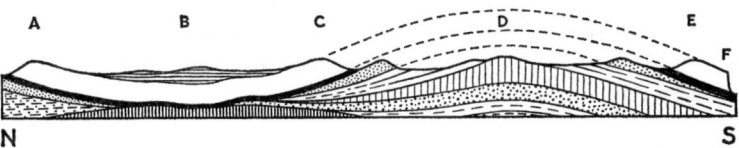

FIG. 17. A simplified section across the London Basin and the Weald from north (N) to south (S), showing the folding of the Chalk (white) and its Gault underlay (solid black). The position of the Chalk over the Wealden dome, before its erosion, is shown by broken lines. A, Chiltern Hills. B, Hampstead, London. C, North Downs. D, Forest Ridge. E, South Downs. F, Beachy Head. (Note how the Gault under the London Basin rests directly on the top of a much older sunken island of ancient rocks.)

Wealden dome, no doubt surrounded by chalk cliffs, stood in its midst as an island.

On top of the chalk which was submerged beneath the sea, layers of sand and beds of flint pebbles washed out of the chalk cliffs and brought down by rivers were first deposited, and then, in the deeper waters, about 400 feet of London Clay, followed by more sands. The 'Eocene Sea', as it is called, was inhabited by sharks, rays, crocodiles, turtles and other tropical creatures whose fossilized remains may now be found.

The Wealden Island may have risen two or three thousand feet above sea-level at one time, but its surface was fairly rapidly eroded by rivers which flowed down it on all sides and eventually carried away all the chalk from the central region. Here, the core of older rock was exposed to form the Weald as we know it today. They also brought down all the flints that were in the Chalk, depositing them in extensive gravel-beds in the London and Hampshire Basins. These rivers cut deeply into the Chalk and established their valleys before the greater part of the dome had disappeared, and this is why there are deep gaps* in the surviving edges of the dome, which now form the escarpments of the North and South Downs.

The Eocene Sea disappeared about 37 million years ago, with a renewed elevation of the land, and there were at least two more submergences and re-elevations affecting parts of south and south-east England before the Great Ice Age ushered in the present period. But this is as far as we need go in the story of the Chalk to make our account of derived flints in Chapter 4 intelligible, and here it remains only to describe briefly a section through the English Chalk as it exists today.

The English Chalk

The English Chalk rests on a bed of dark-blue or nearly black clay known as the Gault, but in some areas there is a transition zone of Upper Greensand (which is often very nearly as white as the Chalk), averaging about 100 feet in thickness. In Norfolk, the Gault is replaced round Hunstanton by a gritty, red, fossiliferous limestone, formerly called the 'Red Chalk' but now distinguished as the Red Rock. The Chalk itself, which follows these deposits with remarkable abruptness, is divided into three series, the Lower, Middle and Upper, the boundaries between them being marked by slight lithological changes and their fossil contents. They vary in relative thickness in different parts of the country, but the total maximum is about 1,580 feet. Fig. 18 shows a generalized section.

The basal beds of the Lower Chalk, being the first to be laid down, are mixed with a considerable amount of clay and sand gathered from the neighbouring lands by the advancing Chalk Sea. Right at the bottom they contain as much as 50 per cent of extraneous

---

* The chief gaps are occupied by the rivers Wey, Mole, Darent, Medway, Adur and Arun.

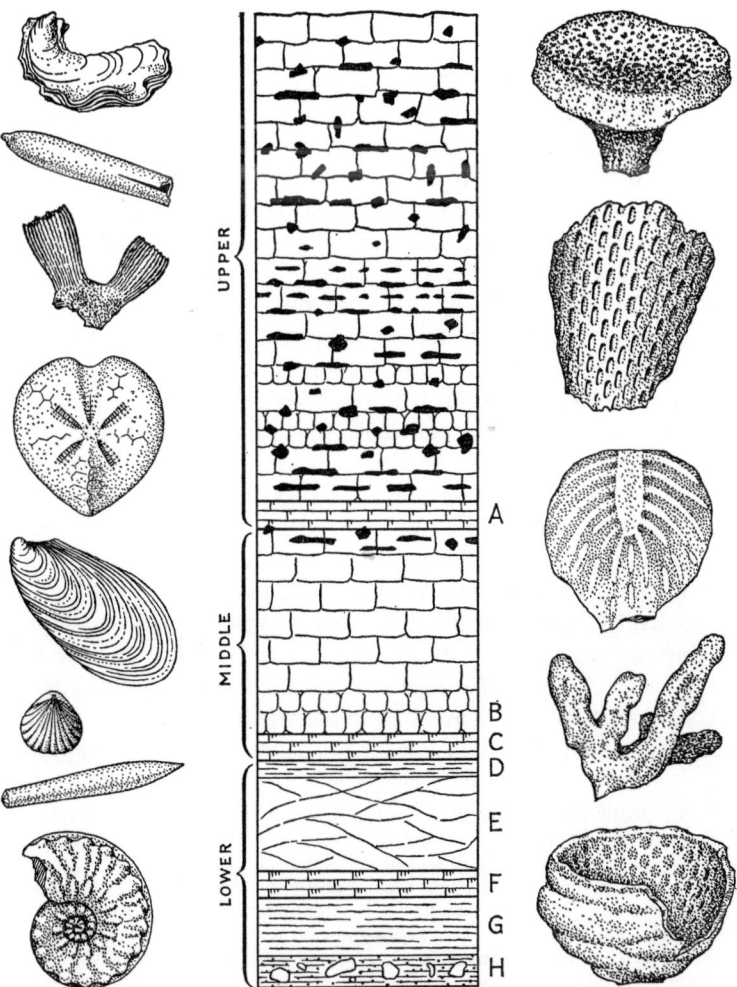

FIG. 18. A generalized section through the English Chalk, showing the occurrence of the flint. The proportions vary greatly in different localities, the Upper Chalk being often twice as deep as here shown. A, Chalk Rock. B, Nodular chalk. C, Melbourn Rock. D, *Plenus* (or Belemnite) Marls. E, Grey Chalk. F, Totternhoe Stone. G, Chalk Marl. H, Glauconitic ('Chloritic') Marl. Of the typical Chalk fossils illustrated, those on the right are all sponges. (The names of the fossils are given in Appendix III.)

material, including the mineral glauconite and phosphatic nodules*. Above this comes a zone called the Chalk Marl, in which the proportion of clay grows steadily less. Where there is still about 30 per cent of clay, the Chalk Marl is used for making cement by simply grinding and roasting it, but at higher levels the necessary clay has to be supplied from other sources.

The greater part of the Lower Chalk consists of a massive grey chalk, sometimes with a pinkish tinge, containing at its base a hard nodular band known as the Totternhoe Stone. This was once widely used for building, especially in the interiors of churches, and many examples survive, even in London†. The top of the Lower Chalk is marked by another belt of marl, containing fossil belemnites. Nodules of marcasite occur sporadically through the Lower Chalk but, except for occasional nodules in the Chalk Marl, there are no flints. The Lower Chalk is therefore sometimes called the 'Grey Chalk without Flints', but since its most distinctive fossils are ammonites it is also known as the 'Ammonite Chalk'.

The Middle Chalk begins with another hard band, called the Melbourn Rock, which has also been used for interior building. This is succeeded by bedded shelly chalk containing calcite crystals representing the fragments of *Inoceramus* and other shells. Above this comes a thick layer of massive white chalk containing scattered brachiopod shells, which are used to identify it. Right at the top are a few seams of marl and, in some regions only, the first flints appear.

---

* Phosphatic nodules are hard, rounded concretions of small or moderate size, generally grey or black. They consist of clay or fine rock-fragments cemented together by calcium phosphate and sometimes contain fossils. They frequently show borings by marine organisms and evidently spent long periods on the sea-floor. The source of their phosphorus is unknown, but similar nodules being formed today off some Pacific islands appear to derive phosphates from guano (bird excreta) and possibly the skeletons of dead birds. Fish excreta, dead fish and decayed seaweed could all provide phosphates, and nodules could be formed by the break-up of a hardened bed of cemented ooze, but it is not known that this occurs. Some or most of the phosphate may very well have a magmatic origin, as described on page 59, but its concentration into nodules probably implies the initial presence of nuclei of organic origin.

† For example, in the cloisters leading from Dean's Yard at Westminster Abbey, in the crypt of St. Saviour's, Southwark, and in parts of the outer walls of the Tower of London. The old builders' name for this and the other chalk building-stones mentioned below is 'clunch', a term used also by miners in the north of England for any hard, stiff or lumpy clay.

They sometimes assume a tabular form but are not very abundant, so that the Middle Chalk is often referred to as the 'White Chalk without Flints', or the 'Brachiopod Chalk'.

The Upper Chalk begins with the hard nodular band known as the Chalk Rock, often yellowish but containing glauconite grains and green-coated phosphatic nodules[35]. This is the third and last of the chalk building-stones. It is followed by massive white chalk with abundant nodular and tabular flint, containing fossil sea-urchins of the genus *Micraster*. Above this comes a white chalk with seams of marl (often pinkish or yellowish) and rather less flint, but with fossil belemnites. Both ammonites and belemnites became extinct during the deposition of the Upper Chalk, which is sometimes called the 'White Chalk with Flints' and is roughly divided into '*Micraster* Chalk' and 'Belemnite Chalk'. The highest zone of the English Chalk is present only in Norfolk and the Isle of Wight, and is distinguished by a fossil oyster, but in Denmark this appears near the base of the cliffs with several hundred feet of younger chalk above it.

The distribution of the exposed Chalk in England (see Figs. 16 and 68) may be seen detailed in the maps published by the Geological Survey, in which the Lower, Middle and Upper Chalk are distinguished by different shades of green and the code letters $h^{5'}$, $h^{5''}$ and $h^{5'''}$, respectively. Similar maps are obtainable in most other countries.

3

The Segregation of Flint

THERE SEEMS NO room for doubt that a vast number of flints consist of the silica which was once dissolved in the waters of the ancient Chalk Sea around 80 million years ago. Much of this silica was secreted organically as sponge spicules and deposited on the sea-floor as the sponges died. Some was possibly precipitated by other means, but eventually it constituted about 1·4 per cent of the bottom ooze. But flint itself occurs in the form of heavy stones embedded in the Chalk limestone at more or less distinct levels. In the original deposit the silica was opaline or colloidal in character, but in the flints it is micro-crystalline. The great mystery of when and how these changes took place is known as the 'segregation of flint', but of the many explanations suggested none can be regarded as definitely established.

The proposed theories fall into three groups. Those which assume that the silica was deposited as gelatinous lumps on the Chalk Sea floor are described as 'syngenetic'; those which consider that the silica gathered into lumps much later in the deeper layers below the sea-floor, where the ooze was gradually being changed into chalk, are called 'penecontemporaneous' theories; and those which attribute flint to the action of water percolating through the Chalk after it had been raised high and dry above sea-level are denoted 'epigenetic'[27].

Syngenetic theories

A hundred years ago it was widely assumed that all flints are simply fossilized siliceous sponges, some squashed out of shape but others still recognizable. To explain why flints often occur in well-marked bands in the Chalk, Richard Owen (1804–1892) suggested that there

SYNGENETIC THEORIES

must have been a bumper crop of sponges on the Chalk Sea floor every 600 years, the intervals being comparatively barren. This was the first syngenetic theory, but it was little more than a general idea tied to a ridiculously inadequate time-scale. Since then, a number of much more plausible theories have been proposed, some making no special reference to sponges, but others regarding them as the chief source of the silica or at least as causing its precipitation. The extremely slow rate of deposition of the chalk ooze must certainly have allowed large quantities of sponge spicules to accumulate in some areas, like the carpet of dead pine-needles in a forest. Here and there, the united network of a complete skeleton might survive, and some have certainly been preserved in flint. The delicacy and fragility of such structures is held to imply that they must have received some sort of protection long before they could possibly have become covered by the ooze. This protection is presumed to have been afforded by the jelling around them of silica thrown out of solution in the sea-water.

This type of theory maintains (with variations—and even contradictions—of detail) that as soon as the flesh of a dead sponge began to decay, it produced ammonia and other substances which reacted with the silica in the sea-water. Some accounts of the process require the ammonia to cause precipitation of the silica, but this must be in error because the solution of silica has been shown experimentally to be substantially increased by the presence of ammonia[43]. Other accounts more reasonably invoke ammonia to facilitate the solution of the opaline silica of the surrounding sponge spicules and so produce exceptionally strong concentrations.

Silica in a strong solution forms a colloidal 'sol', in which the particles of silica are not individual molecules or ions but small clumps of molecules joined to water molecules and held in suspension. Assuming that sufficiently strong solutions exist in the sea, these clumps of molecules would eventually coagulate by the electrolytic action of the dissolved salts in the water, forming particles large enough to sink to the bottom like particles of mud. But in the neighbourhood of sponges or other living organisms it is supposed that the coagulation was inhibited by the presence of other substances —perhaps organic colloids—so that the water locally became supersaturated with silica.

This heavier 'silica-sol' would sink to the bottom and, when the inhibiting agents were removed or ceased to be supplied, the excess silica would be rapidly precipitated*. It would come down as 'silica-gel', or jelly-like lumps of silica impregnated with water. In the spongebeds it would settle over and around sponges of all kinds on the bottom, thickening and strengthening their delicate skeletons in some places but forming structureless clumps in others. It would fill brachiopod shells and sea-urchin tests, and eventually become buried. Finally, it would slowly lose water under the increasing pressure and harden into cryptocrystalline lumps of flint.

This type of theory was proposed in general terms by W. A. Tarr in 1917[28] and again in 1926[29]. He assumed the source of the silica in the sea to be the rivers flowing over siliceous rocks and that, after 'considerable dispersion', it was precipitated by 'alkalic salts' in more or less globular lumps. A more sophisticated version was published in 1949 by Henning Illies[30], who suggested the formation of oxidizing and reducing layers near the surface of the ooze, and the precipitation of the silica at the interface between them. He further maintained that clay would prevent the deposition of free silica by adsorbing it, and that the silica could therefore be deposited only where there was insufficient clay to bind it. The general—but not universal—absence of flints from the marly bands is cited as evidence that this is what happened.

This type of theory would certainly account for much of what has been observed, and particularly for the preservation of delicate sponge skeletons and such marvels as fossil brachiopod shells in which the positions of the larger muscles can be traced by slight colour-changes in the flint. In such cases, the silica must have been deposited before the muscle tissues had decayed. These shells were reported from Germany, but there is good reason to believe that the

* Another suggestion attributes the required excess of silica to submarine vulcanicity, though W. A. Richardson[40] objected that magmatic sources were excluded from the English Chalk because there was no vulcanicity in the British area. However, R. Casey suggested in 1968 (in a Special Lecture to the Geologists' Association, entitled *Four Dimensions of the Cretaceous*) that vast quantities of silica could have been poured into the sea during the opening up of the North Atlantic Ocean by volcanic action along the mid-Atlantic Ridge, and then carried over north-west Europe by ocean currents for which there is independent evidence in the contemporaneous distribution of phosphates. (See page 59.)

occasional deposition of gelatinous silica on the sea-floor has more than once preserved similar delicate tissues in formations other than the Chalk.

Evidence of the oldest known examples was found quite recently in pre-Cambrian formations about 3,000 million years old* in Africa and nearly 2,000 million years old† in Canada. It was gathered by Elso S. Barghoorn[131], working with J. William Schopf, from the Fig Tree cherts in the Transvaal and the Gunflint cherts in Ontario. Both these cherts contain microscopic fossil plants (primitive Algae and bacteria) preserved 'much as a modern biological specimen is preserved by being embedded in plastic'. Even the soft tissues (now hard silica) still stand in their three-dimensional arrangements, while there are single plant-cells showing internal details when magnified 2,500 diameters, and bacteria which still have clear outlines when magnified 30,000 diameters in an electron microscope.

It seems that there is no plausible alternative to the view that these delicate plants were first completely surrounded and penetrated by water rich in silica, and that they were then fairly rapidly 'fixed' by the silica's setting to a gel and holding them fast. 'The process of deposition had emplaced the organic material within a silica-rich matrix before the silica was crystallized into chert. There was no evidence whatever that the silica was of secondary origin'.‡

Well, if this sort of thing could have happened when the earth was little more than 1,500 million years old, is there any reason why it should not have happened time and again through the next 2,900 million years? A totally different kind of evidence that flint was formed in the Chalk in very much this way was offered by R. M. Brydone[31] as long ago as 1920, and his interpretation of it is still regarded as worthy of consideration, if not beyond question. It has, indeed, been invoked to explain the brachiopod shells referred to above, and the reader may substitute 'brachiopod' for 'sea-urchin' in the following paragraphs without invalidating the argument.

Brydone pointed out that the Chalk contains some millions of

---

* By radioactive dating of contemporaneous rocks.
† By radioactive dating of micas in overlying rocks.
‡ That is to say, there is no reason to believe that the fossils were first preserved in some other material and that this was later replaced, molecule by molecule, by silica (as has sometimes happened with the wood of trees).

fossil sea-urchin tests of the genus *Echinocorys*, and that many of these are entirely filled with chalk while others are entirely filled with flint. The tests have only two small openings, a mouth and a vent, and could have been filled only by a thin liquid or semi-liquid such as the chalk ooze or soft gelatinous silica.

As soon as a sea-urchin died and decomposed, its test—if it is now filled with flint—must have received its silica then and there. Otherwise, it would certainly have become quickly occupied by the chalk ooze. It could not have been first filled with chalk, and this later replaced by silica, for in tests which contain both chalk and flint the demarcation between them is always sharp and complete, and there is no sign of sporadic silicification in the chalk.

At first sight this is a very convincing argument, but when it is examined more closely it appears less plausible. Plate III shows several typical flint echinoderms as they are found in the Chalk, and they usually occur thus unattached to extraneous masses of flint. Think what this means. To fill their tests thus cleanly with silica in the manner described by Brydone, a small funnel would be needed and means provided to cut off the supply the moment they were exactly full to prevent overspill. It is impossible to picture anything like this happening on the bottom of the Chalk Sea.

The only reasonable possibility would seem to be the rapid chemical precipitation of silica directly from the sea-water by some substance produced by the decay of the sea-urchin's body, for this would be confined to the interior of the test provided it were resting upside-down. But it is very doubtful that there could have been anything like enough silica available in the water for rapid precipitation, or that there would be enough of the precipitating agent unless initiation of the process is all that was required. If this was so, however, a gentle infiltration of silica-charged water could be allowed to continue for a very long time because of the extremely slow deposition of the chalk ooze, but absolute stillness of the bottom water would have to prevail to prevent the entry of adventitious chalk. This is perhaps the least incredible view to take if a syngenetical deposition of this 'confined' flint is insisted on.

Sea-urchins in flint are sometimes found attached to, or forming part of, a large nodule, as illustrated in Plate IV. The nodule here is clearly not an overflow, but we may wonder whether this sea-urchin got caught in a blob of silica-gel while wandering about on the sea-floor. However, sea-urchins crawl very slowly indeed, and though the record speed among living urchins is about 1 inch per second[37], the usual rate is more like 1/20 inch per second or 3 inches per minute. It therefore seems very unlikely that an urchin afoot could ever get fatally entangled in a blob of silica-gel. It is more likely that a dead and empty test wafted by currents came to rest on a blob of silica-gel, or that the gel formed accidentally over a derelict test, and such events may very well have happened sometimes, especially if a fairly wholesale precipitation of silica was taking place.

The evidence offered in support of this group of theories does suggest that a great many flints did have a syngenetic origin, but at the same time the somewhat delicate balance of conditions required is unlikely to have been maintained continuously on a world-wide scale for some thirty million years. It is more reasonable to suggest that there were waves of excessive silica-precipitation at intervals, and that the flints found in chalk belonging to the barren periods had a different origin. There are, in fact, six good reasons why this type of theory cannot be invoked as an exclusive or even general explanation of the occurrence of flints in the Chalk.

First, one might expect the process to be taking place on at least some areas of the present sea-floor, but not a single case has ever been observed. The natural rejoinder to this objection is that the crust of the earth is at present quiescent and the oceans are not at the moment receiving excessive floods of silica from magmatic sources. But that is to admit that special—not general—conditions are necessary.

Second, when sponge skeletons are preserved in flint they are invariably of either the 'united' or the 'interlocked' kinds, and no reason has been offered to show why the looser skeletons are not also sometimes preserved. If the silica is so deposited that it can replace and preserve soft tissues like the muscles of brachiopods and the cells of Algae *in situ*, without disturbing them, it ought also to enshrine the loose spicules of Monaxonid and Choristid sponges in their original positions.

Third, whereas loose spicules are not notably plentiful in the layers of chalk which contain abundant flints, they are most numerous in layers which are completely devoid of flint. It may be noted that not all forms of the theory lay particular emphasis on sponges, yet they cannot be ignored for they were easily the most abundant siliceous organisms to decay on the Chalk Sea floor.

Fourth, if flints were formed on the sea-floor they ought always to occur in layers parallel with the bedding of the Chalk, but in fact the layers frequently cut through the bedding at an angle which is often steep and may be a right-angle. Tarr explained this by postulating deep fissures in the Chalk Sea floor which afterwards closed up, but there is not the remotest evidence of any such fissures. The flints are found in quite characteristic faults and joints in the rock, which could not have been produced until after the ooze had been consolidated and the folding of the strata begun. (See Plate I.)

Fifth, the pressure of overlying oceans and sediments would not have been nearly great enough to squeeze out the water from the silica-gel and convert it into flint. (See page 76.) However, not all forms of the theory rely upon pressure to accomplish this. The material in which the delicate fossils already referred to were embedded could hardly have lost its water by being squeezed, but no other way has yet been suggested of getting rid of water without loss of volume, or of replacing the water by more silica.

Sixth, the syngenetic theories all require silica to be precipitated from solution by the presence of ions (see page 98) of some kind in the sea-water, but in 1960 G. Millot[129] showed that this sort of thing could not normally happen with any likely concentration of silica in natural water. The reasons he gives are based on experiments with silica solutions and the actual concentrations found in natural water. (See Appendices I and II.) It turns out that the strength of the solutions occurring in nature is far too low for the silica to form a colloid, and that the dissolved silica is not in any way affected by ions, and in particular by the ions in sea-water. Even with excessive supplies from temporary magmatic sources, the necessary concentrations (around 0·012 per cent) are extremely unlikely to occur.

There is thus no reason for supposing that the precipitation of silica-gel on the sea-floor was ever a common phenomenon, and if we feel obliged to allow it in the cases of the Fig Tree and Gunflint cherts, and some of the fossiliferous flint in the Chalk, we should suspect that the local or temporal conditions were anomalous. But we should look at this word 'anomalous' for a moment and see what it implies in the geological time-scale, for it by no means implies that syngenetic flints should be regarded as rarities.

If a set of conditions holds good through 99 per cent of a period, but is interfered with by odd factors during only 1 per cent, we should be justified in referring to the 1 per cent state of affairs as 'anomalous'. Now, by way of example, consider the period during which the Chalk was deposited. If this totalled 35 million years, then we might have anomalies occurring during a total of 350,000 years. If each occurrence required no more than 1,000 years for initiation and climax, the climax being a sudden dumping of gelatinous silica, we could still have 350 'crops' of syngenetic flints!

Now, if there were a band of flint every 10 feet through 3,000 feet of the Chalk (which there is not), that would make only 300 bands and our 350 'crops' would be more than enough to account for all the flints. But there are nothing like 300 bands of flint, and some bands are very wide apart, the volumes between them often containing scattered flints which an anomaly of credible duration could not explain. These conceptual difficulties, together with the other five 'objections', dictate a smaller role for syngenesis than its advocates have claimed.

Penecontemporaneous theories

The general basis of the early theories of this type is that as the Chalk ooze became more and more deeply buried, the water in it was squeezed out but the particles of colloidal silica presumed to be suspended in it remained behind. That at least some colloidal silica is always present in sea-water was never doubted, but even if there were none, that would not necessarily rule out a penecontemporaneous origin for flint. In fact, any process leading to the concentration of silica in the ooze itself could lead to the *subsequent* formation of colloidal particles, so that some of these theories might need only a small time adjustment to make them true.

It is, in fact, maintained by some that the masses of silica sponge skeletons on the Chalk Sea floor would have produced a much less pure limestone had not the silica become segregated into lumps before the ooze consolidated. And this might well have happened a foot or two below the surface of the ooze by the steady solution of the opaline spicules in the static water at that level. A sort of slow fusing together and final jellification of clumps of spicules can be pictured, but this is perhaps too fanciful, even if we suppose unlimited time to accomplish what can never be achieved in the laboratory.

'Clumping' of some sort must have occurred if this type of theory is to explain nodular flint. It has been suggested that irregularities in the texture of the ooze, such as those caused by the currents responsible for the nodular chalk, and by the occurrence of incidental beds of shells, chemical residues from decayed organisms, uncollapsed burrows and boreholes, etc., could conceivably result in local accumulations of the silica which might eventually become flint nodules.

A modification of this idea is that at a somewhat greater depth below the sea-floor, the pressure would be sufficiently great to cause the complete solution of the sponge spicules, forming locally concentrated or even supersaturated solutions of silica. Two possibilities would then follow, the first being that as burial continued and the pressure still further increased, the water-content would be reduced and the silca redeposited. The second is that the silica would also be deposited if the pressure were relieved, and this certainly happened when the Chalk was finally raised above the sea.

These ideas were, perhaps, worth considering when the Chalk Sea was presumed to be a deep ocean, but the solubility of siliceous structures does not increase appreciably in sea-water until the pressure is something like 4 tons per square inch. This implies a depth of about 24,000 feet, or twenty-five times as great as modern estimates of the maximum depth of the Chalk Sea*. Further, R. S. Dean[32] showed by experiments with several colloids that water can be squeezed out of them only by pressures ranging from 40 to 67 tons per square inch. Nothing like this pressure could ever have occurred in the Chalk, even at the very bottom of the ooze where it was thickest, either before or after its elevation above the sea. Such pressures occur normally in the crust of the earth only at depths exceeding 25 or 30 miles.

But, however the silica is supposed to have been deposited in the consolidating ooze, some flint was—according to these theories—

---

* At the present time, the siliceous tests forming the Radiolarian ooze vanish by solution at about 24,000 feet.

still being formed when the earth-movements responsible for raising the sea-bed began. This, it is suggested, accounts for the occurrence of flint along joints and fracture-planes without reference to the bedding. The occurrence of tabular flint and bands of nodules parallel with the bedding are accounted for by periodic variations in the composition of the original ooze, resulting in lithological changes along the bedding-planes in the hardened rock.

This type of theory supposes that most of the flints in the Chalk had been formed long before the end of the major period of uplift, and R. Liesegang considered that the precipitation of flint was a direct consequence of the draining of the sea-water out of the chalk as it rose. F. M. Van Tuyl[33] came to similar conclusions with silica deposited in limestones as chert, but arguing from the evidence of fossils and especially silicified corals, he favoured a replacement of the calcium carbonate by silica, molecule for molecule rather than simple deposition.

William Hill[4] thought that the formation of flint began in a partly consolidated ooze saturated with silica in colloidal solution. It was solid enough to permit the preservation of moulds of sponge spicules but was still beneath the sea. Flints were formed as the Chalk rose and sea-water was replaced by rain-water. This happened 'not long after the elevation of the Chalk', but more silica was deposited on the flints in later times. (See Appendix VI.)

The chief weakness of all these theories is that they rely on somewhat artificial afterthoughts to explain the segregation of the silica into nodules, and they really are not nearly as good as the syngenetic theories at explaining the preservation of delicate tissues. We should expect from them a more general deposition of silica throughout the Chalk, as a sort of gritty impurity, and local occurrences of this kind —with intriguing variations—have certainly been found.

The classic example was discovered by A. J. Jukes-Browne and W. Hill[34] in the Lower Chalk of Berkshire and Wiltshire, where minute globules of opal occur scattered through the rock. There were also some 'hard, bluish-grey nodules with an earthy fracture quite different from that of flint'. In their opinion, 'this globular silica was precipitated from solution before the consolidation of the beds, and while they were still permeated by sea-water'. They attributed this to 'organic agencies', adding that: 'It seemed clear to us that the precipitation of the chalcedonic silica of the cherty nodules was a secondary and subsequent operation' (left unexplained).

The view has also been expressed by many writers that the nodules, and even the opaline globules, are merely incipient flints and might have grown into typical black nodules had more silica (or more time) been available[4]. There is certainly abundant evidence that flints grow by the accretion of silica and were not necessarily of their present sizes when first formed. This will be further discussed in the following sections.

R. G. Bromley[6] also seems to favour a penecontemporaneous origin, suggesting that the majority of flints were formed in the soft infillings of crustacean burrows by some process of silicification of the chalk. The *effect* of this would be just the solution and removal of the chalk, and its simultaneous replacement by deposited silica, but though the process could not occur in that simple fashion it need not necessarily demand the precipitation of colloids. Some possible processes of chemical silicification are discussed on pages 97 ff. and in Appendix VI.

Bromley points out that all stages or degrees of silicification are to be found in the crustacean burrows, from a soft siliceous 'grit' to whole flint nodules. Since the burrows were often bored and inhabited after the sea-floor had been consolidated and hardened, their soft chalk infillings must have arrived even later, and the siliceous nodules have been formed yet later still.

On this theory, flints could not be merely hardened lumps of silica-gel formed on or in the sea-floor ooze, but must have grown from imperceptible beginnings at random sites within the burrows. The soft chalk filling these was washed in as ooze and provided excellent 'packing' for the delicate organisms carried in with it. Thus, the rapid silicification required by the syngenetic theories for the safe preservation of fine detail would not be necessary*. Protected from currents and other disturbances in the hardground burrows, silicification could proceed at a much more plausible rate.

It occurred, however, while the Chalk was still submerged, because

* It would, though! The finest tissues preserved in flint could not possibly survive packing in soft chalk, though this theory would probably be adequate to account for the preservation of intricate sponge skeletons and explain why the loose spicules of inarticulated sponges are always found scattered.

some flints bear on their surfaces flint casts of the tubes left in the ooze by the probing tentacles of marine organisms. These 'trace-fossils' (*Chondrites*) often indicate that tubes which follow the surface of a flint run straight off into the surrounding chalk (though they are not traceable there). This implies that the tentacles probing the ooze beneath the Chalk Sea floor found the flints already present and blocking their way. If this interpretation is correct, it is a persuasive argument for the penecontemporaneous origin of a great many flints.

Evidence which it is difficult to reconcile with either the syngenetic or penecontemporaneous theories is afforded by specimens like that shown at the top of Plate XI. Here is a flint nodule which has clearly been formed round a large piece of a thick *Inoceramus* shell, the edge of which is visible as the broken white band crossing it. The shell runs right through the nodule and shows again on the other side, but it has been completely replaced by flint and now forms an integral part of the nodule. The significant details are the short white strokes crossing the band, for they indicate the cleavage-panes of the calcite crystals into which the original shell must have been transformed before silicification took place. Several of the strokes, especially where the shell has obviously been broken, are perfectly straight and form accurately measurable angles with the surface of the shell. In every case the angle is 78°, which is exactly the *apparent* cleavage angle for rhombohedral calcite when a crystal is broken and laid flat on one face*.

Now, the transformation of the substance of the original shell into rhombohedral calcite almost certainly required some few millions of years, for other fossil shells in limestones known to be at least 20 million years old still show their original laminar structure and are often still nacreous. It therefore seems very unlikely that this flint nodule could have been completely formed in Cretaceous times, and perhaps it was not formed at all until the Tertiary era was well advanced.

Attempts to explain away this implication by a fantastic curtailment of the time required for the crystallization have not been

---

* The angle as measured in a plane at right-angles to the edge at which the adjacent faces meet is 75°, but there is no way of obtaining this angle in the specimen referred to.

convincing. The heavy *Inoceramus* shell may have taken a shorter time than other shells to crystallize, but hardly a short enough time to complete the job on the contemporary sea-bed. That it could have been done in anything like as little time as that required to envelop a sponge skeleton in jelly or 'fix' a brachiopod muscle is quite out of the question, and this alone removes this particular nodule from the ambit of that kind of theory.

Epigenetic theories

A type of theory for which much of the evidence is very difficult to deny assumes that the Chalk was formed with its embedded sponge spicules intact and unaltered, and that the major deposition of flint happened after it was raised high above sea-level. As it emerged, it was subject to percolation by rain and river-water, and any trace of sea-water or sea-salts it may have contained was contemporaneously leached out.

It thus appeared as a nearly pure and more or less homogeneous limestone, and the only silica it contained (apart from the scattered sand-grains in some areas) was in the form of opaline spicules. Rain and ground-water continued to percolate and very slowly dissolved the silica of the spicules from the upper layers, redepositing it as cryptocrystalline silica lower down in layers at definite levels or along planes of weakness. The hollow moulds of spicules which have been removed in this way from the Upper Chalk, and even from the Middle Chalk, have often been found[35,36].

That the silica in flint is derived from sponge spicules was first suggested in 1905 by W. J. Sollas[36], and it is regarded as significant that the amount of soluble silica in the Chalk varies inversely as the amount of flint. Further, the proportion of total silica increases on the whole (there are reversals in detail) from the top of the English Upper Chalk down to the base of the Lower Chalk, where it is from ten to thirty times as abundant. The average percentages of soluble silica in the English Chalk have been estimated at various levels for comparison with the percentages of silica as flint, and W. A. Richardson[40] gives the results shown in Fig. 19. It will be seen that the flint disappears just where the soluble silica begins to increase rapidly. Though R. M. Brydone has objected that Richardson's data were

PLATE IX. Fossil sponges in flint, about natural size. *Above: Raphidonema. Below: Siphonia koenigi.*

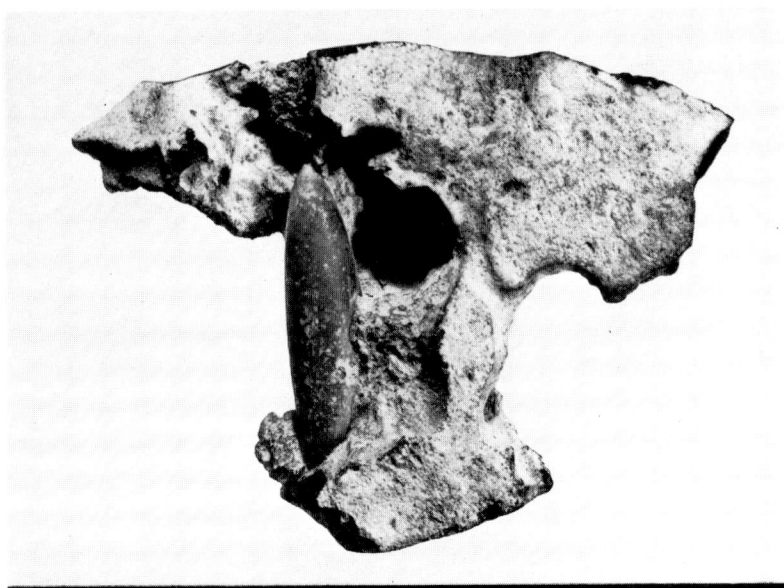

PLATE X. *Above:* A rotted or desilicified flint from the debris of an old chalk-pit, containing the fossil belemnite *Gonioteuthis quadrata* (*Actinocamax quadratus*) preserved in calcite. *Below:* A large flint nodule enclosing tunnels which probably represent the burrows of small crustaceans.

too meagre, the diagram is nevertheless interesting as showing the sort of distribution that has been found in at least some regions.

The occurrence of sponge spicules in the meal inside hollow flints is of no significance in this diagram because the total quantity is

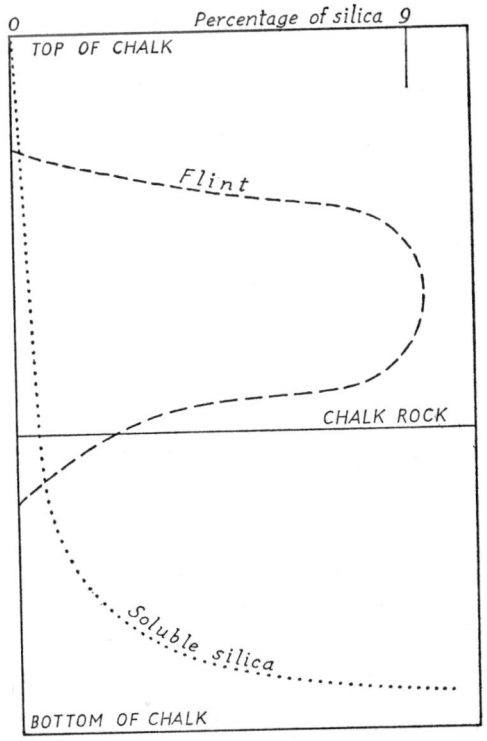

FIG. 19. The relation between the percentage of flint and soluble silica in the English Chalk, according to W. A. Richardson.

negligible in comparison, but it has been observed that the spicules are very much more abundant inside such flints than outside. As many as forty species have been found in a single nodule (from Norfolk), and on the back of the 'lion's head' in Plate II there is a small hollow containing more than twenty spicules, all converted to flint and forming part of the cortex of the nodule.

THE SEGREGATION OF FLINT

A problem of another kind is to explain why the flints in the Chalk show widely different degrees of cortication in different regions and at different levels. For example, in parts of Hampshire the flints of the *Micraster cortestudinarium* zone have very much thinner rinds than those of the succeeding *M. coranguinum* and *Marsupites testudinarius* zones. In the zone of *Gonioteuthis quadrata* (*Actinocamax quadratus*), which lies higher still, there are some bands of flints showing remarkably thick rinds, but above them, in the same zone there are flints showing the merest film of cortication[14]. There are thin-skinned flints again in the higher zone of *Belemnitella mucronata*, but thick-rinded flints occur in the same zone a few miles away[52].

Such characteristics are generally consistent throughout any particular locality, but comparison between localities does not suggest any direct association between the degree of cortication and the lithology of the beds. It is at any rate clear that the thickness of the cortex has nothing to do with the chronological succession of the strata, and it is more natural to suppose that flints showing wide differences in the degree of cortication are of different ages, and that these are independent of the age of the chalk in which they are found. But it is also possible that flints of the same age may show differences because of local variations in the supply of silica, with consequent differences in their rates of development. That variations in the supply of silica have frequently occurred can be inferred from at least some types of 'inclusion' (page 23) and 'zoning' (page 88). It is not unreasonable to assume that flints grow as black (or grey) nodules until the supply of silica runs out, and that then the process of cortication begins.

However, there is another possibility. This is that a flint nodule begins as a small, friable white nucleus composed of grains of silica, and that this next becomes rigid by cementation with new waterborne silica penetrating inwards into the nodule. The water finally locked inside produces first a grey and then a black core. If this is true, we should talk of the 'nigrification' of white flints rather than of the 'cortication' of black ones, at any rate regarding the early stages of formation. Cortication by 'drying out' certainly occurs in soil-flints, and it is likely that loss of water alternates with periods of water-absorption, even in the same nodule, according to the ambient conditions. (This will be discussed further in connection with 'zoning'.)

EPIGENETIC THEORIES

The evidence of epigenesis is extensive and various, but before more is offered the reader should be warned against the assumption that there is only one 'correct' theory and that, when found, it must automatically exclude all others*. Circumstances alter cases, and the most that science can usually say of any discovered process is that 'this is evidently the sort of thing which happens as a general rule', for it is almost a fundamental law of nature that anything which conceivably *can* happen *has* happened—somewhere or at some time.

If we examine the objections raised to the syngenetic and penecontemporaneous theories, we shall see that they apply to separate and limited aspects of them, and are competent only to discount their universal validity. It may well be, therefore, that the processes they describe have all taken place in some localities or at some levels. Again, it is possible that flints which were engendered by one process were later added to by another, and some of the evidence cited for epigenesis may be accounted for in this way. This evidence is concerned with the fact that the flint in different parts of the same nodule is often clearly of different ages.

Oakley[27] draws attention to the fact that flints are sometimes found to have been broken and then cemented together again with fresh flint, and that other flints have clearly been added to since their first formation as hard nodules. Again, a secondary thickening of the outer surfaces of flints is sometimes observed, while the tubular hollows in some flints may be lined or even filled with successive layers of flint which are quite distinguishable. Some unusual flints observed by William Hill[4] at Ballard Cliff, in Dorset, show a pinkish-white layer covering the black core *beneath* the cortex, but how this came about it anybody's guess.

These curious facts, and others described in the section on *Secondary silica* at the end of this chapter, suggest that the traditional belief that flints 'grow' is based on observation older than the science of geology, and sometimes very convincing specimens are found. For

---

* Many examples could be given of mineral specimens which are quite indistinguishable, yet are known to have totally different origins. For example, the orthoclase felspar formed chemically in the Chalk of the Paris Basin is in no way different from that of igneous origin found in the granite of Dartmoor. On the other hand, the flints from different regions may vary considerably, and to demand that *these* must all have been formed in the same way seems a little rash, particularly when that 'same way' is still a mystery!

THE SEGREGATION OF FLINT

example, Plate XI shows an 'agate-skinned' or 'agate-rinded' flint in which a thick rind has been added to an old core with a distinct surface of its own. This is traceable beneath the rind on the broken surface of the nodule by a slight but sudden change of colour from black to dark brown. A pale narrow line separating the colours suggests that the core was thinly corticated before the rind was added.

The additional growth may have taken place in three or more stages, the division between them being indicated by the thin black lines visible in the photograph, though these could have a different interpretation. They appear to cut across inclusions in the new flint and may therefore have been produced after the rind was formed by an inward diffusion of water. Clearly-demarcated layers or courses of this kind are frequently called 'zones' and such terms as 'onyx-zoning' or 'agate-zoning' are sometimes used to describe this sort of phenomenon. It is discussed further on page 88.

In whatever way new flint is added to old, a distinction should be made between a primary nodule and all subsequent additions to it, for the deposition of the secondary flint may have been caused in a completely different way. For example, it could conceivably be greatly facilitated by, and perhaps wholly dependent upon, the presence of an already-formed nucleus. Any such nucleus might be expected to grow if washed in a solution of silica, much as crystals will grow readily in solutions of their own substance, and this principle is invoked in one form or another in all the epigenetic theories. It could certainly account more plausibly than Brydone's theory (page 71) for the neat and exact filling of sea-urchin tests with flint, for they may often contain siliceous nuclei when there are none in the immediately surrounding chalk.

Not only do sea-urchins eat sponges (among other things)[37] and thus accumulate spicules not easily got rid of, but their tests, though mainly calcareous, contain about 0·13 per cent of silica[38]. Other modern echinoderms (sea lilies, starfish) contain up to 0·64 per cent of silica and the Cretaceous sea-urchins may have been more siliceous than the modern species since they lived on a sea-bottom bearing vast sponge-beds through many millions of years of their evolution. Further, sea-urchin tests are comparatively rich in the sesquioxides of iron and aluminium[38], and these substances can remove silica from solution very effectively by adsorption (Appendix II).

EPIGENETIC THEORIES

Another general observation said to favour an epigenetic deposition of flint relates to its broad-scale distribution with reference to water-levels in the Chalk. Chalk is pervious to water, and rain falling on chalk hills penetrates through the pores, fissures and cavities to a great depth. Here it disperses slowly, replacing water lost elsewhere

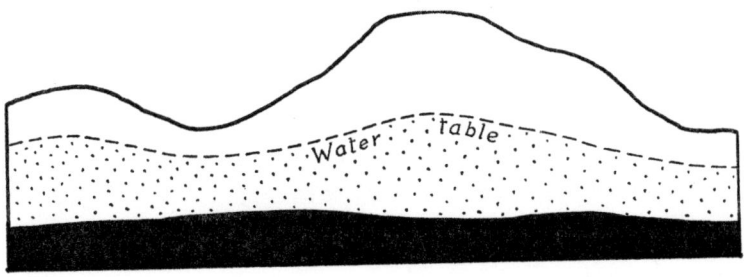

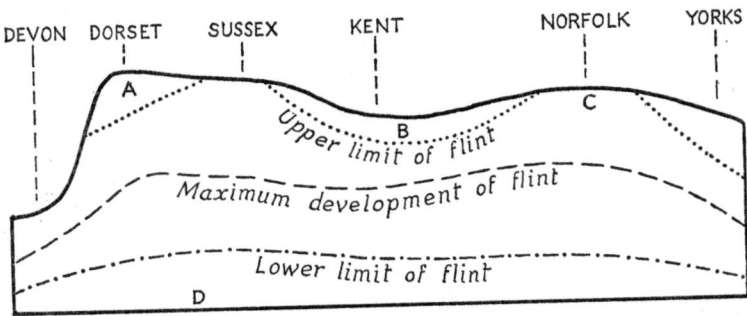

FIG. 20. *Above:* The form of a typical water-table in a hill. Wells sunk below this level will always contain water. *Below:* A generalized section of the English Chalk on a traverse running from Devon to Kent to Yorkshire, showing the levels of occurrence of flint. The zones in the Chalk are identified at A, *Belemnitella mucronata;* B, *Gonioteuthis quadrata (Actinocamax quadratus);* C, *Liostrea lunata (Ostrea lunata);* D, *Schloenbachia varians.* (*After* W. A. Richardson.)

through springs and by surface evaporation, but at a certain depth the average supply keeps pace with the average loss and there is a permanent 'reservoir' of water. Wells and bore-holes are sunk to this level—called the 'water-table'—to obtain water-supplies. It is well established that the water-table in undulating country is not level, but to some extent mimics the surface contours, as shown in Fig. 20

THE SEGREGATION OF FLINT

(*top*). It rises and falls with the seasons, the average fluctuation in a typical area (in England) being of the order of 40 feet[39]. Its form is not always satisfactorily explained by dispersion and evaporation from the surface, particularly where it stands at a great depth, but this is another question. (See Appendix IV.)

Below the lowest level, the chalk remains permanently saturated with water, and wherever there is water a great deal of it is held in the pores of the rock by capillary attraction. Because it is held, this water is not available for supplies but may be regarded as static. It fills the chalk to slightly above the level of the water-table and is not easily displaced by other water. In effect, it makes the rock containing it virtually impervious and not subject to continual percolation.

If flint accumulates silica from constantly percolating water, therefore, it would be expected to appear above the contemporary water-table, and in belts which conform more or less to the form of the water-table. The lower strata would not be expected to contain any flints at all, except where they have been raised well above sea-level and all the overlying chalk removed. This has happened in many areas but must have taken a considerable time, delaying the initiation of the flint-formation. The incipient flint nodules in the Lower Chalk of Berkshire and Wiltshire already referred to (page 77) may possibly be attributed to this delay.

All this would sound very hypothetical were it not for a remarkable observation of the general occurrence of flint made by W. A. Richardson[40] about 1919. This is that the upper limit of flint in the English Chalk, its level of maximum development, and its lower limit, all tend to mimic the contours of the exposed surface of the Chalk, and therefore the water-table. (See Fig. 20, *bottom*.) The interesting feature in this diagram is that although the surface is about 200 feet higher in Dorset than it is in Norfolk, the surface-chalk in Norfolk comes some 500 feet* higher in the Upper Chalk series than

---

* A somewhat equivocal figure, for the total thickness of the Chalk is very different in the two regions. For '500' the reader may prefer to read 'a few hundred' and, further, to take into consideration that the traverse of the section wanders around the country in wide leaps and is open to the charge of selectivity —objections which were, indeed, duly made by R. M. Brydone. However, the measurements of the section and its discontinuity are less important than the general picture it gives. This is supported by the indications of the zone fossils and is of broad significance.

EPIGENETIC THEORIES

the chalk in Dorset. Richardson's lines of flint evidently have little or nothing to do with the bedding, which is represented as zonally level at the bottom, but everything to do with the geomorphology.

Many details of this must be of comparatively recent origin, but the initial folding and determination of the major lines of drainage may certainly be traced back to Miocene, or even Eocene, times and have merely been accentuated (with small modifications) through the past twenty million years. The division of the Chalk outcrops into hills and valleys is, of course, mainly the work of rivers and general erosion, but the form of the water-table may also be affected by the folding of the strata (Appendix IV).

One of the chief objections to this type of theory is that there is evidence that at least some flints are as old as the youngest chalk. For example, the 'Bull Head Bed' (page 114) consists of loose nodules resting on top of the eroded surface of the surviving Upper Chalk, and must have been derived from still higher beds. On the Continent there are abundant flints in the very highest levels of the Chalk, and even in the *Cerithium* Limestone ('Coccolith Chalk') which lies above them and belongs to the Tertiary era[41]. The silica of these flints could not possibly have been derived from Chalk sponge spicules.

However, an even more prolific source of soluble silica is to be found in the overlying soils, particularly where these support Pteridophytes such as the horsetails (Equisetaceae) and all kinds of grasses (Gramineae)[42]. Such plants extract silica not only from solution but also directly from solid silicates and deposit it in their tissues as opal. When they die they return it to the soil in minute globules called 'opal phytoliths', and under grass as much as 1 or 2 per cent of the weight of the soil may consist of opaline silica in this form[43]. There is thus a 'silica cycle' in which comparatively insoluble silica, and the silica locked up in silicates, is extracted by vegetation, converted to soluble silica, and then returned to the soil, from which it is constantly leached by water percolating down to the rocks below. The annual silica turnover for good grassland averages about 50 tons per square mile*, and of this perhaps 10 tons is removed by drainage—enough to make a million tons of flints in 100,000 years. This would mean a fist-sized flint in every cubic foot to a depth of 70 feet throughout

* From figures communicated to the author by Dr. L. H. P. Jones, of the Grassland Research Institute, Hurley, Berkshire.

the square mile—if all the silica did, in fact, become flint. (See Appendix V.)

The supply of dissolved opaline silica to the very highest levels of the Chalk therefore presents no real obstacle to the epigenetic theories, though its subsequent deposition as flint is still open to debate. The several theories which have been proposed to account for this involve such factors as the relative solubilities of silica and calcium carbonate, the availability of carbon dioxide, the dispersal of percolating water in the Chalk, and the varying density and lithology of the chalk itself. They may be divided into 'physical' and 'chemical' theories, according to the nature of the dominant processes involved.

Physical theories

The phenomenon which first led to the development of detailed epigenetic theories was the frequent occurrence of the flints in more or less well-marked bands in the Chalk, the relative distances between which could be displayed as a fairly simple mathematical curve. When this was first observed the 'rhythmic deposition of flint', as it was called, was studied from many angles by both geologists and physicists.

A search was made for other mineral phenomena with which the deposition of flint from solution might be compared, but nothing on the same large scale was observed. However, even miniature examples would have been interesting if they clearly showed the deposition of substances from solution within the body of porous minerals in bands or zones separated by barren zones. There is a sandstone in Dumfriesshire in which iron hydrates have been deposited in zones, and the purple slates at Penrhyn sometimes show green rings from a similar cause. Other examples include agate (Fig. 29) and onyx, in which the bands seem to have been produced by the inward diffusion of coloured solutions from the surface*.

---

* Bands are produced artificially in agate and onyx by this means to enhance their market value. A stone may be soaked for many weeks in a solution of a ferric salt, and then in a solution of potassium ferrocyanide. Where the salts meet in the pores a deposit of Prussian blue is formed. Green zones can be produced with salts of nickel or chromium, red zones with iron, and so on. The black zones of onyx are produced by keeping the stone for several days in a solution of sugar and honey at just below boiling-point. After that, it is washed, dried and soaked in hot concentrated sulphuric acid, which releases black carbon from the absorbed carbohydrates[70].

The formation of such bands seems to have been first studied in the laboratory by R. Liesegang, who observed a curious phenomenon in 1896. Having placed a drop of silver nitrate in the centre of a plate of gelatin containing a trace of potassium dichromate, he found that as the silver salt diffused outwards a series of concentric rings of silver dichromate were precipitated. (See Fig. 21.) These 'Liesegang rings', as they are now called, appeared close together near the centre

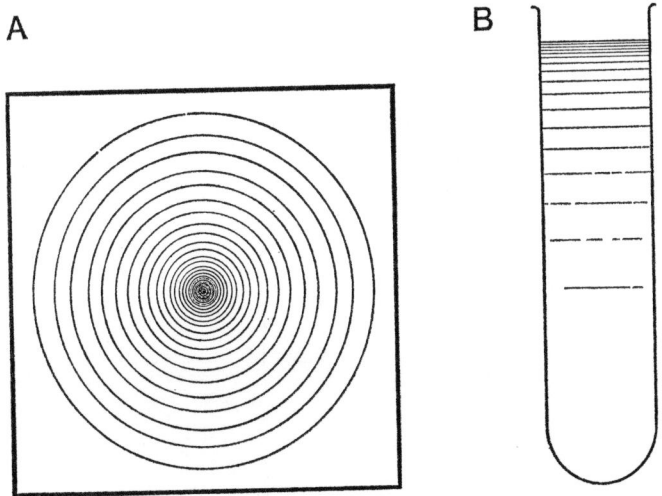

FIG. 21. A, The general appearance of Liesegang's rings, seen in plan. B, Similar zones produced in a vertical column of gelatin.

of the gelatin but at wider and wider intervals towards the edge. In an experiment with silver nitrate and ammonium dichromate, he noted that at certain concentrations the precipitated crystals of silver dichromate were each surrounded by a barren zone.

On other occasions he produced overlapping rings, a flat spiral like a watch-spring, and some curious tubular deposits suggesting miniature paramoudras (page 22). Liesegang suggested that the zones in typical agate might have been produced by a similar diffusion of iron salts through the chalcedony (at that time thought to consist chiefly of silica-gel), and that other rhythmic mineral deposits, including the flints in the Chalk, are probably caused by similar processes. He published an important paper on the mineralogical significance of diffusion phenomena in 1913[44], and a further note on the production of spirals in 1914[45].

An able summary of Liesegang's work, in English and with illuminating comments, was produced by G. A. J. Cole[46] in 1917, and in

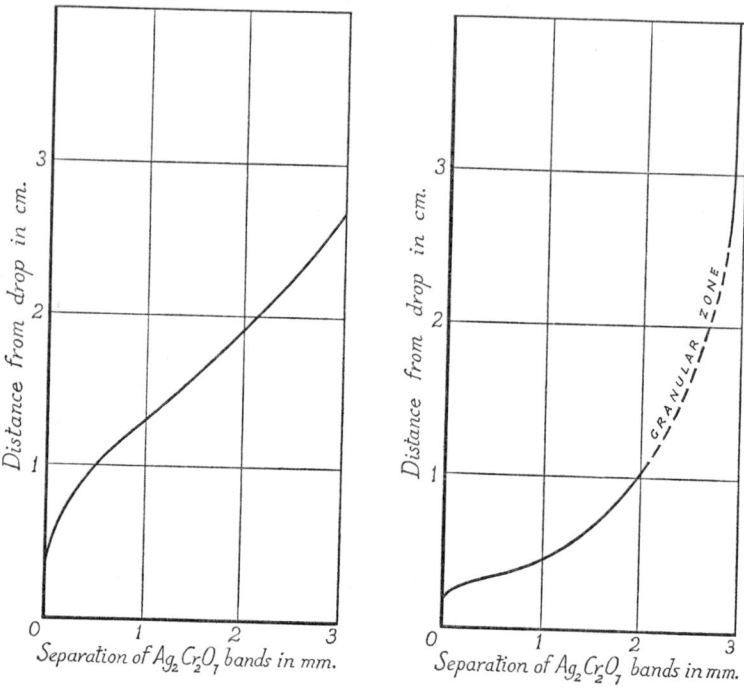

FIG. 22. The distribution of bands of silver dichromate deposited from a solution diffusing through gelatin. *Left:* According to R. Liesegang. *Right:* According to J. Stansfield.

the same year J. Stansfield[47] reported his repetitions of Liesegang's experiments and some comparison tests made with solutions of different strengths. Working largely with lead nitrate and gelatin impregnated with potassium dichromate, he attributed the different spacing between the rings to the progressive dilution of the reagent as it diffused from the centre.

Meanwhile, similar experiments were being made by several other workers[48], the most interesting method being to drop solutions of

PHYSICAL THEORIES

coloured salts on to columns of gelatin or agar-agar in test-tubes. In these circumstances, the precipitation occurred in bands or zones which were close together near the top of the gelatin but wider apart towards the bottom. (See Fig. 21.)

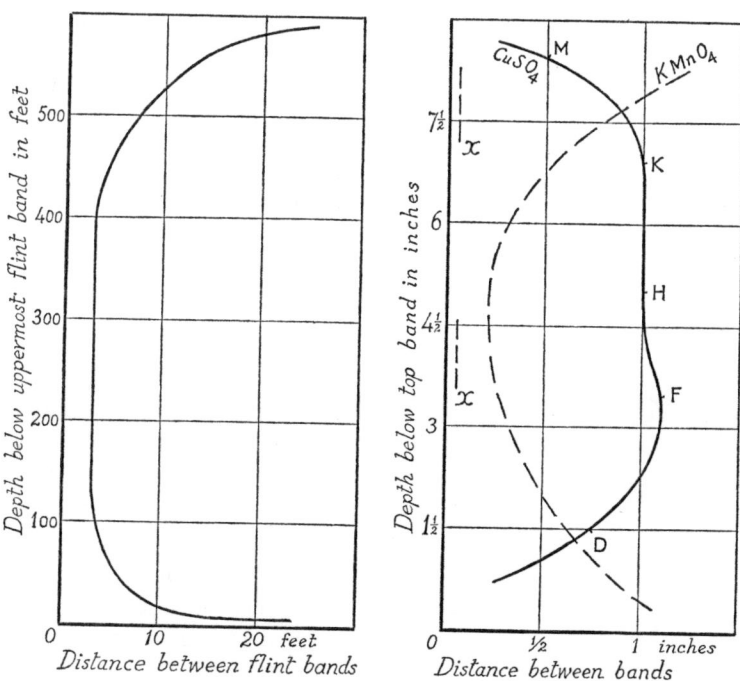

FIG. 23. *Left:* The distribution of bands of flint in the English Chalk according to W. A. Richardson. *Right:* The distribution of bands of copper sulphate ($CuSO_4$) and potassium permanganate ($KMnO_4$) deposited from solutions percolating through chalk.

In 1919, W. A. Richardson[40] constructed curves comparing the sequences of Liesegang's and Stansfield's rings with the bands of flint in the English Chalk. These are shown in Figs. 22 and 23, where the distance between any two consecutive rings (or bands) is plotted against their mean distance from the point of the drop on the surface of the gelatin or, in the case of the Chalk, from the level of the highest recognizable band of flint.

91

THE SEGREGATION OF FLINT

It will be seen that all the curves are smooth, but otherwise the differences between the laboratory curves and that for the Chalk are more striking than the similarities. For example, the bands of flint in the Chalk are widest apart at the top and the bottom, and are more or less regularly spaced throughout the middle section, whereas the silver dichromate bands occur close together near the 'top' (i.e. the centre of the rings) but become progressively wider apart towards the 'bottom' (i.e. the periphery).

Further, Liesegang's and Stansfield's experiments can show no gravitational effects, such as might well appear in vertical percolation through the Chalk, and the arbitrary 'top' of Richardson's Chalk section must be a long way below the original exposed top of the Chalk and not fairly analogous with the centre of the rings. The only common feature appears to be that, in both the Chalk and Stansfield's experiment, below a definite level the bands settle down to a uniform distance apart. It might have been more interesting had Stansfield's 'granular zone' fallen within this section, but the plain fact is that these experiments are not sufficiently parallel with what is known of the conditions maintaining in the Chalk*.

In 1932 the author carried out somewhat similar experiments but using columns of chalk instead of gelatin, and obtained much more striking results. About an ounce of copper sulphate was first pounded to break up the crystals and change it from dark blue to a fine, very pale-blue powder. This was intimately mixed with about a pound of precipitated chalk and then compressed into a block in a rectangular case about a foot high, with three wooden sides and one of plate-glass (for observation). The compressed mixture appeared absolutely white and represented the Chalk with its content of soluble silica. A concentrated solution of copper sulphate was then dripped on to the top surface to represent the percolation of silica-bearing water through the Chalk.

The immediate result was the formation of a deep-blue patch beneath the drip, and the growth of separate copper sulphate crystals in the chalk just below it. The chalk surrounding them was stained pale-blue, and darker streaks began to grow downwards from the crystals so that they looked like very small blue tadpoles. Their lower

* These diffusion experiments would seem to be much more appropriate to the problem of 'banded flints', which are discussed on page 124.

PHYSICAL THEORIES

portions were evidently redissolving, but the blue stain then faded instead of intensifying and below it was a dead white band showing no changes at all. A little lower still a second band of crystals began to appear. This also developed streaks and was followed by a broad belt of separate blue crystals scattered in a pure-white matrix. A white band devoid of crystals came next, and then the whole cycle was repeated three times, when the bottom of the block was reached. This took about four days, but percolation was allowed to continue for a week and, towards the end, two of the white bands began to show scatterings of large crystals.

It should be explained that the 'crystals' were crystalline nodules of no particular shape, and not single copper sulphate crystals. However, there were two anomalies: in one place a large hollow nodule formed, possibly by the fusion of contiguous crystals, while in the bottom band all the larger crystals were surrounded by blue haloes and might eventually have developed into hollow nodules.

Finally, the block was laid on its back and the glass cover removed. The exposed surface was then 'developed' by a brief exposure to ammonia vapour, which changed the pale diffused copper sulphate into the strong blue cuprammonium sulphate and intensified all the features. These were then photographed, but unfortunately by this time the block was becoming over-charged and the clear distinction between some of the bands was getting blurred by a general rash of deposits. However, careful notes and detailed sketches were made throughout the experiment and the most complete sketch is shown on the left in Fig. 24. The notes of times and quantities, nearly all the photographs and all the negatives were lost during the last war, but the best surviving photograph is reproduced in Plate XII. Both sketch and photograph should be imagined as printed in pale blue with the larger nodules darker.

The distances between the bands were measured and a curve prepared for comparison with Richardson's curve for flint bands in the Chalk, but it will be seen in Fig. 23 that they curve in opposite ways. That is, whereas the flint bands are closer together in the middle, the copper sulphate bands are wider apart at the corresponding level. The letters on the curve refer to the zones lettered in the same way in Fig. 24, and it will be noticed that there is a reverse tendency in the curve between F and H.

THE SEGREGATION OF FLINT

Two other experiments were performed with copper sulphate and precipitated chalk. In one (Fig. 24, *centre*), the mixture was rammed tightly into a long glass tube and plain water was allowed to percolate through from the top. The sulphate was completely leached out from the top half-inch, below which the mixture turned a pale diffused blue and contained very small blue dots with streaks running downwards. This zone was followed by a longer zone in which large angular nodules appeared in a completely white matrix. These zones all grew in length until, after three days, a new pure-white band appeared and the whole cycle began to be repeated.

The other experiment was simpler still. The mixture of copper sulphate and precipitated chalk was pressed tightly into a perfectly dry test-tube, where it appeared a uniform white. It was then stood on one side in a dry place, during a spell of hot summer weather, and merely observed two or three times a day. In spite of the total absence of perceptible moisture, angular blue nodules began to appear evenly distributed throughout the white matrix, except for the top inch, which remained dead white. (See Fig. 24, *right*.) After five days the tube was emptied and the grains examined. Those in the top inch were still invisible to the naked eye and had undergone no change, but the visible nodules lower down measured up to a sixteenth of an inch across and some were hollow. The material was still as dry as when it was put in, yet there had clearly been some migration of molecules or ions to build up the nodules. The materials had not been desiccated and must have contained a trace of moisture, but it is difficult to see how there could have been enough unless the water of crystallization in the copper sulphate was in some way available. A very striking feature in both these experiments was the absolute sharpness of the boundaries between the zones. There was no visible gradation at all between the white top and the diffused blue, or between the diffused blue and the white matrix containing the nodules.

Plate XII also shows yet another experiment. In this, a strong solution of potassium permanganate was dripped on to a rectangular block of natural chalk cut from the Upper Chalk of Purley (Surrey). The permanganate reappeared on the surface of the block in zones which can be clearly seen in the photograph. Two sets of zones may be distinguished, the broad zones being themselves divided into sets

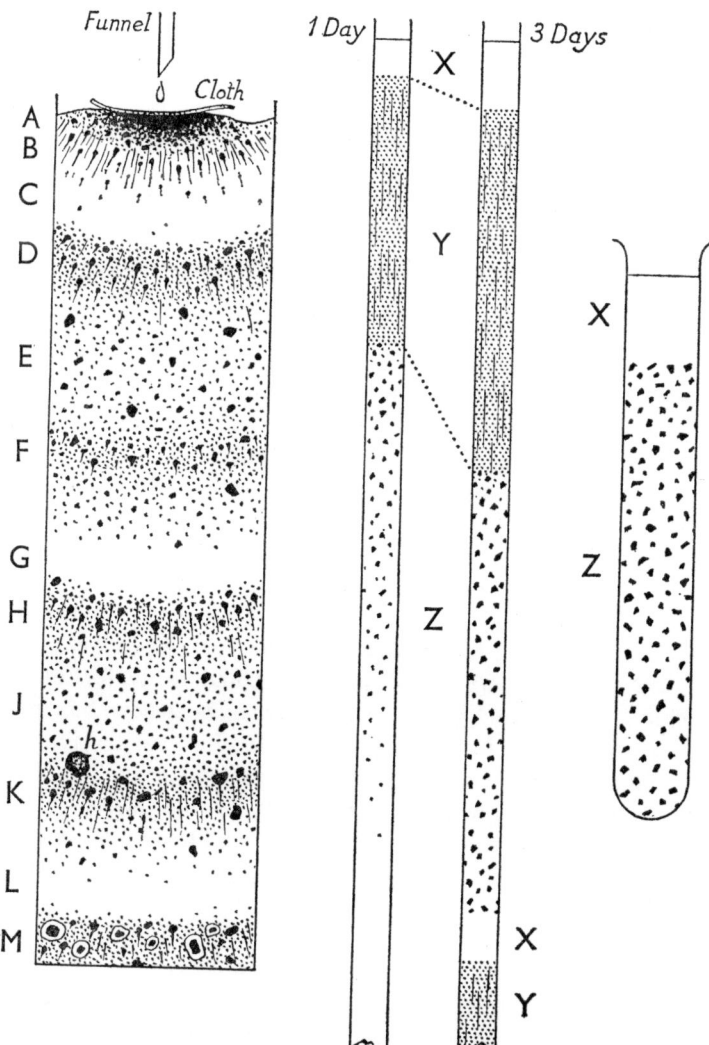

FIG. 24. *Left:* The distribution of copper sulphate nodules from a solution percolating through precipitated chalk. Band H was formed after 3 days, and band M after 4 days.; *h*, large hollow nodule. *Centre:* Bands of copper sulphate distributed by percolating water in an initially uniform mixture of powdered copper sulphate and precipitated chalk. *Right:* Self-segregation of powdered copper sulphate disseminated through precipitated chalk in the dry. X, Pure white zone. Y, Diffused pale blue with streaks. Z, small angular nodules.

THE SEGREGATION OF FLINT

of miniature zones and the pattern being repeated at two levels. The curve based on the broad zones, shown in Fig. 23, is seen to be of the same general character as the curve for the bands of flint in the Chalk.

If the segregation of flint in the Chalk is a purely physical phenomenon, in some way comparable with these experiments, it is perhaps worth noting that the solubility of potassium permanganate is about 1,700 times greater than the solution of silica in riverwater (see Appendix II). If the separation into zones is proportional to the solubility, this would make the fine zones (x in Fig. 23) equivalent to zones of flint from 8 to 10 feet apart in the Chalk. This agrees remarkably well with Richardson's data for the Chalk, though the coincidence is probably fortuitous.

The cause of the zones would appear to relate to differences between the water molecules and the molecules of potassium permanganate. The water evidently dispersed into the chalk faster than the permanganate, so that the permanganate was precipitated. More water then washed through the precipitated permanganate and carried a dilute solution further down, but the water again went faster and left a more concentrated solution behind ready for another precipitation. It would appear that the permanganate can be separated from the water, to some extent, by filtration, but the filtration is through a thick porous rock where the passage through the pores is long and tortuous and involves a great deal of surface contact. More probably the separation does not depend upon the size of the molecules so much as on variations in concentration due to adsorption, but potassium permanganate is an inorganic salt and the detailed explanation is unlikely to be simple*.

The bearing of all these experiments upon the segregation of flint remains an open question. What they do demonstrate is that a solution percolating through a porous rock deposits its solute in zones, and so we should expect a solution of silica percolating through the Chalk to do the same. There remains, however, the problem of finding

* Though the experimental set-up and photographic results resemble those of chromatography the process is clearly not the same. In chromatography the various substances in a mixed solution are separated by their different rates of adsorption, each being carried by diffusion a characteristic distance through the adsorbent. In the present experiments a single substance is repeatedly deposited at irregular intervals and travels for no particular characteristic distance.

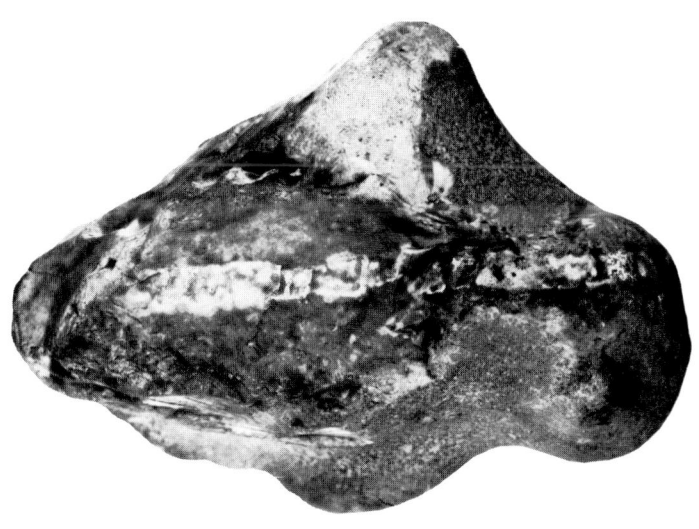

PLATE XI. *Above:* A flint nodule with a completely silicified piece of a large lamellibranch shell, *Inoceramus*, forming part of its substance. *Below:* An 'agate-rinded' flint nodule, showing several stages of apparent growth.

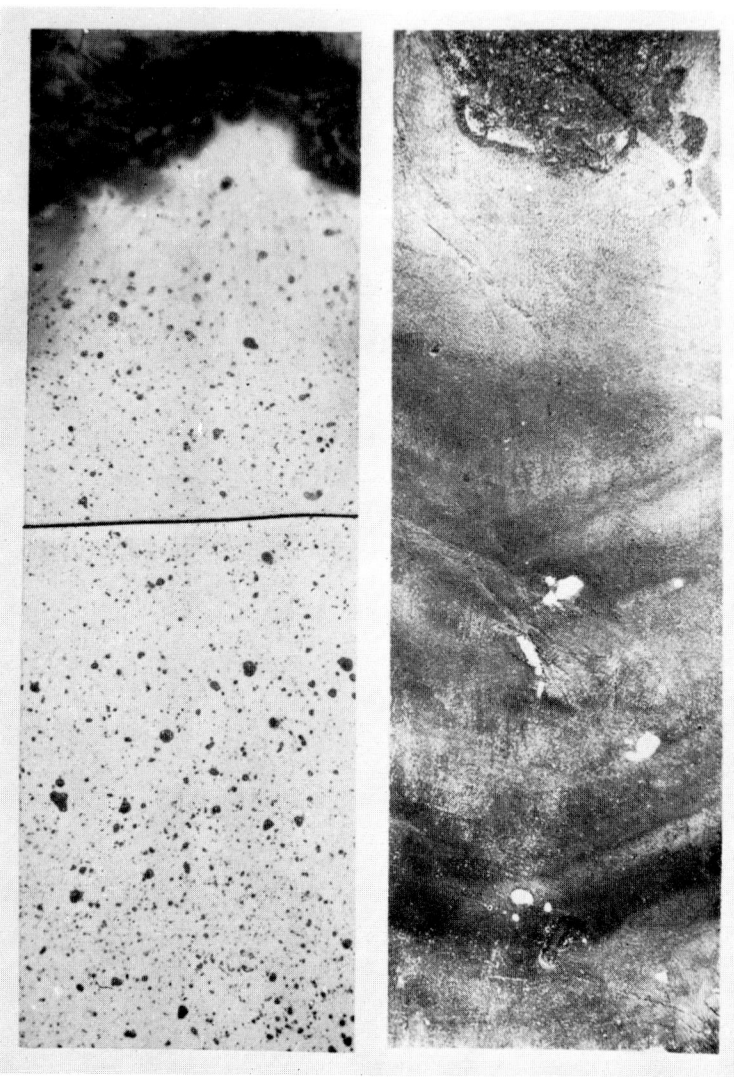

PLATE XII. Experiments in the deposition of substances from solution in the body of chalk blocks. *Left:* Copper sulphate in compressed precipitated chalk (advanced stage: see Fig. 24). *Right:* Potassium permanganate in a block of natural chalk.

room for it. How can room be found for a ton of flints in 130 tons of chalk without obviously disturbing the chalk? In the experiments described above, the matrix of precipitated chalk was undoubtedly compressed by the development of the crystals of copper sulphate, while the potassium permanganate formed micro-crystals in the pores of the chalk and grew larger crystals on its surface like whiskers. Some of these surface crystals can be seen at the top in Plate XII.

Two explanations are possible in the case of flint. The first is that the nodules are disposed to grow most readily where the rock is soft and able to be compressed. The second is that the water takes up chalk in exchange for the silica, so that no significant change of volume is involved. In adopting this theory, W. A. Richardson further suggested that the chalk thus removed is redeposited as calcite at a lower level, where it acts as a cement to form the extra-hard bands in the Chalk. The idea of a simple, direct exchange of silica for calcium carbonate is, however, attended by difficulties, and it seems that if an exchange does take place some sort of chemical reaction must be involved.

Chemical theories

The best-known of these theories depend upon the conversion of normal calcium carbonate into the bicarbonate (or hydrogen carbonate, as the chemists prefer to call it) by the action of carbon dioxide in solution (carbonic acid):

$$CaCO_3 + CO_2 + H_2O = Ca(HCO_3)_2$$

The general principle is that suggested in 1918 by R. S. Dean[32] for the formation of chert nodules from solutions of mineral silica. Having no convenient supply of sponge spicules to call on, he first invokes the chemical action of the carbon dioxide in ground-water on the silicates in shales. This provides a double solution of opaline silica and carbon dioxide for percolation through beds of limestone ($CaCO_3$). He then suggests that when the carbon dioxide reacts with the limestone, the silica is precipitated by the release of positive calcium ions from the bicarbonate produced. He claims to have demonstrated this reaction experimentally, and to have observed that the precipitation always starts around nuclei (in suspension in his solutions).

The chief modern objection to this theory must be the general absence of colloidal silica from natural water (see Appendix II), but Dean's chief mistake may have been only in requiring his silica solution to be colloidal. One of the 'chemical' systems described below would have served him better. The old objection was the inadequacy

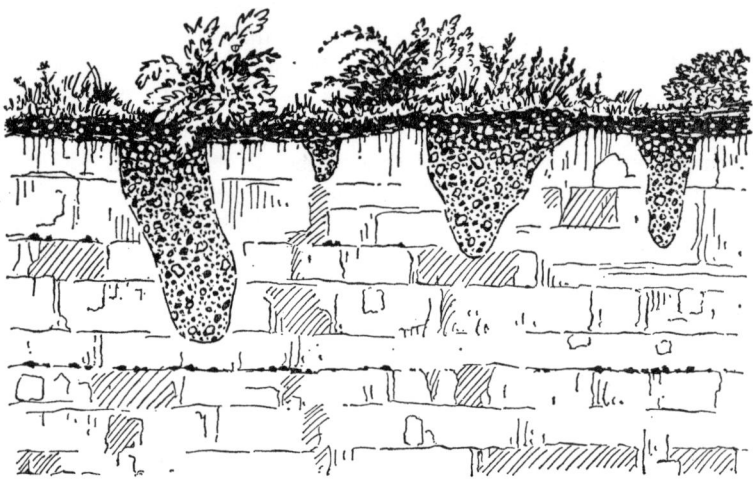

FIG. 25. Solution-holes or 'pipes' in the top of a chalk-pit.

of the supply of carbon dioxide in ground-water. This we shall discuss when we come to the more elaborate theory of Volkmar Wroost.

Calcium bicarbonate is about 140 times as soluble in water as the normal carbonate and is chiefly responsible for the hardness of water in limestone districts. Most chemical reactions at ordinary temperatures take place most readily (and often exclusively) in solutions, where the dissolved substances separate into groups of atoms called 'ions', which bear electric charges. Thus, the solution of calcium bicarbonate charges the water with the ions Ca^{++}, H^+, HCO_3^{--} and CO_3^{--}.

Now, the rain-water, river-water and ground-water which percolate through the Chalk certainly dissolve some of the chalk. Solution

CHEMICAL THEORIES

occurs extensively near the surface and in such fissures as can swallow up the ground-water fairly quickly, for large holes in the Chalk caused by solution are quite common. For example, there are more than twenty such 'swallow-holes' in the bed of the river Mole between Dorking and Leatherhead, and upwards of fifty in the basin of Mimmshall Brook, a tributary of the Colne. Solution-holes or 'pipes' may also be seen sectioned along the tops of many chalk-pits, where overlying beds of gravel or clay-with-flints have generally filled them in. (See Fig. 25.) Less frequently, subterranean caves are found to be dissolved out of the chalk, as at Polesden Lacy (Surrey), but they are not as large or as extensive as those found in harder limestones (e.g. in the Carboniferous Limestone of the Cheddar Gorge).

Theories which rely on the solution of chalk by carbonated water are concerned with its slow percolation through the pores of the rock, and the most important is that proposed by Volkmar Wroost[49] in 1936. According to this theory, the CO_3 ions are first taken up by the water adsorbed on the surfaces of the embedded sponge spicules. The silica would thus be converted from a gel into a sol (page 70), dissolve in the water, and be carried downwards.

Meanwhile, the loss of the CO_3 ions would make the bicarbonate solution less stable and cause a precipitation of the normal carbonate. This is supposed to account for the replacement of some siliceous sponges by calcite, while the precipitation itself would cause the liberation of more CO_3 ions. This reciprocal action would regulate itself so that the relative amounts of silica and bicarbonate dissolved in the water would achieve a balance and the double solution would continue to percolate downwards.

There would then be no change until the amount of *normal* chalk taken into solution suddenly increased. This could happen, for example, inside the test of a sea-urchin, or in a crustacean burrow, where the chalk is less compact and its grains present a greater surface-area to the percolating water. If this happened, another set of changes would be started.

First, the dissolved silica sol would lose its adsorbed CO_3 ions and become silica gel, being precipitated and eventually converted to flint (by dehydration and a change to the cryptocrystalline structure). Second, the released CO_3 ions would convert the adjacent chalk into the bicarbonate which would then dissolve, and thus there would be a direct replacement of the chalk by the silica. It is in this way that Wroost would explain the infilled sea-urchins discussed by R. M. Brydone (see page 72).

The occurrence of the flint in bands is explained by the increase of the solubility of the chalk under pressure. The pressure increases with the depth, but the amount of bicarbonate dissolved would not rise uniformly because of the capture of CO_3 ions by the spicules of opaline silica encountered on the way. But at certain critical pressures the chalk would claim all the CO_3 ions and pass into solution, dumping the silica as a gel. Once started, the silica would gel to excess, releasing even more CO_3 ions to form bicarbonate with the chalk.

The process would then be repeated at a higher level of concentration until the next critical pressure was reached, but there would be a special tendency to deposit the silica where opaline silica was already present, and this is held to explain the preservation of sponge skeletons inside flint nodules. The distance apart of the bands of flint is, in this theory, held to depend upon the local solubility of the chalk, which must be less in the marly bands, for example, and on both the rate of percolation of the water and the amount of silica present.

Now, there is a very great difference between the solution of chalk to form swallow-holes here and there, or to widen underground fissures, and its distributed solution through the enormous body of the Chalk. The chief objection to Wroost's theory is that there would not be nearly enough carbon dioxide in the percolating water. It has been suggested that bacterial activity in the soil covering the Chalk as it rose from beneath the sea might have supplied what was needed, but this is catching at a straw. The effects of the meagre yield from the thin soil which generally covers the Chalk would not be measurable.

Moreover, the theory does not explain the restriction of the flint to the Upper Chalk. To account for this, appeals have been made to the water-table hypothesis (page 86), but they fail not only because the water-table at the time of the uplift is quite unknown, but also because the requirement that it maintained a steady line between the Upper and Middle Chalk for at least a million years is quite incredible. Nevertheless, it is still possible that Wroost's theory contains elements which are valid.

CHEMICAL THEORIES

It is suggested here that insufficient attention has been paid to the direct solution of the normal carbonate in soft water. The direct solubility of chalk is usually treated as negligible, since less than 3 ounces can be dissolved in 1,000 gallons of cold water, which is about 0·0014 per cent. However, as much as 400 million tons of rain fall over the London area (for example) per year, and this would dissolve 8,600 tons of normal calcium carbonate by direct solution. Now let us compare this with the quantity likely to be dissolved by the conversion of the chalk into calcium bicarbonate through the action of dissolved carbon dioxide.

The carbon dioxide dissolved in water forms the weak carbonic acid, H_2CO_3, and the estimation of carbon dioxide in solution is ascertained by estimating its acidity ('pH value'). Hard surface-water has already had its acid neutralized, so that the maximum power for dissolving chalk by its conversion into calcium bicarbonate will be found in soft water such as rain or, better, rain-water which has been standing for some time in a lake. Normal surface streams are often found to be neutral except after heavy rain, and even in large reservoirs the quantity of dissolved carbon dioxide is extremely small. The Welsh water impounded for the Birmingham water-supply, for example, is slightly acid but can be completely neutralized by adding half a grain of chalk per gallon[39].

The maximum acidity in soil-water (peat-bog water) may require as much as 5 grains of chalk per gallon for complete neutralization, but this is far above the average. For ordinary ground-water one grain of chalk per gallon is certainly excessive and more than adequate for the water from the sand and gravel coverings, and shallow soils, over the Chalk*. If we adopt this double figure, it still means that only 380 tons of chalk can be converted to calcium bicarbonate by the 40 million tons of annual rain over London.

This is 8,220 tons *less* than the direct solution of the unaltered chalk! And even if the Chalk were everywhere covered with peat-bogs of maximum acidity, the corresponding figure would still be 6,320 tons less. Thus, though the solubility of the unaltered chalk is almost negligible compared with that of the bicarbonate, it is very far from negligible when the means for producing the bicarbonate are so

* Half a grain per gallon neutralizes an acidity of pH 4, which is the maximum figure given for rain-water by A. Holmes[50].

poorly supplied. It is, in fact, 20 times as great. Moreover, solution of the normal carbonate is very slow and many continue through a great thickness of the Chalk, whereas the rapid effect of the carbonated water must cease within a few feet of the top.

A simple calculation shows that typical surface-water percolating through and dissolving the chalk should acquire 184 times as many CO_3 ions from the normal calcium carbonate as from all the bicarbonate its acid can produce. This might be enough to meet the main objection to Wroost's theory, if not to make it 184 times more probable. His reasons for the deposition of the flint in bands are less plausible, in the author's view, than the cycle of attenuation and concentration exemplified in the experiment with potassium permanganate described on page 94 and illustrated in Plate XII.

Wroost's theory, however modified, at least allows the *replacement* of the chalk by silica, and there is independent evidence that can be interpreted in this way. For example, there is the soft, whitish siliceous chalk containing blue-grey nodules in Wiltshire and Berkshire already referred to (page 77), and there are the curious nodules of 'silicified chalk' found near the top of the Middle Chalk in the Isle of Wight[51]. These look like white flints but have the texture of chalk and appear to represent chalk in the process of being replaced by silica, grain by grain.

Examples occur in the Upper Chalk of typical flint nodules with the cortex grading into the surrounding chalk over at least part of their surfaces. A nodule with a graded cortex looks like an ordinary white flint and its surface feels quite hard, but at certain points a penknife will cut readily into it to a depth of perhaps half an inch before meeting the genuine hard flint. For convenience it is proposed to call this zone the 'soft cortex', but it is not always present and should not be confused with the cortex proper.

In 1950 the author undertook an examination of this soft material, searching in particular for some transition compound (if one existed) between the external calcium carbonate and the internal silica. Nothing was found by either chemical or microscope techniques, but since a transition compound needs to exist only momentarily, and that in very dilute solution, this result did not prove anything. What had been hoped for was that 'relics', left over from sporadic imbalances, might be common enough for detection. Theoretically, the most likely intermediate substance was some form of calcium silicate ($CaSiO_3$), and the unstable form known as pseudowollastonite was favoured because of its crystal habit. Equations were devised (see Appendix VI) and the views of others were sought, but the surviving correspondence suggests that nobody else was interested—at that time.

In 1969 the author re-examined the problem, using a specimen from Amberley, Sussex. A small slice of the soft cortex was cut out perpendicularly to the surface of the nodule. It was divided into outer, middle and inner portions, and these were then separately treated with dilute hydrochloric acid. All three effervesced, the outer most vigorously, the inner only slightly, and it was evident that the proportion of calcium carbonate in the soft cortex diminished from the outer surface inwards.

The residues were presumably pure, or almost pure, silica, but there was just the possibility of a tell-tale trace of calcium silicate. They were therefore very thoroughly washed and submitted, first, to electron-probe examination. This was kindly done (in December, 1969) by Dr. P. J. Goodhew, of the University of Surrey. He found abundant silicon but no other metals, and therefore no silicates, but this did not rule out the possibility of a trace of calcium less than 0·1 per cent by weight. Such a trace (possibly very much less) *was* then found by spectroscopic examination. Now, traces of calcium have been found before in flint, and have always been attributed to calcite crystals, but here the treatment with acid and the extremely thorough after-washing should have been adequate to rule out this source. However, there was the possibility of the inclusion of microscopic calcite crystals inside comparatively large grains of silica, which would have protected them from the acid but not from the spectroscopic arc, and it was felt that much more rigorous tests should be made and repeated before any claim to the discovery of calcium silicate could be made.

This inconclusive story would scarcely have been worth telling were it not for the fact that P. Buurman and L. Van der Plas[132], of the Agricultural University at Wageningen, Holland, have since, and quite independently, arrived at a closely similar chemical explanation of the silicification of chalk. They state that their paper, published in 1971, is a sort of follow-up to G. Millot's demonstration that silica cannot be precipitated from natural water as a gel by the action of ions. They realized that a purely chemical process must now be sought, and they undertook a very much more thorough investigation than the author's tentative probings.

The methods they used included: (a) X-ray diffraction patterns, (b) differential thermal analysis, (c) the polarizing microscope, (d) the scanning electron microscope (at ×9,000), and (e) X-ray spectroscopy. Some details of their findings are given in Appendix VI, but their general conclusion is that, although they found no calcium silicate, there is a strong presumption that calcium silicate *is* the intermediate compound involved in the silicification of chalk. This falls just short of evidence, and all that can really be positively and unequivocally stated at present is that a chemical replacement of chalk by silica has definitely occurred in some places, at some unknown period, by some unknown process. We must be thus cautious because we are equally certain that a great many other things have also been happening in connection with flint, in other places and at other unknown periods.

Progressive silicification from the outside inwards presents problems of its own, for in the author's Amberley specimen there is a typical hard cortex about a quarter of an inch thick beneath the soft zone. What, then, can be happening? Is the original cortex growing from the outside by accretion of silica, as well as inwards by deprivation of water? Or does the process of silicification of chalk *first* produce the white cortex-substance, which *later* becomes black flint? Or is the whole explanation of silicification a reversible process, so that in the Amberley specimen the soft cortex is not chalk being silicified but the cortex proper being *de*silicified? Desilicification does occur in soil-flints, as described on page 109, though by a physical rather than a chemical process. In the author's view, black flint nodules may be formed in a number of ways and eventually acquire a cortex. But whether possessing a cortex or not, they may then behave as nuclei encouraging the silicification of the chalk in contact with them. This would accommodate the fact that not all flints have a 'soft cortex' and those that do may have one on some parts of their surface but not on others*.

* The Amberley specimen has its soft cortex on only a part of one large projection. The rest of the nodule has a normal hard cortex with no signs of silicification in the chalk in contact with it.

SECONDARY SILICA

On any view, aggregation or accretion round a nucleus of some kind is quite essential to account for the formation of discrete nodules, though progressive silicification of the chalk along a soft layer or other suitable bed could conceivably produce tabular flint. But in this case, we should be obliged to regard the cortex proper as an intermediate stepping-stone to black flint, instead of a sign of its decay, and this is not tenable unless we believe that there are different kinds of cortex, hard to distinguish but originating in diametrically opposite ways. This, strangely enough, is by no means impossible to believe and deserves further consideration.

Secondary silica

This term refers to any silica deposited on or in a flint nodule after the nodule itself was formed and apparently 'finished'. While this has often happened in the geological past, there is abundant evidence that it is still taking place at the present time, and it is possible that the phenomenon of the 'soft cortex' described above is an example of it. The new silica is sometimes deposited as secondary flint, sometimes as chalcedony, and sometimes as quartz crystals. Further, original flint occasionally appears to have become changed to chalcedony, and chalcedony to flint, and these products are also referred to as secondary silica.

Where secondary flint has been deposited on top of original flint in the body of the Chalk, it can hardly be distinguished as 'secondary flint' unless the original flint has a clearly demarcated surface of its own. Such a surface can be traced in the 'agate-rinded' flint illustrated in Plate XI, and in certain flints showing 'a curious secondary growth' found in Dorset[52]. Another possible case of renewed deposition is seen in the 'thin coating of blue and white agate' on the fractured surfaces of flints at Keston (Kent)[35], while L. Cayeux[53] gives detailed descriptions of secondary silica deposited on flints from the Middle Chalk (zone of *Inoceramus labiatus*) in the Vallée du Cher in the Paris Basin. Nodules found on the very top of the exposed chalk in Kent 'appear to have been shattered and re-cemented by secondary flint'[54], but these do not appear in the body of the Chalk but form part of the Bull Head Bed to be described in the following chapter.

THE SEGREGATION OF FLINT

The author found a somewhat similar phenomenon near the top of a small, long-disused and overgrown chalk-pit on Riddlesdown (Surrey) in 1935. Here, a large nodule *in situ* in the upper Chalk had been cracked and splintered, probably by a quarryman many years since, and the crack was in process of being filled with chalcedony and flint. This was clearly being deposited by trickling water, and a splinter of flint just above it showed similar distributions of chalk sediment. (See Plate XIII.)

In the upper photograph, the white ribbons of chalcedony (on one side zoned) show where the silica-bearing water had trickled across the face of the flint. The ribbons are about half a millimetre thick and are sparsely dotted with minute papillae. Towards the top they merge with the flint and are indistinguishable from it. Since there was nothing above the specimen but about three feet of chalk capped by a foot of clay-with-flints and soil, the silica in the water almost certainly came from the soil, which supported rough grass, and was no doubt deposited by simple evaporation.

The secondary silica deposited inside hollow flints usually lines the cavity but sometimes fills it. In many cases the percolation of water from outside seems to be impossible, but the deposits could then result from the rearrangement of the molecules by a trace of water trapped in the nodule. Three examples are shown in Plate XIV. The clear-cut, sparkling quartz crystals are usually about the size of pin-heads or match-heads and have here been magnified. The chalcedony is reproduced natural size and its waxy appearance is quite characteristic. In this specimen it is honey-yellow but often it is creamy, mauve or bluish.

The deposit shown at the top on the right is certainly of silica and probably of chalcedony, but consists of clusters of perfectly spherical, opaque white balls, some in contact but others separate. There are upwards of 300 of them and they are firmly attached to the surface of brown, cauliflower-like chalcedony lining an enclosed cavity in a dark-grey flint beach-pebble from Seaford. They measure about one-hundredth of an inch in diameter and through a hand-glass look like spiders' eggs, but in the photograph they are magnified about ×30.

They are difficult to account for unless they are silica replacements of perfectly-formed coccospheres, but the author has been unable to find a record of any other such occurrence. The chalcedony on which

SECONDARY SILICA

they stand has been sectioned and has a curious vesicular structure. It seems to have developed outwards from the surface of the flint and in places appears to represent sponge-structure. This specimen has been described in detail here mainly as an illustration of the remarkable forms secondary silica may take in flint nodules.

Secondary silica is also occasionally deposited on the brown flints of old gravels. In such cases the silica could not have come from the Chalk but is easily accounted for by overlying soils supporting vegetation, as described on page 87. The author has a large specimen from the lower terrace of the Old Blackwater river (in the valley now occupied by the Wey) at Farnham, Surrey, which is peculiar in bearing secondary silica apparently derived from rocks (or their soils) very much older than the Chalk and therefore lying stratigraphically beneath it.

What evidently happened is that the flint fell from the terrace into a very old sand-pit in the Folkestone Sands and there became buried. It may have lain in the sand a century or more, during which time it acquired a partial but thick coating of dark-brown limonite (hydroxide of iron), which is abundant in the sands. This substance is even less soluble in water than silica but it is soluble in humic acids, which could have been brought down from the overlying soil together with a solution of silica. The layered limonite coating has firmly cemented numerous sand-grains to the flint, and round its edge there is a sort of fringe of brown secondary silica, faintly glittering in places with microscopic quartz crystals but elsewhere resembling the flint beneath.

The interesting thing is that the stone must have fallen into the sand-pit (or into a well of which no record remains) in comparatively recent historical times, and received both its limonite and its silica in a remarkably short period. The possibility that it fell from the terrace into a later valley in the sands at a much more remote period, and there became buried in a cliff-fall, is precluded by the situation in which it was found. Secondary silica is also well-known as a cementing agent, and the example of the Hertfordshire puddingstone will be described in the following chapter.

4

Derived Flints

So LONG AS flints remain in the Chalk where they were formed they are said to be 'native' or 'raw' and *in situ*. Once they have been freed from their original surroundings they are said to be 'derived'. They may attain this status in a variety of ways. A quarryman may dig them out, the chalk in which they are embedded may disappear by solution, attrition or the action of plant roots, they may fall from a cliff or be dislodged by rivers or the sea. And once they are free they may be transported many miles by gravity, water, ice, a Stone Age implement trader, or the quarryman's cart—these last two having consequences to be described in the following chapters.

However they go, from the moment they become exposed they undergo new sets of changes, some superficial but others affecting their entire structure. The type of change will depend upon the environment, but we may distinguish between changes caused by water or mineral solutions entering or leaving the flint by its natural pores, and mechanical changes caused by rough usage.

Residual deposits

To begin nearest home (from the flints' point of view), the first exposures in many areas could have been in the soil on the recently emerged chalk landscape. We find abundant flints today on the top of the chalk hills, where they accumulate in the soil as the chalk itself is slowly removed by sub-aerial erosion. Here they lie through the centuries, first becoming white all through and then slowly 'rotting' and turning a dirty grey.

Since these flints have not travelled, except downwards as their

RESIDUAL DEPOSITS

supporting surface was lowered, they form a 'residual deposit'. They may be found by scratching away the turf, where many are entangled in the grass roots. The chalk soils are 'dry' and the flints are mostly white from loss of water through their pores, for while evaporation from their surfaces draws out the water extremely slowly, it continues for a much longer time than they ever remain wet. The plant-roots, too, help to extract water and exercise a bleaching action. All this accelerates the slow change to a white cortex (which goes on even in the chalk itself), and prepares the surface for the processes of patination and staining discussed in the following section.

The whitening of the exposed flints proceeds so rapidly that not only have many flint implements become white throughout in two or three thousand years, but even flints broken by the plough in modern times may show whitening on their new surfaces after less than a century. The process does not merely involve loss of water. The outgoing water takes silica with it, enlarging the pores of the flint and finally leaving it nearly as porous as pumice.

Flints in this state are usually grey with dirt and are said to be 'rotted' or 'desilicified'. The decay generally goes on very irregularly, eating out hollows and following lines of exceptional solubility such as may occur round old sponge structures. This accentuation of fossil structures by differential solution often causes such micro-fossils as sponge spicules and Foraminifera to stand out strikingly above the general surface. A typical rotted flint is shown in Plate X.

The process of desilicification is often said to be assisted by the acids produced by soil organisms, but there appears to be no evidence for this although other substances produced by organisms may play a part. Years ago somebody seems to have cited 'acids' at a venture and nearly every later writer to have repeated it, and this in spite of evidence to the contrary. For one thing, the presence of acid would be more likely to precipitate silica than to dissolve it, but the evidence is the frequent occurrence of calcite crystals in the flint. A freshly-broken surface sometimes shows minute square or oblong crystals, relics no doubt of fossil shells, those in the specimen shown in Plate X measuring about one-thirtieth of an inch long. This specimen also contains a Belemnite guard in calcite, and it is difficult to see how these objects could have resisted the attack of acid water. The small crystals of calcite dissolve right away in dilute hydrochloric acid in about four seconds, and one can only suppose that the acidity of the soil-water washing over them was always quite negligible.

It is certainly extraordinary that these conditions should persist through the immense period of time that the specimen must have lain buried, but similar examples are quite common. The large square patch on the cheek of the 'lion's-head' in Plate II is also of calcite and actually stands out above the surface, yet this specimen was taken from directly beneath the turf. (On the other hand, the beach-pebble at the top of Plate XVIII, on the right, bears rectangular holes from which calcite crystals have been dissolved out.) Moreover, the desilicification of soil-flints can be explained both by the simple solution of the quartz crystallites and by the action of plant-roots without invoking acids at all. A flint subjected to the solvent action of pure water could lose a quarter of its substance in only 9,000 years. (See Appendix I.)

The solubility of calcite in pure water is not very different from that of quartz, but the calcite would be expected to last much longer than the flint because its crystals present a smaller surface-area in proportion to their volume than the microscopic quartz crystallites in flint. We may suppose a cubic millimetre of calcite to present a surface of about 6 square millimetres, but the crystallites in the same bulk of flint might well present upwards of 1,000 square millimetres of surface to solution. This is a staggering figure, yet perhaps conservative*, and it does help to account for the solution of the silica while the calcite is preserved. Thus, the desilicification of flint, no less than its segregation in the Chalk, is better explained by the action of pure water than by invoking acids, but plant-roots probably also play an important part.

It has been shown that such 'silica accumulator' plants as grasses and horsetails can obtain their silica directly from the soil-rock where their roots are in contact with it, and may do so in the complete absence of either dissolved silica or humus[42]. The action of the roots

* Using the measurements given by Meldau and Robertson[13], the volume of a single crystallite is of the order 0.0003 μ^3, and the area of its prismatic surfaces 0.03 μ^2. If we assume that 90 per cent of the flint consists of crystallites, the number of crystallites in 1 mm^3 of flint is 3×10^{12}. If they were all free, the total surface-area of their prismatic sides would be 10^5mm^2. Supposing only one-hundredth of each crystallite is exposed to a water-filled pore, then the area exposed would be 1,000 mm^2.

is to produce organo-silicon compounds in which carbohydrate groups play an important part, and the saps of horsetails and maize have been found to be highly supersaturated with silica attached to organic complexes of this kind. (See Appendix V.)

The structure of desilicified flint naturally varies according to the stage reached, but Meldau and Robertson[13], G. Nagelschmidt and others have measured the constituent particles in a number of specimens. The results indicate that they may be reduced to one-quarter their original volume in the raw flint. This would (ideally) enlarge the volume of the pores by a factor of about two and one-third, but it would also connect them together by new spaces. Since such flints do not fall into a powder, these volumes require to be redistributed so as to reduce the number of pores but greatly enlarge them, and many are in fact visible to the naked eye in the solid parts of the specimen in Plate X.

Soil-flints, whether on the chalk hills, in gravel soils elsewhere, or on exposed road-surfaces, are liable to mechanical damage by frost, pressure or shock. The pressure of stone against stone may be concentrated at a single point of contact, and if it is sharply applied, as by the hoof of a galloping horse, one of the flints may crack. Ploughs and harrows also sometimes break flints, and in deep soils the weight of the overlying layers may initiate conical cracks or break off slender projections. If the cracks, even though they are invisible, become filled with water which afterwards freezes, the flints may be split and produce the fractures described on page 39. Some examples of frost-damage are shown in Plate XV.

When the chalk landscape first emerged from beneath the retreating Chalk Sea, it may or may not have contained a great many flints, but as it rose and began to bear soils and vegetation, the percolating rain-water inevitably carried soluble silica down to levels where new flints could be deposited and old flints could grow. In the author's view (though some would disagree) this was probably the grand period of flint-production*, but a million years may have passed before flints began to be abundant in chalk soil. Flints seem to have

---

* W. A. Richardson[40], after agreeing that there was more than one generation of flint, cites evidence from Belgium of flints which could not have been formed *before* the last stages of Upper Chalk times, nor *later* than the deposition of the Thanet Sands. This is more or less the period referred to here.

been in plentiful supply when the Eocene Sea began its invasion of south-east England some fifty-five million years ago, but by then at least 2,000 feet of the Upper Chalk had vanished over enormous areas, leaving vast numbers of flints in residual deposits.

The calcium carbonate comprising the bulk of the lost chalk had been carried away in solution and by the other agents of erosion, but wherever the land was fairly level the comparatively insoluble flints and the clay from the marly bands were left stranded on the continually descending surface. Such deposits are described as 'clay-with-flints' and may measure 30 feet or more in thickness. In many areas the quantity of clay is too great to have been derived entirely from the chalk marls and has been attributed to the old overlying Tertiary rocks in some regions but to glacial deposits in others[35]. The chalk on which the clay-with-flints rests is frequently pitted with solution-holes or pipes (Fig. 25), which fill with clay-with-flints as they deepen.

Though the oldest of these deposits certainly date from Eocene times, they have continued to accumulate in suitable places ever since. They often cap the flat tops of the chalk hills, where they enable trees—chiefly beeches—to grow. Such clumps are, in fact, a characteristic of the chalk landscape, well-known examples including Chanctonbury Ring in Sussex, Cherhill Down in Wiltshire, and St. Catherine's Hill near Winchester. Much of the woodland along the top of the North Downs (including St. Catherine's Hill near Guildford) is growing on the residual deposits of clay-with-flints.

The flints in them come in all sizes and shapes and are usually more or less broken by frost and desilicified. They are frequently stained, nearly always dirty from contact with the humus of the soil and, where exposed, green with the growth of microscopic Algae (*Protococcus*, etc.). They may also show black patches as if they had been splashed with tar. These are generally superficial deposits of either limonite (hydroxide of iron) or some form of psilomelane or wad (hydrated oxides of manganese[35]), probably derived ultimately from the seas in which the vanished overlying sediments were laid down.

Mixed with the clay-with-flints there is usually a good deal of grit or sand. Black flint pebbles and pieces of a hard indurated sandstone known as sarsens or greywethers may also be found. None of these could have come directly from the Chalk but are derived from

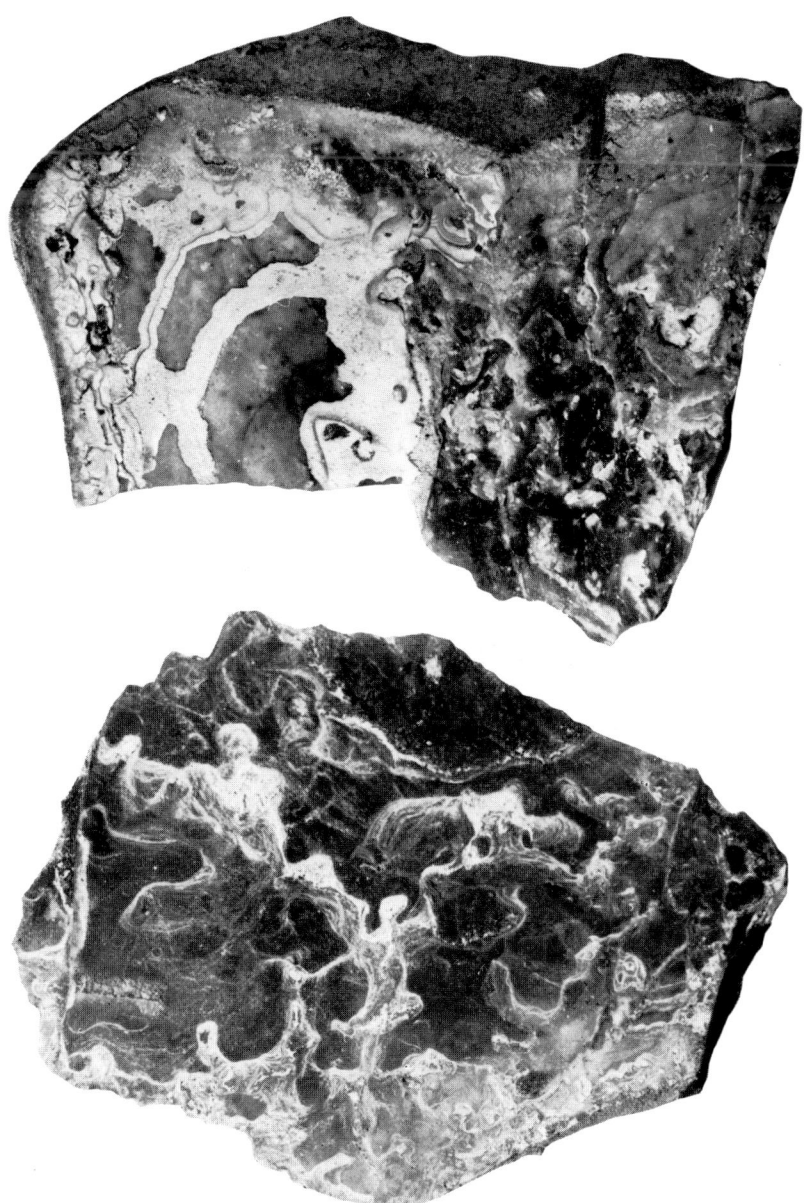

PLATE XIII. *Above:* Part of a shattered flint nodule showing recent deposition of silica from runnels crossing the broken face. *Below:* The deposition of fine chalk sediment on another shattered fragment —*not* a picture by El Greco!

PLATE XIV. Secondary minerals deposited inside hollow flints. *Top* (*left*): Mammilated chalcedony, honey-coloured; (*right*) opaque white spheres, probably chalcedonic, magnified ×30. *Below* (*left*): Quartz crystals, ×20; (*right*) calcite crystals of an unusual acicular form, ×2.

RESIDUAL DEPOSITS

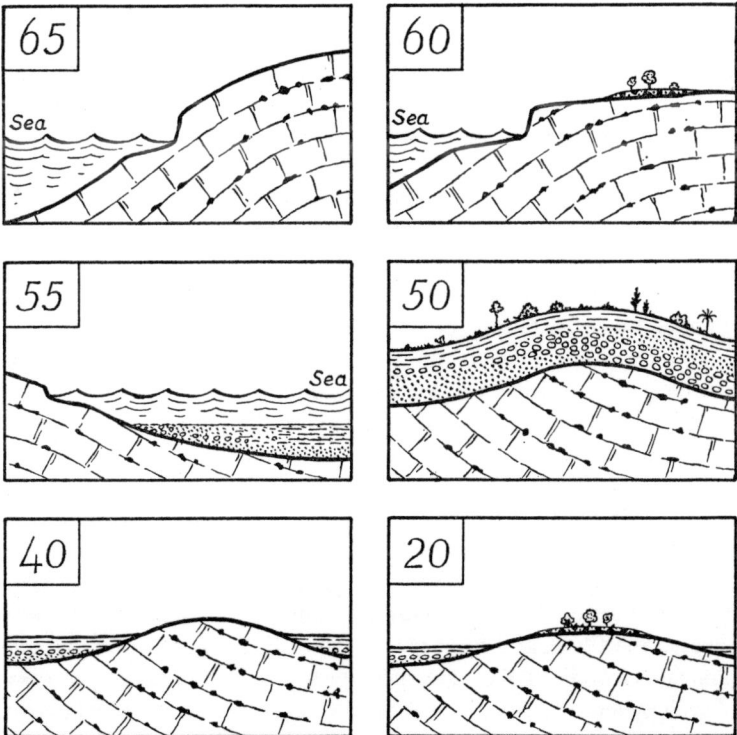

FIG. 26. A series of token diagrams of the history of the Chalk in a typical region since its formation. The numbers indicate millions of years ago. 65, The Chalk emerges from the sea containing some flints, but others begin to grow. 60, The surface of the Chalk is lowered by erosion and the older patches of clay-with-flints appear. 55, The Chalk is folded downwards and a new sea deposits fresh sediments upon it. 50, The land again rises, supporting a landscape on the new rocks. 40, Erosion removes most of the new rocks, once more exposing the Chalk. 20, The surface is again lowered by erosion and more recent patches of clay-with-flints appear.

sediments laid over the Chalk during later incursions of the sea or by rivers. Several thousand feet of these once lay on top of the Chalk over very wide areas, but today few traces of them remain except in the synclines or basins where the Chalk has been depressed below sea-level, as it is beneath London (see Figs. 17 and 26).

DERIVED FLINTS

The earliest deposit to be laid over the Chalk of the London Basin is the Thanet Sand, and in Kent and Surrey this covers a very curious deposit known as the Bull Head Bed. When the sea encroached over the Chalk to lay down these sands, it appears to have swept over an extensive sheet of (now) reddish clay-with-flints resting on an exposed band of flints in the chalk itself. At the bottom of the Bull Head Bed, these flints project from the chalk, their upper halves being coated with a green silicate of iron. Above them are other flints entirely coated in this way, the whole bed being about a foot thick. Some of the flints have been cracked and recemented with silica, or have been rounded by encrustations of secondary silica on their surfaces, and some—known as 'marbled flints'—show curious brown zones which will be mentioned again in the next section.

Other residual deposits of flint, having the general character of clay-with-flints but with little or no clay, include the Brown Flint Drift, also of north Kent, in which the flints are chocolate-brown, the Angular Flint Gravel on the higher parts of the Chalk Downs in the Isle of Wight, and the Pebbly Clay and Sand found chiefly on the Chiltern Hills. These formations all contain a much higher proportion of residual material derived from the lost strata which once covered the Chalk and from glacial deposits. Some of those marked 'Plateau Gravel' on the older geological maps, may consist entirely of such material[20], though most high-level gravels are relics of ancient drainage systems.

Patination, gloss and staining

Before considering flints which have been derived by transportation, it will be convenient to look into the general question of the colouring and patination of flint. The original straw-yellow or brownish tinge of thin slivers of raw flint was judged by W. J. Sollas[36] to be 'due to the carbonaceous pigment, the last residuum of the living protoplasm once present in the chalk'. The whitening of cortication of flint has already been described, and green-coated, black-coated, blue-tinted and chocolate-coloured flints have been referred to. Osborne White[14] notes violet and carnelian-tinted flints in Hampshire, and Dewey et al.[35] describe bands of pink and green-coated nodules in the Upper Chalk of Kent. In fact, all flints are liable to bleaching or coloration of one kind or another.

Colours caused by physical changes are to be distinguished from colours caused by pigments, but often the physical changes are necessary to permit the entry of the pigments. The relevant physical changes are the loss of water which causes cortication, the loss of silica causing desilicification, the fractures caused by frost, and the mechanical damage resulting from impact, scratching, rolling and chattering. These changes are all described on other pages; here it will be convenient to consider the type of change known as 'patination' and certain minor phenomena associated with it.

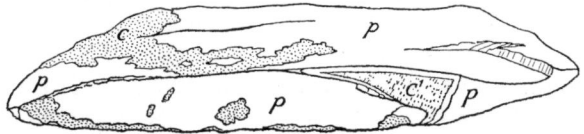

FIG. 27. A piece of white tabular flint, corticated to some extent right through and bearing a dense pale cream patina. The patina, p, has been abraded away in patches, exposing the (much soiled) white cortex, c. The flint has been chipped at c' to show the cortex and patina in section, the thin line indicating the grey 'thread' at the base of the patina.

The term 'patina' (as applied to flint) is today used somewhat differently by antiquaries and geologists. In its older sense, it referred to a curious glazed surface-layer comparable with the patina on old marbles or bronzes. This is quite distinct from the whitening of the surface of a flint, which is simply the beginnings of cortication, and while some corticated flints are also patinated, others are not. Staining is something else again, all forms of flint being able to take up stains.

A patinated flint can usually be recognized by its curious 'greasy' appearance and feel, and though the patina is often too thin to show any other characteristics, its thickness is usually visible in the broken edge of a patinated white flint (taken from the soil). The waxy-looking surface is here seen to belong to a slightly yellowish layer of greater density than the deeper cortex, from which it is sometimes separated by a thin grey line. Its appearance suggests the enamel of a tooth, but the case-hardening of a ball-bearing might make a better comparison. (See Fig. 27.) The broken edge of a rough, unpatinated white flint (Plate I, *foot*) shows no such layer, but the only invariable sign of genuine patination is the characteristic waxy lustre*. (This should not be confused with the polish or 'gloss' to be described below.)

This is not always made clear by geological authors, who often seem to confuse patination with soil-cortication. However, the question can no longer be dismissed as a mere matter of terminology, for the process of patination, in the original sense, now turns out to be almost the exact opposite of cortication.

The confusion arose out of the mistaken notion—it was never anything more—that black flint necessarily contains opaline silica, and that this could be removed by acid rain-water to produce whitening of the flint. No other idea was seriously considered, so the term 'patination' began to be used to distinguish its supposed occurrence in broken or derived flints from the original 'cortication' of flints still embedded in the Chalk. This seemed reasonable, because flints which have lain for a long time in the soil usually do acquire a genuine patina which adds a 'finish' to any whitening or staining, but the prime importance of the finish itself does not seem to have been realized.

Thus, in 1919 W. A. Richardson[40] was already describing the cortex as a kind of 'coarse patina', and in 1935 E. Gehrke[55] gave an explanation of patination which was identical with the old explanation of the cortex. The same interpretation is given in the British Museum booklet on flint implements[56] (1956), though the earlier handbook on the Stone Age[81] followed the old tradition and emphasized the 'more or less lustrous' surface, which it ascribed to 'chemical or molecular changes'. As recently as 1957 H. Alimen[76], the French anthropologist, referred to the patina on old flint implements as a 'brilliant varnish', but to that on later ones as 'dull and greyish'. With all due respect to Madame Alimen, could confusion be worse confounded?

But there is no need for the confusion to continue, for since the cortex has been known to result from simple loss of water, patination (in the classical sense) can be perfectly accounted for by the partial

* The author well remembers being instructed in the significance of this lustre by the late Arthur Leach, who, as long ago as 1928, was deploring the growing misuse of the term 'patina' for mere incipient cortication—or even simple staining.

PATINATION, GLOSS AND STAINING

or entire refilling of the emptied pores with silica derived from soil-water (see Appendix II). This not only explains the observed skin of increased density, but also the waxy or chalcedonic lustre. The 'grey line' illustrated in Fig. 27 probably marks the level at which the infilling becomes complete, either with silica or silica *plus* water some measure of the blackness of a flint core being thus restored.

The following two sets of specific gravities provide positive evidence of the increased density of the patina in common white-coated soil-flints:

	A	B
Black core	2·56	2·60
White cortex	2·44	2·44
Cream patina	2·58	2·56

It will be noted that in specimen A the patina gained slightly more than the core lost during cortication, the gain being in silica and the loss in water. In specimen B, the patina has not entirely recovered the original density of the core, but the degree of cortication was here proportionately great and there may have been some degree of desilicification. The loss apparently due to cortication amounts to about 6 per cent by weight, as against a loss of only about 4·7 per cent in specimen A, which is similar to the mean loss of water when black flint is calcined (see page 205). However, this does not affect the point being illustrated here, which is simply that patination involves an increase in density.

Some degree of cortication is evidently a necessary preliminary to patination, but it may be only a few molecules thick and quite invisible, yet sufficient to allow the greasy appearance of a patina to develop. A thicker cortex may take up stains and so provide for the coloured patinas described below. Since the process of patination is a sort of clogging up of the pores, it brings itself to a standstill after forming a skin which seldom exceeds a millimetre in thickness. Deeper penetration does occasionally occur, with the production of a very hard, dense crust, but to describe any substantial white nodule as 'patinated right through'—as is sometimes done—is to do violence to both language and sense. However, a *very thin* flake may really become patinated right through, and then it resembles porcelain and may be translucent. Patination is a slow process and is generally

DERIVED FLINTS

relied on as a sign of great age, but it is easy to obtain evidence that natural cortication may occur within years rather than centuries.

Some interesting attempts have been made to imitate the whitening of flint with the idea that this would explain patination. In one method, black flint is boiled for a long time in a strong solution of caustic soda. The slight whitening produced in this way is probably caused by the solution of crystallites in the surface, thus widening the pores and facilitating the escape of water. An incipient solution-gloss (page 121) which mimics the waxy lustre of patination may also be produced by this means. In another experiment, black flint was exposed to rain-water and the gaseous products of vegetable decay in the presence of chalk, and after twenty-two months a white film 0·01 millimetre thick was found[56]. In both experiments the result recorded was incipient cortication—a mere whitening of the surface—though it has often been referred to as 'artificial patination'.

It will now be appreciated that the various coloured 'patinas' which have received special names are sometimes found in flints which are not patinated. Among the most common is the pale filmy blue assumed by black flint when it first begins to whiten. This is not due to pigment but to an optical effect depending solely upon the extreme thinness of the white layer, which is thus rendered transparent. The blue rays are reflected from this but all colours of longer wave-length pass through into the translucent flint beneath, where they are absorbed*. The white layer will absorb oil and, if very thin, will become transparent enough for the black flint to show through.

Sometimes a pale-blue flint is marked by small black strokes resembling writing, showing where the whitening has been inhibited, possibly by included sponge spicules (which would not so readily lose water). Whatever their cause, these marks form 'graphic patination' and in the example shown in Plate XIX (*bottom*, *left*) it is difficult to believe they have not been made by a pen. This specimen is also irregularly whitened elsewhere, showing that the soil-cortication has

---

* It is sometimes stated that the red rays reflected from the upper surface of the film interfere with those reflected from the under surface, resulting in the cancellation of the red light, as in a soap-bubble. However, this is doubtful because either one or both of the surfaces is 'matt' and the light reflected from it is scattered. Also, it is known that white flint transmits red and yellow but not blue rays (see page 34), so that there is no need to invoke interference to explain the effect.

proceeded very unevenly. 'Toad-belly patination', common especially in Suffolk, in which soil or gravel flints are speckled with yellow and green, is also caused by uneven whitening. In this, the white film is thin enough in some places to show the blue tint, but the whole is stained yellow by iron and appears green where it would otherwise have been blue.

Uneven whitening is not always due to inhomogeneities in the flint, for it can often be traced to the vegetation growing on the soil in which the flints are found. An example is afforded by the illustration of 'basket patination' shown in Plate XVI. This specimen is a grey flint with a pattern of white lines. It was found in a roadside bank and very carefully examined *in situ* to put beyond reasonable doubt that its pattern is simply a bleached print of old grass-roots. The surface of the flint is no smoother than blotting-paper and shows no signs of patination. It was probably tossed into the bank when the road was made up no more (at a guess) than ten years previously.

White marks caused in this way are called 'reduction patches' and and they are quite common on flints of all colours. They may be bleached out by almost any kind of plant-root or the soil-organisms associated with it, and the small specimen of brown flint at the top of Plate XVI was marked by the 'holdfast' or attachment of a seaweed (bladder-wrack) in the estuary of the river Test.

At the bottom of the same Plate is a square block of black flint bleached in the centre by adhering soil (in part still present). Bleaching of this kind by substances in the humus is often a literal bleaching of coloured pigments, but black flint has little colour to bleach and cortication by abstraction of water generally predominates. The lustre of patination may afterwards supervene, and few such objects will ever be found to go completely and exclusively into a single phenomenological category.

Basket patination is also frequently caused by more direct cortication along a criss-cross of microscopic cracks—not, as was formerly thought, by the ready percolation of water but by the facilitation of its escape. It may also occur on surfaces which have suffered scratching through movements against other stones in the soil. Old flints usually acquire at least the beginnings of a patina or protective skin, and this may develop before cortication gets a visible hold. But if the thin skin gets scratched the whitening is soon renewed along the scratches or 'striations' and a basket patination may result. When the striations are very fine and sparse a 'spider's web' patination is produced.

A flint decorated in any of these ways may acquire the waxy appearance of a final patination, but this must never be confused with what is known as a 'gloss'. The waxy lustre has a dull and greasy appearance, but the term 'gloss' is applied to a very high polish, usually with specular reflectivity. It occurs in all types of derived flint, generally in very small patches, and there are at least three principal causes, so that we may speak of fracture-gloss, friction-gloss and solution-gloss. There is also an evaporation-gloss, evident in calcined flint and possibly elsewhere.

Fracture-gloss is, perhaps, the most puzzling although it is the most familiar. When a block of flint is struck a sharp blow with a hammer, it breaks with a conchoidal fracture the surfaces of which generally have the velvety appearance of a matt photograph. But sometimes the region near the point of impact is as smooth and shiny as glass. Very rarely the whole fracture-surface has this quality, and the author has a specimen in which the mirror-like gloss measures about $11\frac{1}{2}$ square centimetres ($1\frac{3}{4}$ square inches). Now, conchoidal fracture is also a characteristic of glass, the fracture-surfaces of which are always shiny, so we may suppose that fracture-gloss has something to do with this type of fracture. The mirror-like surface remains unexplained, but it is certainly quite unlike that on the cleavage-planes of crystals for there is no ordered arrangement of molecules or atoms in either flint or glass.

Friction-gloss is also common, though it is seldom noticed because the shiny patches are often of only pin-head size. They are simply spots polished by friction between two stones and are quite easy to produce artificially. If two flints are rubbed together, the contact being maintained in the same small area, mirror-like facets may be formed in a very short time. In the soil, this sort of polishing may be caused by almost any kind of repeated motion, such as the vibration following an earth-tremor, the vibrations caused by heavy traffic, or even the repeated hoof-beats of horses over the turf. Fifty rubs on the same spot can produce the gloss, but they can be delivered at wide intervals spread irregularly through years or even centuries, provided the stones are not otherwise disturbed. The piece of tabular flint in Fig. 27 bears a creamy patina over most of its surface, but when held at various angles before a lamp, some six or seven tiny patches of mirror-like gloss are revealed by their glitter. They clearly mark the spots where soil-pebbles rested on the flint surface. A similar friction-gloss is also produced on flint sickle-blades by the corn or grass stems, as described on page 164.

Solution-gloss is something else again. When a high gloss is found at the bottom of a hollow in the surface of a soil-flint, it is impossible to attribute it to contact with another flint. In the author's view, it is probably an effect of partial solution of the surface, which, as in the electrolytic polishing of metals, would first remove all the microscopic projections that make the surface rough. The stone might have to remain both wet and undisturbed for a very long time to produce a specular finish, but this presents no conceptual difficulty. It will be noted that both the solution-gloss and the friction-gloss are produced in an opposite manner to the lustre of a patina. In the glosses, the smooth surface is formed by removing the projections, while in the patina a similar result is achieved by filling in the hollows.

The gloss produced on the white surface of calcined flints, between the cracks, is fine and satiny, and sometimes almost specular. The most probable explanation seems to be the following. The water being driven from the pores by the intense heat of the fire would instantly become vaporized on reaching the surface, and since it must be saturated with dissolved silica it doubtless deposits some in the surface-pores as it leaves them. Since such a gloss may be fully developed by exposure to a temperature of 600–900°C. (1,100–1,650°F.), this is a much more plausible explanation than the supposed fusing of the surface silica, the melting-point of quartz being about 1,600°C. (2,850°F.). There seems to be no reason why, in certain circumstances, an evaporation-gloss should not also occur on cold flint surfaces, and this might be worth considering when any puzzling gloss is found.

One other type of glazed surface should be mentioned, namely that known as 'wind-polish'. It is rather less brilliant than a gloss and often has a waxy appearance very similar to a thin patina. However, it is produced by the fine dust blown across deserts, where it must be almost impossible for a true patina to be acquired, or, if acquired, to survive. In the same environment, blown sand gives stones of all kinds a surface resembling ground-glass, and when the prevailing wind is fairly constant, flat facets are found to be first ground on the pebbles and later polished. Such stones are called 'ventifacts' or 'dreikanters' (see Fig. 38), but this is a general desert phenomenon and has to do with flint only where flints are found in deserts (as in the Sahara and Kalahari).

All forms of flint may become stained by iron, manganese and other minerals, and three possible modes of staining may be recognized. A flint may receive its colour during the process of its formation and, though it is none the less stained thereby, it is usually referred to simply as an originally 'coloured' flint as distinct from a 'stained' flint, which begins its existence as a normal black flint but becomes stained later. It is, however, preferable to distinguish between 'primary' staining or coloration and 'secondary' staining or coloration, the secondary staining being either of the cortex or of the core.

Yellow, orange, brown, pink and red primarily-stained flints have been found, and they show the usual translucency and textural quality of normal black flint[57]. Secondarily-stained flints, on the other hand, may be of any colour and are liable to changes in their physical properties.

Of the two kinds of secondary staining, that of the cortex is simply a matter of the percolation of pigments in solution into the empty pores, where they are deposited frequently—but not always—along with the silica of a patina. The staining of a black flint core is a much slower process, for here the pores are already filled with water and the coloured ions have no means of access except by diffusion. Since the black of the flint is merely an optical effect, depending upon its translucency, the introduction of any opaque pigment readily colours it. Desilicified flints, rather surprisingly, seldom retain stains at all, except for a dirty whitish-green which may be produced by microscopic soil organisms in the enlarged pores.

White flints in ploughed fields are often seen to be stained with iron rust on their prominent edges where they have been struck by a ploughshare, and flints spotted with rust-stains are common on roads or fields where iron-shod horses or cart-wheels frequently pass. This staining of flints by contact with iron has often been queried and the evidence alternatively attributed to microscopic Algae or lichens, but it certainly happens sometimes. The larger flint at the top of Plate XVI is crossed by a deep-red bar undoubtedly produced by a rusty wire hawser which lay pinned across it at the bottom of a tidal pool. However, there are small rust-spots in some of the cracks and hollows of the calcined flint shown in Plate XVII which are less easily explained and may be caused by iron bacteria (e.g. *Leptothrix*) in the soil.

When water containing iron compounds washes or drains over flints, it penetrates most rapidly through cracks and planes of weakness, disseminating at different rates and producing different concentrations according to the varying qualities of the flint. The beach-pebble at the left-centre of Plate XIX is stained yellow, brown and red in this way, the regular pattern being quite fortuitous. The chip at the bottom reveals the black flint within, and its edge shows the depth of cortication. Lying over this like a skin, there is a paper-thin layer of true patination which can be discerned easily enough in the specimen, and this bears a lustre clearly enhanced by a solution-gloss where it covers the adjacent hollow. Elsewhere, the flint is rough from friction with other beach-pebbles.

The water responsible for the staining of flint need contain very little iron and, indeed, the most likely compounds (the hydroxide, carbonate, silicate and sulphide) are all so slightly soluble that only rarely does the proportion of dissolved iron exceed 0·0001 per cent. Even this minute quantity may affect the taste of the water, discolour whisky and tea, and cause iron-mould in linen[39], so it is not really surprising that such solutions are able to dye flint gravels yellow, brown and red, even to their very centres, if they wash over them for a few hundred thousand years.

The penetration of the iron is accompanied by chemical simplification so that it usually ends up as yellow or brown ferric hydroxide deposited in a colloidal state among the crystallites, but sometimes it exhibits the deep-red colour of rouge (ferric oxide). Two or three colours appear together in the small pebble shown in the frontispiece (*top, left*), and here there appears to have been separate staining at different periods, inhomogeneities having developed in the flint (by shock or pressure) in the intervals. It should be added that the minutest imaginable traces of iron may be responsible for quite strong colours, and they never form an appreciable proportion of the stone.

Other colours which sometimes appear include lilac-pink (caused probably by manganese), blue (possibly from copper), and green (usually from iron again). The blue stain should not be confused with the blue of incipient whitening, described above. The penetration of the stains, the weathering, and the mechanical shocks—weak but repeated—to which derived flints are subject, gradually change their physical properties so that they lose the characteristic conchoidal fracture of raw flint and break in a splintery or hackly manner like chert. Old fractures of this kind gradually become smoothed over and may show new signs of patination, often with new patterns of staining.

Banded, furrowed and spiral flints

The broken surface of some flints, and particularly of brown gravel flints, sometimes shows a remarkable pattern of parallel lines. These are generally thin and close together, but often broaden and become farther apart towards one end of the series. They may be straight but are usually curved, and the ends of the lines are often cut off abruptly in a baffling way. Stones showing such patterns are called 'banded flints' and some are illustrated in Plate XVII. The lines are usually of the same colour as the flint but of a darker or a lighter shade. Those in Plate XVII are darker, but in Plate XVI the reader may just be able to see the series of faint, curved, light bands near the lower end of the specimen showing basket patination.

The cause of such bands is still not certainly known, though S. P. Woodward[58], who studied banded flints as long ago as 1864, claimed to have found conclusive evidence that the bands are produced by infiltration of water charged with iron or manganese, and compared them with the zones in onyx (a mineral similar to agate, illustrated in Fig. 29). He observed that the bands may cross fossil inclusions, and because they sometimes cross each other he concluded that separate series could be produced at different times in the same stone. He seems, however, to have been mistaken in assuming that the bands always present a convex surface towards the source of diffusion, for wavy and straight bands are equally common.

More recent studies have compared them with the diffusion bands in gelatin produced by Liesegang and Stansfield (page 89 ff.). The diffusing agent in flint, however, may be only water which settles in zones determined by molecular forces, and there causes some change which renders the zones visible*. It is known that when water diffuses into certain other minerals it forms rhythmic zones of water-concentration, and these have been studied in zeolite† crystals by Arne Tiselius[59]. Comparative measurements of the zones of water-concentration shown in his photographs are certainly very similar to those in typical banded flints.

When plotted in the manner of Liesegang's silver dichromate bands in gelatin (Fig. 22, page 90) they produce the kind of curve shown on the left in Fig. 28. Here, the 'datum' is the crystal-face at which the water is absorbed, and the curves differ in general direction from Liesegang's because the bands get closer together, instead of wider apart, as they recede from the source.

However, some experiments similar to Liesegang's have also shown a reversal of order, the bands being most widely separated in the region of the drop. E. S. Hedges and R. V. Henley[60], for example, obtained this result by diffusing either ferric chloride or aluminium sulphate into agar-agar containing arsenious sulphide, and L. N. Mukherjee and A. C. Chatterji[61] found that diffusions of zinc, nickel and ferrous cyanides, nickel ferricyanide, and cobalt ferrocyanide, all behave in the same way. The progressive decrease in the spaces between the bands in these cases was found to be caused by increasing concentration, which is also what we should expect with water infiltering into flint.

It should, perhaps, be explained that varying degrees of water-concentration in a substance implies spaces in that substance able to contain more or less water, and in the case of flint, where the pores already contain water, a variation in concentration requires at least one of five conditions: 1, there may be a zonal *loss* of water; 2, the pores may become enlarged by solution and so hold more; 3, the crystallites may change their form so as to occupy less space; 4,

---

* Appendix VII may suggest possibilities though it contributes nothing specifically to this problem.

† Zeolites are hydrated double silicates of aluminium and sodium or calcium, and are usually found as glassy crystals in cavities in altered igneous rocks, where they represent the original felspar. They have the power of absorbing water and yielding it up again on heating. Some zeolites are used in water-softeners of the 'base-exchange' type.

the silica may become opaline*; or 5, the water itself may become more dense, as it does in powdered quartz (Appendix VII).

If the zones are caused by loss of water, the diffusion would need to be outwards instead of inwards. In black flint the bands appear

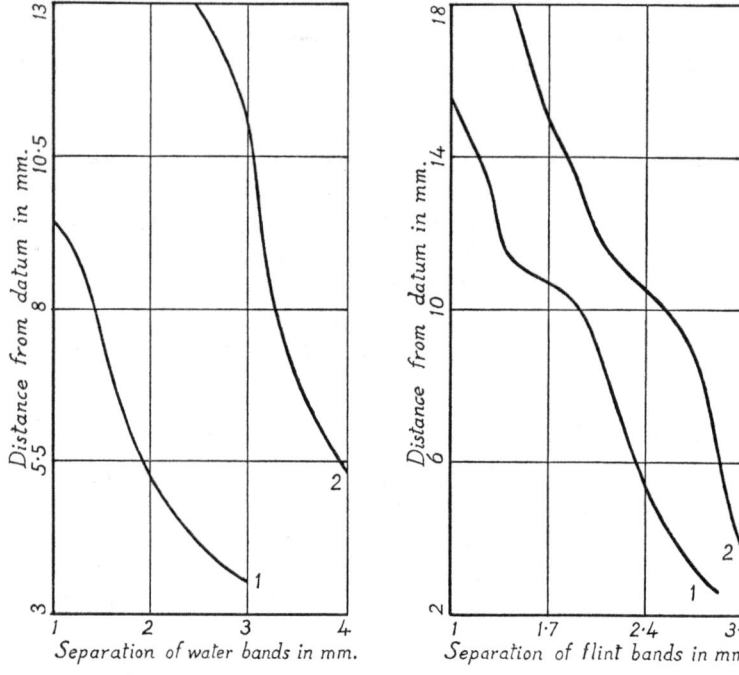

FIG. 28. *Left:* The type of curve produced by zones of water-concentration in zeolite crystals. *Right:* Corresponding curves for the zones in banded flint.

grey, and this could arise from loss of water, from a change in the form of the crystallites (see Fig. 4, page 34), or from opalization. Nobody knows the answers to these questions, but if the phenomenon in banded flint is related to the water-concentration, and if the

* Opaline silica is sometimes found in flint and in agate, where it forms the light or white zones which do not take up stains[70]. (See Fig. 29.) Now, zones of opal may be described as zones of water-concentration, and it may be that the visible zones in either agate or banded flint are merely indicators of the rhythmic occurrence of opal.

diffusion also starts at the broad end of the series (as S. P. Woodward maintained), then we cannot but be impressed by the form of the curves shown on the right in Fig. 28.

These are taken from the banded flints shown at the top of Plate XVII, No. 1 being the uppermost, and while they agree in general form with the water-concentration curves, they show irregularities which may be attributed to inhomogeneities in the flint. They agree strikingly below about 11 millimetres from the datum (a convenient point of reference outside the widest band), and in any case compare very much better with the water-curves than they do with Liesegang's.

FIG. 29. Section through an agate, showing zones.

Once formed, the bands in the zeolite crystals migrate slowly inwards as a group. They draw wider apart as they go, indicating a general dilution, the two curves representing the same set of bands separated by an interval of time*. A similar inward migration of the bands in flint might explain why they are often found near the centre of a nodule and apparently unconnected with outside influences, though there is another possible explanation of this curious feature.

While there seems little doubt that, as in the 'marbled flints' of the Bull Head Bed, the formation of the bands was often accompanied by fresh iron-staining, in many cases there is no evidence of additional staining and water appears to have been the only agent involved. In such specimens the bands seem to have been produced

* Their separation varies as the square root of the time, as in Boltzmann's diffusion equation, but if there is a corresponding rate for banded flint it is not ascertainable.

by the simple redistribution of an existing stain into lighter and darker zones, and the entire process could have taken place right inside the flint. It is reasonable to suggest that a slight loss of water from the flint as a whole caused the central water to redistribute itself in bands. The ultimate effect of this might well be a certain amount of local chalcedonization and of this there is some evidence.

There is certainly, in some instances, a change in the density or hardness of the flint in (or between) the bands, and this is revealed in the weathered specimens which occasionally turn up in soils and

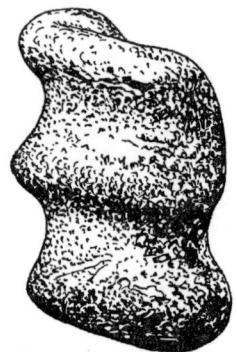 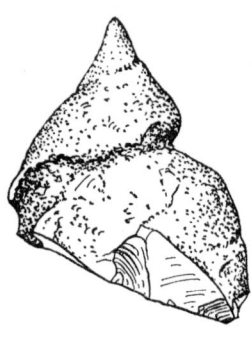

FIG. 30. Spiral flints. *Left:* A specimen from Dorset, in the British Museum. *Right:* A tapered spiral from the soil on the South Downs.

gravels. The surfaces of such flints bear parallel ridges owing to differential weathering, and often show no staining of any kind. They are sometimes called 'furrowed flints' and two are shown on the left in Plate XVII. They are certainly puzzling objects, and at the beginning of the 19th century James Parkinson[62] thought they were the petrified remains of the peduncle of the 'duck-barnacle' (goose-barnacle)! There is, however, no doubt that they—and the more usual kinds of banded flint—are purely mineral phenomena.

The spiral flints mentioned on page 25 and illustrated in Fig. 30 may be a parallel phenomenon in which the flint itself is precipitated by the diffusion of silica solution through the chalk, as in the experiments described on pages 89ff. This was suggested in 1935 by H. Dighton Thomas[63], who drew attention to the fact that similar spiral

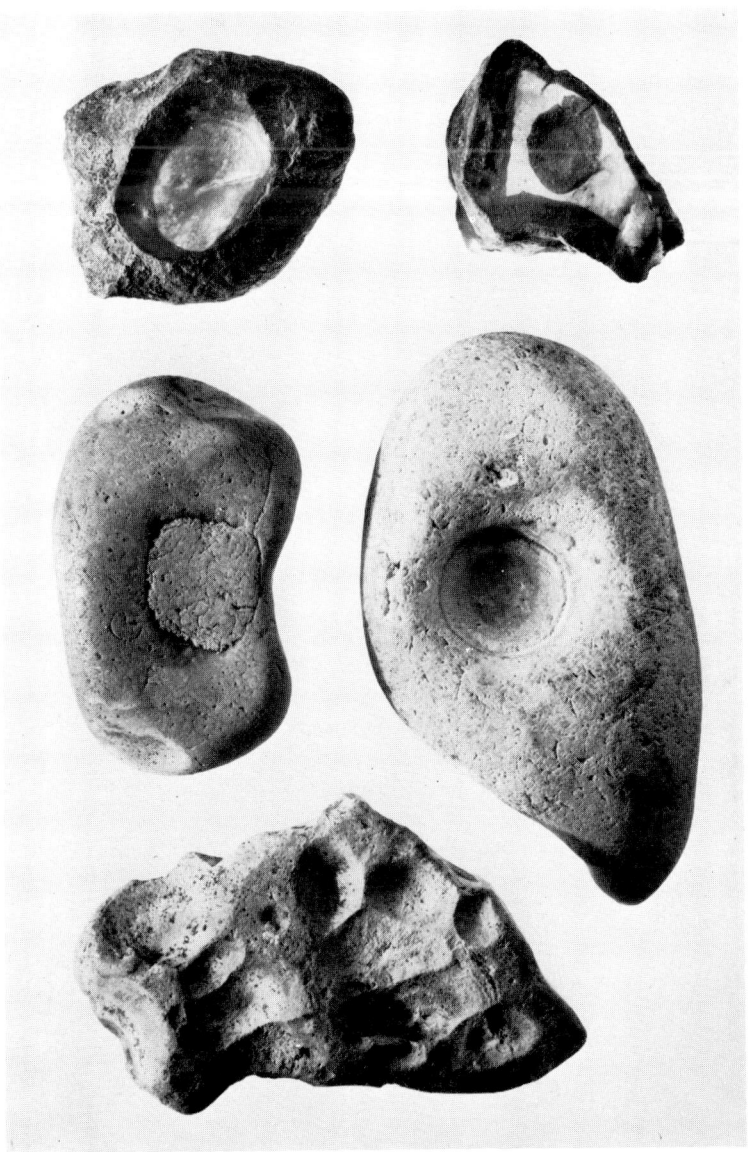

PLATE XV. Derived flints damaged by frost. *Top:* Soil-flints. *Centre:* Beach-pebbles; the apparent frost-pit in the larger one is more probably an abortive attempt at boring by a mollusc. *Foot:* Frost-pitting in a road-flint.

PLATE XVI. Bleaching and staining. *Top (left):* A brown estuarine pebble bleached by a seaweed holdfast; *(right)* brown rust stain on white flint from a steel hawser. *Below (left):* 'Basket' patination, in this case bleached by grass-roots; *(right)* black flint bleached by acid soil.

concretions of considerable size have been formed in iron oxide from solutions percolating through sandstones (Lower Greensand). He pointed out that in experiments of the kind performed by Liesegang, precipitates in gels sometimes form corkscrew spirals instead of bands[45]. E. Hatschek[64] obtained this kind of spiral with both calcium phosphate and lead chromate, and E. S. Hedges and R. V. Henley[60] got the same result with magnesium hydroxide in agar-agar.

Dighton Thomas thought that the author's accidental 'Gastropod', or flint 'Top-shell', was probably precipitated as a tapering spiral, though the tapered specimen in the British Museum shows only a slight narrowing towards one end. He rejected all suggestions that such spirals have an organic origin, and thought that they might occur if there were slight but sudden variations in the thickness of seams in the chalk. This is quite compatible with the view that they are essentially freaks of chance, which is how we should regard them in the absence of other evidence.

Such freaks must constantly occur, but sometimes the degree of special attention afforded them hinders progress towards their proper assessment. Suppose one discovered a number of stones representing every possible form between a misshapen sausage and a bent flattish ovoid. No reason is given why any one of them should be considered more remarkable than any other, yet somewhere in the middle of the series would be a nearly perfect sphere. This would be sure to be picked out as a marvel and some special explanation invented for it. It is true its shape is unique, but that all the other shapes are equally unique is likely to be ignored. The fact is, a perfect sphere should have been expected and its presence is not at all remarkable. Its absence would have been *really* odd, yet nobody would have noticed that!

Gravels

Gravels and shingles are composed of stones that have travelled, and may be of any kind of rock, for example limestones, sandstones, quartzites, slates, schists and igneous rocks. In large parts of England and some Continental countries they are predominantly of flints. In English usage, 'gravels' are inland pebble-beds consisting entirely of water-worn stones, and 'shingles' are pebble beaches along present-day seashores. In America, shingles are usually referred to as 'marine gravels', a term used in England only for examples now found far from the sea. For convenience, the shingles (contemporary marine gravels) are here treated separately from the other gravels.

Flint river gravels consist of nodules which have been washed out of the Chalk by rivers and carried downstream until the water was travelling too slowly to move them any farther. Since the smaller stones can be moved more easily than the bigger ones the gravels usually show grading according to size. When immersed in water, a stone is relieved of about one-third of its weight, and a river moving at two miles per hour can trundle along pebbles as large as a hen's egg over a fairly smooth bed. River-beds are rarely smooth for any great distance, however, and the pebbles are moved chiefly in times of flood.

They commonly move only an inch or two at a time, as a swirl or gush of water catches them, passing thus from one obstruction to the next with long intervals of rest between. There are places where they may tumble over a waterfall or be bumped and scraped along a cataract, and some may get caught among boulders where they are washed round and round by the eddies without a chance to move on. These will finally wear a great hollow or 'pot-hole' in the bedrock, and continue to jostle about in it like eggs being boiled in a saucepan.

Flint is extremely hard; but since one flint is as hard as another, two rubbed or bumped together must abrade each other. During their intervals of rest they are subject to mild bombardment by the smaller stones which are still moving, and to the scratching of sand-grains, while very slow solution goes on all the time. Thus, their corners and edges get chipped off or worn away and after a sufficiently long period they may become completely rounded.

The rate of abrasion is estimated to vary with the square of the velocity of the water, so that if a river trebles its speed in time of flood the process goes on nine times as rapidly. Large irregularly-shaped flints in a slow stream may merely become smoothed over and even retain some of their cortex. Such flints are often described as 'sub-angular' and they often make up the bulk of coarse gravels. Among them fossils may remain perfectly recognizable, as in the upper two sea-urchins on the left of Plate III, and the lower specimen in Plate VI (which is a red gravel-flint). Perfectly smooth round pebbles of black flint are, in fact, comparatively rare—which means that there are only millions of millions of them, instead of millions of millions of millions.

The movements of the stones—and the water—also wear away the river-bed, which becomes deeper and deeper by perhaps a few

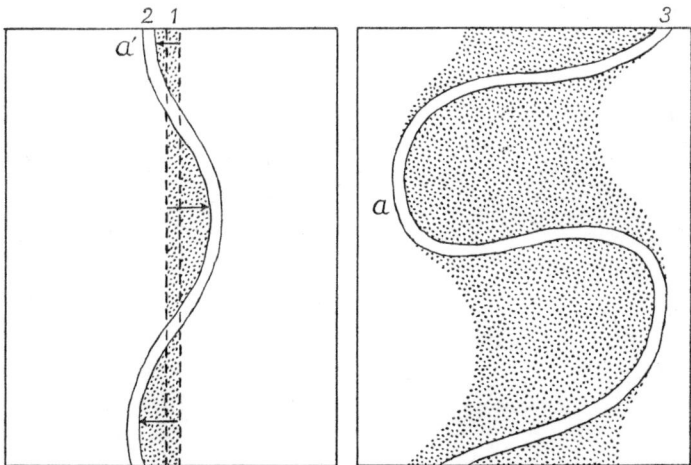

FIG. 31. The area of gravel deposited by a river flowing downwards on the page. In its original straight course, 1, indicated by the broken lines, the gravel (dotted) coincided with the river-bed. In meandering to position 2, as shown by the arrows, the river increased its length by one-twelfth but trebled the area of gravel. The development to position 3 trebled the original length of the river but multiplied the area of gravel by sixteen. During this period (perhaps five thousand years) the meander begun at a' migrated downstream to a. At 1, the gravel-area equals the water-area; at 3, the gravel-area is six times the water-area. (*Note:* In 2 and 3 the gravel also occupies the stream-beds, here left blank for clarity.)

inches every thousand years. In most cases, the banks are continually collapsing into the stream so as to produce a valley with sloping sides. Once a valley has been formed, the river wanders from side to side of it, gradually widening it and depositing gravel wherever it goes. Its windings not only become more and more exaggerated, but the meanders also travel slowly downstream, sweeping the valley from end to end. (See Fig 31.) Eventually, the valley-floor may become a plain a few miles wide, and all of it carpeted with gravel by the action of a small river no broader than a carriage-drive.

Most of the vast sheets of gravel in the London area have been laid down by the Thames and its twenty London tributaries, but some of the gravels are at higher levels than others. They rest, as it were, on shelves and form 'terraces', the most important (in London) being the Taplow Terrace, along which Oxford Street runs. The presence of a terrace indicates that the river responsible for it once flowed at this level, and that at some time in the past it acquired an increase

FIG. 32. A river terrace. The high bank on each side of the stream is part of a bed of gravel laid down when the river flowed at a higher level. An increase in the erosional power of the river ('rejuvenation') caused it to cut a new valley in its old flood-plain and lay down fresh gravels at a lower level.

in velocity owing to the elevation of the land nearer its source, or to an increase in volume through a change of climate or the capture of new sources of water. It then began to cut a new valley in its old plain, leaving terraces high and dry on each side of it. Eventually, it formed a new plain at a lower level than the old, as shown in Fig. 32.

Before the present era there were vast formations of rocks over the present landscape. The extent of the Chalk we have already described, but there have also been sandstones, limestones and clays in various regions, some of them several hundreds of feet thick. And these supported other landscapes at much higher relative levels than the present land-surface and had other drainage systems. Many of the existing high-level or 'plateau' gravels were deposited by the rivers of these systems and bear no relation to the present river drainage. In their day they were all supplied with flints from the contemporary Chalk, and this accounts for the fact that many gravel beds occur far from the present outcrops of chalk, and not only at higher relative levels but also at higher actual levels owing to subsequent elevations of the land. Other high-level gravels may even have been marine shingles deposited during periods of deep regional subsidence of the land, while others again undoubtedly consist of stones brought down by glaciers during the (Pleistocene) Great Ice Age, which may be said to have 'ended' about 10,000 years ago.

The glacial gravels are generally mixed with materials gathered from all the rocks passed by the glaciers on their way down from the ice-cap. Since the Chalk was often cut through or ridden over, the boulder-clay dumped where the ice melted is frequently rich in flints. Where the clay has been washed out these form sheets of gravel. They cover large areas of England north and north-east of the Thames valley and are generally mixed with 'foreign' stones, some of which must have travelled several hundred miles. They include pieces of rock which could only have come from Norway, while chalk containing flints was sometimes transported on the ice-sheet in truly enormous blocks. There are several nearly 500 feet long, and one, about half a mile long, was carried from Yorkshire and dumped in Huntingdonshire, where it now supports the village of Catworth. Elsewhere, the chalk has been broken up with other glacial detritus to form the flint-laden Chalky Boulder Clay, which covers large areas of Cambridgeshire and East Anglia and produces gravel-beds at suitable sites.

The melt-water from deep snows, and sometimes the surface downwash from torrential rain, are also potent agents for producing deposits of gravel at the foot of hill-slopes. The stone-bearing soil becomes saturated and thus lubricated, and under the pull of gravity slides downhill to form a type of deposit known generally as 'head'. The soil then gets washed out, leaving the stones to form a 'head gravel'. There are spreads of flint gravels of this kind in many parts of England, and the flints they contain come from various sources. Some come directly from the Chalk, others from chalk soils and residual deposits, and others again from older gravels. Flints from many different sources may occur jumbled together in the same deposit, as is probable in the sheets of head gravel in north Kent.

In short, wherever there is movement over the surface of the land, whether by water, ice or shifting soil, the loose stones go with it and, being more durable and less easily dispersed than the smaller matter, end up as beds of gravel. During their travels they are subject to all the changes described in the previous sections of this chapter, and to all possible combinations of them. The enormous variety of their forms, colours and modes of occurrence pose endless intriguing problems, and they often tell tales which are truly astonishing.

The four pebbles in the centre of Plate XVIII, for example, bear some very curious spots. The white one has black spots, the black one white spots, and the grey ones both white and black spots. They come from the Blackheath Beds in Surrey, a formation which was probably once a shingle beach on a lagoon. The spots are commonly interpreted as representing the points of contact between pebble and pebble while under pressure from overlying rocks, but this will hardly do without qualification. For one thing, they are not ordinary pressure-marks and show no signs of fracture or comminution. They often have at least one perfectly straight side and are sometimes rectangular, and while some of them appear to be associated with inclusions in the flint, others lie entirely on the surface and resemble chalk-marks. Moreover, they are often too close together to be simultaneous points of contact, and occasionally they lie at the bottom of unlikely hollows. And why are some white but others black?

Perhaps a better explanation could be found in some process of water-exchange through the points of contact. Local effects might be produced by water-bridges maintained by surface-tension, or by pinched specks of argillaceous material. At all events, a white spot of the type observed indicates local loss of water from the substance of the flint, and a black spot either the absorption of water as in the restoration of blackness in the zones of agate-rinded flint, or the unaltered original flint of the pebble. A flint deficient in water in contact with one ready to lose water might well result in a local surface exchange. If so, the factors involved would probably include capillarity on an almost molecular scale, where the tensile strength of water is so great that transferance would probably be complete within any isolated zone. (See Appendix VII.)

Problems of this kind are continually turning up. What are we to make of the soil-pebble at the top right-hand of Plate XV, for example? This has a black core with a white cortex, but this is surrounded again by black flint one boundary of which is as straight as a ruled line. It could be some sort of infilled hollow flint, but it is difficult to imagine how the infilling could have occurred. The pebble to the left of it is also black outside and nearly white within, and there are signs of banding on the edge of the lighter part. The hollow is the work of frost and the light colour could be a reduction-patch caused by the hollow's remaining filled with vegetable soil for a long time, but it is a puzzle, nevertheless.

The pebbles of a gravel are sometimes cemented together by other minerals to make a sort of natural concrete called 'conglomerate'. The binding material or 'matrix' is carried into the interstices between the pebbles by percolating water, and is usually gritty. It may be a hardened clay, an iron compound like limonite, some form of calcite, or a deposit of silica. In conglomerates of flint pebbles it is sometimes a siliceous grit firmly set by partial solution and united to the flint by the same process. The matrix is thus as hard as flint itself, and in the example from the Hertfordshire 'pudding-stone' shown at the bottom of Plate XVIII, it will be noticed that when the specimen was broken from the rock, the pebbles did not part from the matrix but were themselves cracked across.

The cementation is, indeed, so complete that it is likely to have occurred during a prolonged influx of exceptional quantities of dissolved silica. This is not difficult to account for if we assume the cementation to have taken place beneath a land-surface supporting forests of Pteridophytes or grasses. A soil consisting largely of silicates and only a foot or two thick may contain 2,000 tons of silica (in combination) per acre. In about 5,000 years the whole of this will have been converted to soluble opaline silica by such plants, and all but the 100 pounds or so maintained constantly above ground by the living vegetation could have been carried downwards by drainage. (See Appendix V.)

This could have happened over the Hertfordshire deposits (and elsewhere) at any time since their elevation above the sea, and since they are of Eocene age and lay beneath dry land during the succeeding Oligocene and Miocene periods, there was ample opportunity for their induration with silica. The landscape in Miocene times, in particular, seems to have consisted of vast grasslands or prairies and the process could have gone on at a maximum rate for several millions of years. The hard, indurated sandstone or 'quartzite', of which only the boulders known as 'sarsens' or 'greywethers' now remain, may well have been formed in the same way. Detailed research into the geomorphology, climate and drainage of these periods might disclose when and where the optimum conditions prevailed, but only the general suggestion can be offered here.

Shingles

The Hertfordshire pebbles once formed a shingle beach and constitute a sort of fossil seashore, but the present-day beaches also abound in problems. Their rounded flint pebbles must all have come originally from the Chalk, but when the sea attacks a chalk cliff the flints fall to the beach as irregularly-shaped black and white nodules of all sizes. It takes time for them to get knocked into smooth shapes, and in the process they may become stained almost any colour by the normal minerals in the sea-water, and by those derived from seaweed and dead sea-creatures. Iron again predominates as a staining agent, but lead and zinc are present in almost equal abundance while copper and manganese are adequately represented. But the most noticeable effect of the sea is the mechanical damage it accomplishes.

The sea is a very much more powerful agent of destruction than a river and constantly drags the stones up and down the beach. During storms the beach becomes, in fact, a veritable ball-mill and, in addition to being rolled violently along, the stones are subject to shattering blows by the breaking waves. A breaking wave falling on a hundred yards of beach may weigh about 300 tons. This rams the top layer of stones against the lower ones, and sets up a general vibration or 'chattering' in the surrounding shingle.

The water falling on a single flattish round pebble about 3 inches in diameter may weigh 20 pounds, spread over a second of time. But this pebble rests on another round pebble, their point of contact measuring, say, a mere sixty-fourth of an inch square. (See Fig. 33.)

PLATE XVII. *Above:* Three furrowed and two banded flints (drawings *after* S. P. Woodward[58]). *Below:* Calcined flint, a Neolithic 'pot-boiler' from Hayes, Kent.

PLATE XVIII. *Top (left):* The back of the coloured pebble shown on the right in the frontispiece; *(right)* a beach-pebble containing small rectangular holes once occupied by calcite crystals. *Centre:* Typical spotted pebbles from the Blackheath Beds. *Below:* Hertfordshire puddingstone.

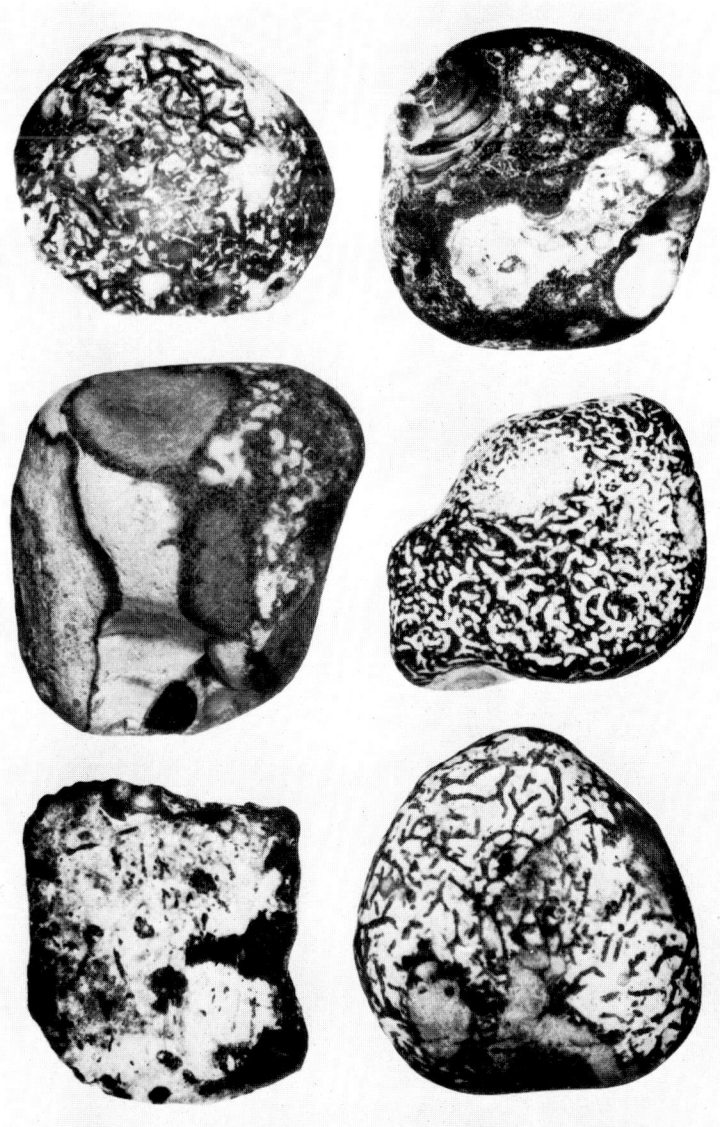

PLATE XIX. Beach-pebbles showing wave-battering, differential staining and (*right*) organic patterns possibly reflecting sponge structure but more likely the work of small marine worms. The specimen at the bottom (*left*) shows 'graphic' patination.

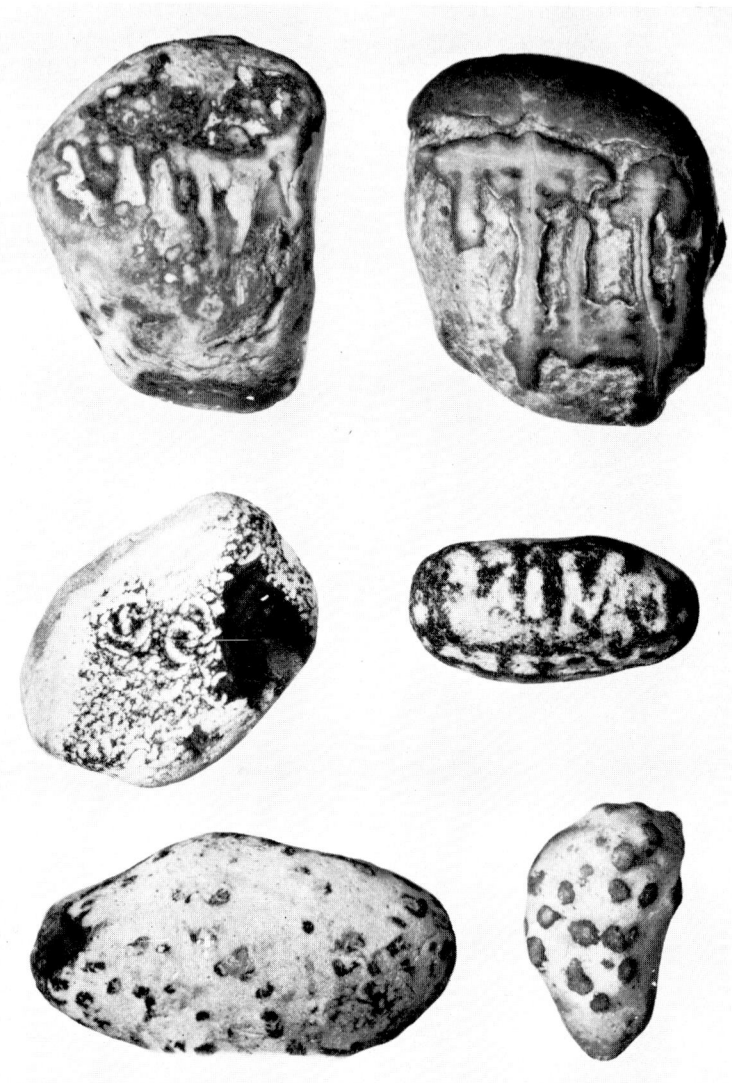

PLATE XX. Beach-pebbles in which differential erosion mimics artificial inscriptions and suggests currant buns. *Top:* Pebbles in which cracks have been sealed up with quartz. *Centre:* Pebbles with local surface alterations, probably by marine worms. *Foot:* Pebbles in which sponge canal-systems have been made more resistant than the normal flint by chalcedonization.

This is where the 20 pounds weight would be concentrated were it not that the upper surface of the top stone is almost certainly convex and sheds some of the water. Let us suppose that the weight at this point is only 10 pounds distributed through 1 second, or 1 pound in one-tenth of a second. On so small an area, this is equivalent to a force of nearly 2 tons per square inch delivered in one-tenth of a second, and with the pressure prolonged through a full second. Both

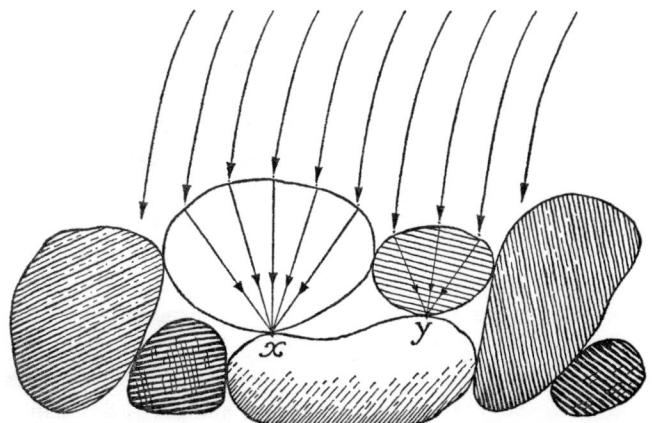

FIG. 33. Water from a breaking wave falling on beach-pebbles. The arrows show how the weight on two pebbles is sustained at the points x and y. The energy concentrated at the point x may equal 80 joules (10 pounds falling 6 feet).

flints are 'bruised' and suffer minute surface-fracture at the point of contact, even if fragments are not actually chipped off.

There is, of course, no precision in these figures, for the random distribution of the stones on the beach must result in wide variations in the damage sustained. Some will get off lightly; others may receive an exaggerated blow that cracks them right through. But in time, every stone on the beach between high and low watermarks will show signs of battering of this sort, and the top two specimens in Plate XIX illustrate the typical appearance of wave-battered pebbles. It has been estimated[65] that during a heavy storm the energy the sea expends on a shore may exceed 70 horsepower for every foot length of the coast!

The centre specimen on the left of the same Plate shows wave-battering at one side, but the rest carries long, isolated surface-cracks enclosing undamaged areas, the cracks having been sealed up with silica stained a dark brown. The separate 'panels' are coloured various shades of yellow, red and brown, each forming a well-demarcated unit. All this is only skin-deep: the bulk of the stone is pure-black flint of even texture, and still yields a conchoidal fracture.

This specimen probably lay face downwards on a sandy bed for a long time, for its back surface is completely covered with the fine mosaic-like pattern typical of wave-battering. Such patterns often appear to be brightly and variously coloured while wet, but as the pebble dries the colours disappear and a sort of greyish bloom supervenes. This is due to the myriad of fine scratches which cover the surface and may be compared with the surface of ground-glass. Indeed, bottle-glass which has suffered in the same way may often be picked up on a beach. The coloured pattern may be preserved by varnishing the stone or by the more arduous process of polishing it.

The two lower right-hand specimens in Plate XIX show patterns of a different kind, and these are problematical. In both cases the white areas are very thoroughly corticated and partly desilicified, for they are full of pores visible through a hand-glass. The black areas are unaltered flint, though scratched by friction and showing very minute scars probably from chattering. In the upper specimen the black marks also carry a high polish very difficult to account for.

The condition of the white marks and their curiously curved forms can be very closely compared with known cases of attack by marine organisms, some of which are described below, but it is difficult to picture how organisms of any kind could completely cover all the surfaces of a pebble with such a dense, uniform pattern. It is, perhaps, possible that the pebbles lay at some time in a small rock-pool which was swarming with polychaete worms or larvae of some kind.

Another suggestion is that the marks follow inhomogeneities in the flint reflecting sponge-structure. If so, the sponges are completely unidentifiable, though it is interesting to compare the spherical specimen in Plate XXI with the *Callopegma* in Plate IX. Three similar specimens are shown in Plate XX, on the left at the top and in the centre. In these the white markings mimic letters of the alphabet and might easily be mistaken for artificial scratches. This, however, is impossible and the resemblances are quite accidental.

Variations in the density of the flint often result in differential abrasion, and Plate XX shows some examples. In the specimen at the top, on the right, the outstanding bars suggesting Hebrew characters or some hanging script appear to be slightly chalcedonized and may conceivably have developed from original sponge-structure. Each bar is, however, divided by a narrow groove which more probably represents an old crack in the flint. The spaces between the bars bear smaller and less-easily-discerned marks of the same general character, but are pitted and scratched in contrast with the polished surfaces of the large bars. It is likely enough that this pebble had once been badly shattered and was afterwards repaired by having its cracks sealed by silica from solution. This could hardly have taken place on Brighton beach, where it was found, but the pebble had a previous history in the gravels on which the sea-front rests.

The two specimens at the foot of Plate XX also show differential abrasion, but their projecting knobs, which have resisted cortication, almost certainly represent the infilled canals of sponges. The left-hand pebble is grey with black knobs, and the other buff with reddish knobs. The reader may compare them with the fossil sponge at the foot of Plate IX, and with the markings in the specimens of *Siphonia* shown in the frontispiece.

All the types of pebbles described in this chapter are very common indeed on shingle beaches of flints. They may be picked up in scores, together with others presenting similar problems, and the beachcomber will find a surprising number which have apparently had holes drilled in them. Plate XXI shows five typical examples of these from beaches on the south coast of England. The holes illustrated are quite different from those described on pages 20 and 29, and are produced by marine organisms.

Holes ranging in size from a coarse hair to a pencil-lead are commonly drilled by polychaete worms of the genera *Polydora* and *Potamilla*, which are bristle-worms belonging to the same phylum as the earthworms (Annelida). They are very minute, seldom measuring more than half an inch long. Their bodies are covered with short bristles and their heads bear long tentacles often kept coiled up like corkscrews. They make short, U-shaped burrows with the two openings side by side, so that their holes may be recognized by occurring always in pairs[66]. (See Fig. 34.) The flint lining the holes and surrounding their openings is strongly desilicified and visibly porous.

These worms will attack almost any kind of rock-material, including limestones, shales, slates and sandstones, but how they manage to bore into such a hard substance as flint is a mystery. Their bodies are soft and bear nothing tougher than the horny bristles, so that some sort of chemical reagent is presumably secreted. This is frequently referred to as an 'acid'*, but though any acid would serve

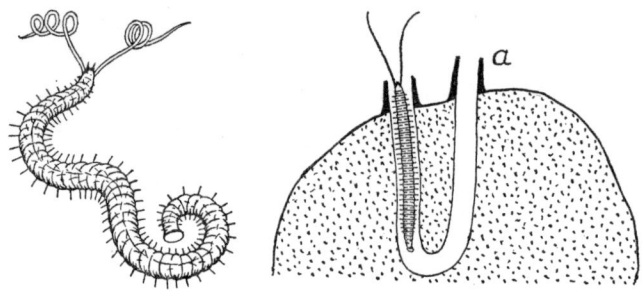

FIG. 34. *Polydora ciliata*, much enlarged. The worm is seen in its U-shaped hole on the right. Note the tubes of mud erected round the openings. (*Adapted from* W. T. Calman[66].)

for boring into limestone, no known acid (except the unlikely hydrofluoric) will attack flint. On the other hand, a strong alkali might be used on flint but would be useless with limestone. It seems more likely that the worm secretes a substance which combines with the rock to form a soluble organic compound similar to that manufactured from silicious rocks by some plants. The remarkable results of such root-action have already been described (pages 87, 110) and a parallel animal process is at least credible.

Larger holes are bored by certain molluscs, though it is not possible to identify all the holes that may be found in flint pebbles. One of the

* The reader may have observed how almost any kind of unexplained phenomenon to do with the disappearance of minerals is liable to be attributed to 'acid', regardless of the chemical probabilities. One should never accept such statements except in cases where it has been demonstrated, for the use of the term is sometimes as glib as the old attribution of all mysterious occurrences to 'electricity', 'rays', or 'vibrations'.

borers responsible is almost certainly *Gastrochaena dubia*, owner of the fragile Flask Shell illustrated in Fig. 35. The flask-like shape of the holes is characteristic but the animal gets its name from a flask-shaped jacket of shell-fragments and sand-grains with which it protects itself when taking up residence in old bivalve shells[67]. Another borer of comparatively large holes is the Wrinkled Rock-borer or Red Nose, *Hiatella* (*Saxicava*) *rugosa*, which makes a funnel-shaped hole about one-third of an inch in diameter at its opening. (See

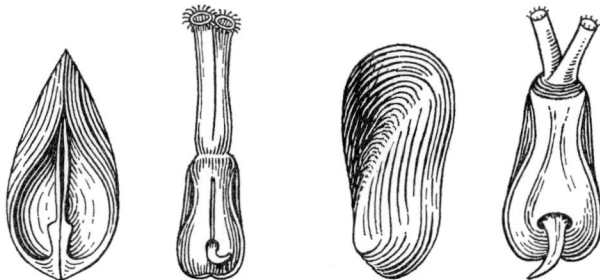

FIG. 35. Small rock-boring molluscs with their shells. *Left:* Flask-shell, *Gastrochaena dubia*; note the enormous oval gape. *Right:* Wrinkled Rock-borer, *Hiatella* (*Saxicava*) *rugosa*, with its curiously misshapen shell. (*After* Edward Step[67].)

Fig. 35.) The large specimen on the right of Plate XV is quite possibly the beginning of such a boring.

There are several other molluscs which bore large cylindrical holes in quite hard sandstones and schists[68] but have not been certainly associated with flint, though some flints have clearly bored holes quite big enough for them. They include the Little Piddock (*Barnea parva*, formerly *Pholas parva*), which also bores into slate and cement-stone. All these molluscs have calcareous shells, often thin and often bearing projections like the teeth of a rasp. They rasp their way into soft rocks, as the worn teeth show, but as they are often found in rocks much too hard for this method alone, they probably also secrete substances which combine with or dissolve the rock-material. It remains to find a flint with such a shell still in its hole, for even the identifiable holes are almost invariably empty.

As with fluviatile gravels, the pebbles of shingle beaches are subject

DERIVED FLINTS

to grading according to size, the smaller ones being raked farther down the beach than the big ones and becoming more and more rounded as they go. Waves are able to throw big stones up the beach, but the rapid dispersal of the water by percolation leaves them stranded and the downflow ('backwash') drags only the smaller stones with it.

Perfectly shaped, smooth, oval stones of very large size are sometimes found, but the big ones at the foot of the cliffs are usually subangular. A small pebble may get caught in a hollow in one of these and, being constantly swirled around as the waves wash over it, wear the hollow into a deep cup and itself into a round marble. The most common regular shapes among the well-worn stones are flattened ovoids and bun-shaped discs; spherical pebbles are rare.

As with fluviatile gravels, also, the pebbles of a shingle beach may travel a long way from the chalk cliffs which first gave them up to the sea. Shingle beaches are often found on flat or marshy coasts many miles from the nearest outcrop of the Chalk, or even at the foot of cliffs of some quite different rock, such as sandstone, clay or shale. That the pebbles travel along the coast is evident on any shore where groynes have been erected. The purpose of the groynes is solely to prevent the migration of the beach, the direction of which may be seen in the difference in the level of the beach on the two sides of a groyne. (See Fig. 36.) The stones are piled up against one side but have been dragged away from the other.

This 'longshore drifting', as it is called, is the result of the raking of the pebbles up and down the beach by waves which approach the shore obliquely. Such waves not only move the pebbles up and down, but sweep them along as well, and if there were no groynes to prevent this the whole beach would eventually disappear. However, the lateral movement of the pebbles will stop where the shore curves round to face the waves, and here they will accumulate to form a shinglebank. This may gradually build out seawards to form a 'spit'.

During its longshore travels a beach naturally gathers fresh stones from many sources, and an originally pure flint shingle may be found to contain stones derived from other rocks before it has travelled very far. Again, stones from distant places may be carried past the chalk cliffs and add their quota to the flints even at the start of their journey. Thus, the flint beaches on the south coast of England contain 'foreign' stones such as quartz and jasper, which ultimately came from the West Country, and those on the east coast contain stones which came from the north.

When pebbles are transported in this way along a clearly demarcated stretch of coast, they tend to become graded along the direction of their motion. The process is not by any means simple. Much depends on the surface over which the stones travel. They behave

FIG. 36. How groynes prevent the pebbles of a beach from travelling along the coast.

differently when resting upon other pebbles and when on smooth sand, and again differently when they are angular and when they are smooth and round. A large spherical pebble can be rolled along over smaller ones, but not small ones over larger ones. With pebbles of mixed sizes the smaller ones generally fall to the bottom through the spaces between the larger ones, so that the larger ones travel farther. On the other hand, very large stones in vast numbers may form an immovable block that only a severe storm can disturb.

Below low-water level, where the beach is always submerged, the movements are produced by currents and the grading tends to be reversed[69]. With a mixed shingle the buoyancy of the smaller pebbles

DERIVED FLINTS

causes a certain degree of 'fluidization' in their bed and the larger ones tend to sink below them because of their greater weight, so that the smaller ones now travel farther. An undertow has been observed to lift small pebbles right out of their bed and carry them along as if they were floating. As a wave passes overhead, they may be seen to 'jump' and are carried sideways before they settle again, and even at a depth of 180 feet stones weighing up to a pound have been found washed into lobster-pots[65]. Stones may also be transported by seaweeds. If, for example, a bladder-wrack attaches itself to a small stone like the one illustrated in Plate XVI, it will lift it and carry it along when caught in a current.

Comparatively rapid elevations of the land, such as occurred at various times as the weight of the ice-cap was removed from northern Europe after each phase of the Great Ice Age, have frequently lifted shingle beaches high above sea-level. Here they form 'raised beaches' formally comparable with the river terraces described on page 132. Some raised beaches are several hundred feet above the present sea-level and in suitable circumstances may form 'plateau gravels'.

All these topics are fully treated in books on physical geography and geology. Here, it has been necessary only to show how derived flints may travel and why they are often found in unexpected situations.

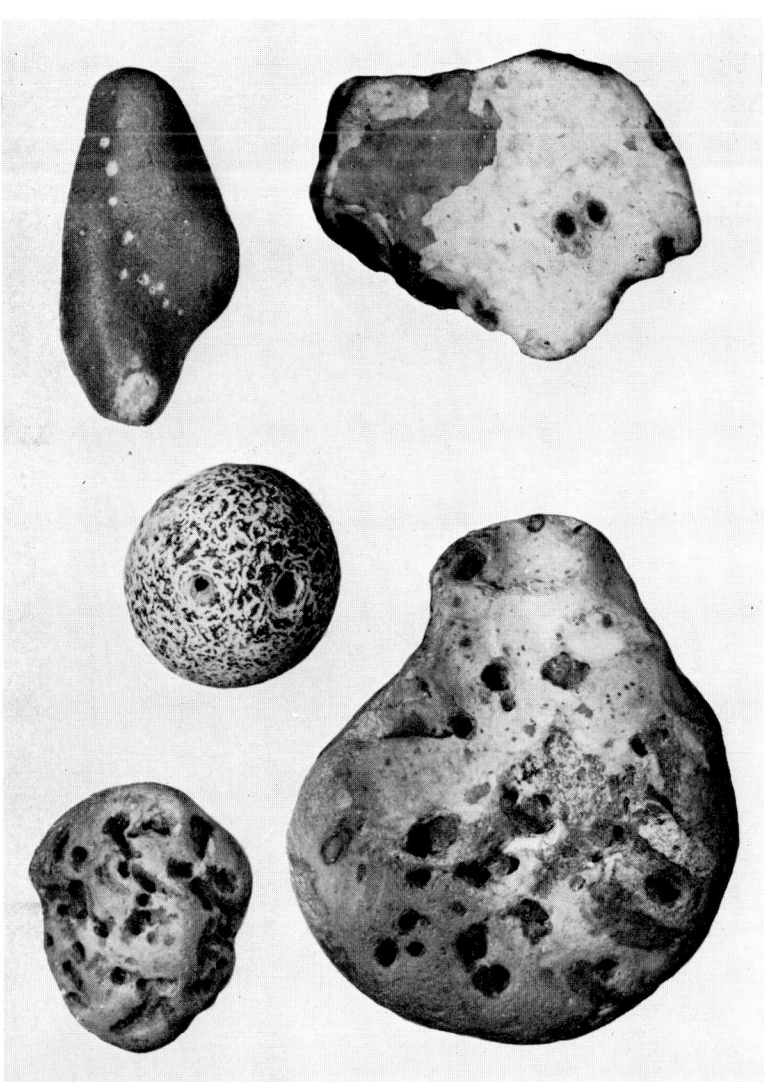

PLATE XXI. Beach-pebbles showing borings by two species of polychaete worms and possibly a mollusc. The worm-holes are always U-shaped so that their openings occur in pairs, but a mollusc makes a single short *cul-de-sac*.

PLATE XXII. Paleolithic flint implements. *Left*: A 'core' implement, an ovate hand-axe about 4 in. long. *Right*: A 'flake' implement, possibly a scraper, 3¼ in. long.

5

Prehistoric Uses of Flint

FLINT WAS SURELY the most important of all the rocks and minerals used as a raw material by Stone Age man, but while this chapter discusses such general questions as the methods of manufacture of flint implements, it does not deal with the origin, distribution and chronology of particular 'cultures'. Such subjects are dealt with in books on archaeology or prehistoric anthropology; they belong to the story of man rather than to the story of flint.

Nevertheless, some sort of broad time-scale must be given since the ageing of artefacts is described, and the development of techniques can hardly be outlined without reference to the broad divisions of the Old, Middle and New Stone Ages and to a few of their characteristic industries. A general time-scale displaying the Stone Ages in relation to the historic period is therefore given in Fig. 37, and the distribution of the major cultures and industries through Europe, Asia and Africa will be found in Fig. 67 in Appendix VIII. In both these diagrams the term 'Eolithic' appears (in quotation marks), and a note on the use of this word is desirable.

'Eolithic' is an adjective formed from 'eolith' (Gk., 'dawn-stone'), a name which seems to have been coined by Gabriel de Mortillet in 1876 to denote man's very first attempts at making stone implements. In England, it was first used by J. Allen Brown in 1892 with reference to some stones apparently showing crude artificial chipping discovered by Benjamin Harrison on the North Downs. These had been described by J. Prestwich in 1891, and other such specimens were then found in many parts of south-east England and in East Anglia. However, their authenticity was disputed and it has since proved impossible to decide whether most of them are of human origin or not. In particular, the form known as 'rostro-carinate' ('beaked-and-keeled'), illustrated in Fig. 43 and at one time considered the most authentic of the eoliths, has been found to occur by natural fracture during the fluid movement of gravel soils after severe freezing in depth, so that few of the classical 'eoliths' are any longer accepted by archaeologists and the term 'eolith' has tended to fall into disuse.

One of the chief objections to the human origin of the East Anglian stones has been their undoubted great age, for they are certainly more than a million years old. However, this objection now carries much less weight because undoubted 'pebble-tools' (pebbles sharpened by slight chipping) which are certainly more than a million years old have been found in Africa[71]. Moreover, these were made by a race of Hominids known as the Australopithecines before modern man had evolved, and the term 'eolith' is surely most appropriate to them. Examples of such pebble-tools belonging to the Oldowan and Kafuan industries are shown in Fig. 43.

It seems reasonable to use the term 'Eolithic' for the period of these earliest experiments in stone, and to keep the term 'Palæolithic' ('ancient stone'*) for the period of the oldest completely-formed implements, which were certainly made by members of the genus *Homo*. This, at all events, is the system adopted in Figs. 37 and 67, but the reader is reminded that all such classifications are merely matters of convenience; they are not concerned with facts but with terminology.

The time-scale in Fig. 37 is approximately that advocated by M. H. Day[71], A. Holmes[50] and others, though it may be noted that I. W. Cornwall[72] and the late F. E. Zeuner[73,74] favoured somewhat shorter periods. In the present context we need only to realize the comparative immensity of all plausible estimates of the times involved. If we condense the whole period from the Lower Palæolithic to the present day into a single year, then we might reasonably think of the Romans as ruling Britain for about 6 hours yesterday, the Ancient Egyptians as building the pyramids 3 days ago, and the Upper Palæolithic or Old Stone Age as not coming to an end until about a week ago.

---

* The terms 'Palæolithic' for the Old Stone Age and 'Neolithic' for the New Stone Age, were introduced by Sir John Lubbock (the 1st Lord Avebury) in 1865.

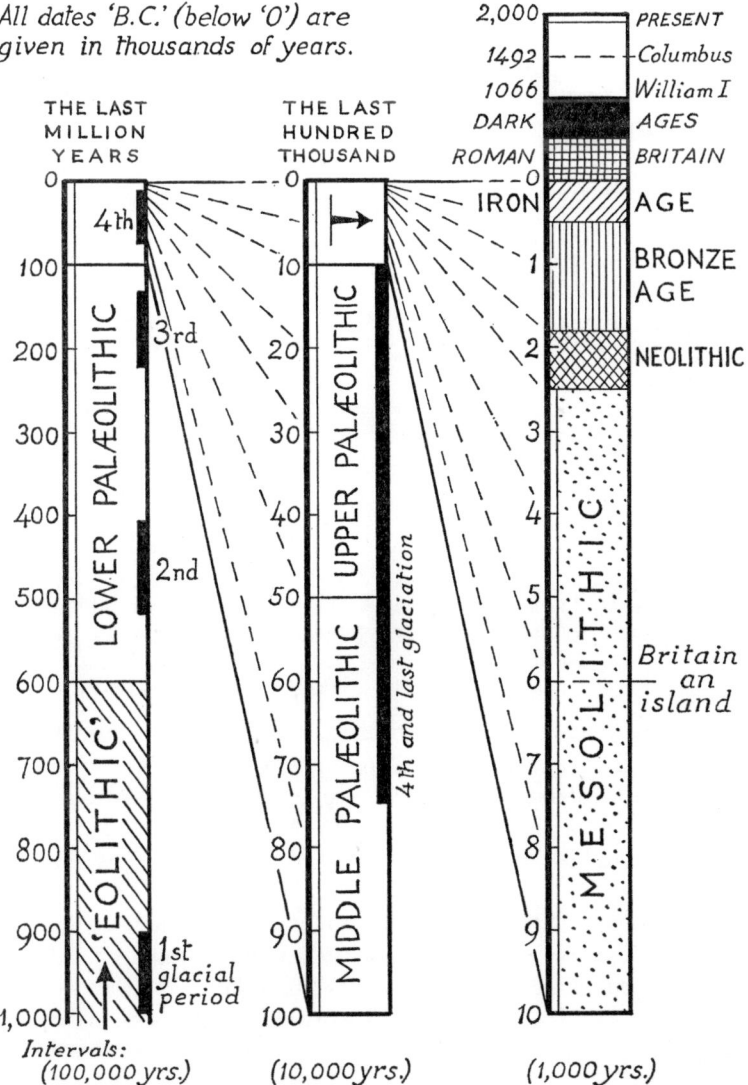

FIG. 37. The cultural periods during which flint has been used by man. Note that the time-scale of each column is ten times greater than that to its left. (E.g., compare the two representations of the 4th glacial period.)

Artificial fracture

The artificial chipping of a flint produces a 'flake' which bears recognizable characteristics, and when these are all present and well-developed we may infer human agency with reasonable—but not absolute—certainty. The nodule or 'core' from which the flake was removed shows the same characteristics in reverse, and if such a core shows that several flakes were removed in a consistent and regular manner, so as roughly to shape the core, then we may be even more —but still not absolutely—certain. It is only when the shape produced by the flaking is of quite unnatural complexity, and shows evidence of design and skilful systematic edge-trimming, that we can positively

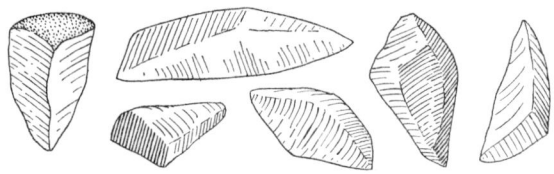

FIG. 38. Dreikanters. Angular pebbles do not roll but tend to remain long enough in one position for the blown desert sands to grind facets on them.

affirm that it was made by intelligent man. Perfect symmetry of shape is not in itself a safe criterion, for natural stones often mimic the shapes of hand-axes, points, and even triangular arrow-heads.

Some typical natural fractures were described in Chapter 1 and illustrated in Figs. 5 and 6. It is easy to see how frost-pitted specimens and pot-lid fractures may sometimes be mistaken for artefacts, but rough shaping of this kind is often followed by much more detailed 'work'. This may occur in subsoils or gravel-beds, and on surfaces exposed to blown sand. We may dismiss these last with an illustration of some typical dreikanters, which were sufficiently described on page 122. Fig. 38 shows how easily these faceted pebbles might be mistaken for such artificially worked stones as the two implements on the left in Fig. 49.

Flints forming gravels or buried beneath soils are subject to what is called 'subsoil pressure-flaking'. This may occur through the sheer

ARTIFICIAL FRACTURE

weight of the overlying beds, but is also caused by movements of the containing bed during adjustments to a disturbed equilibrium. Among such disturbances are those resulting from soil-creep, which is the general tendency of soils to slide down slopes, solifluction,

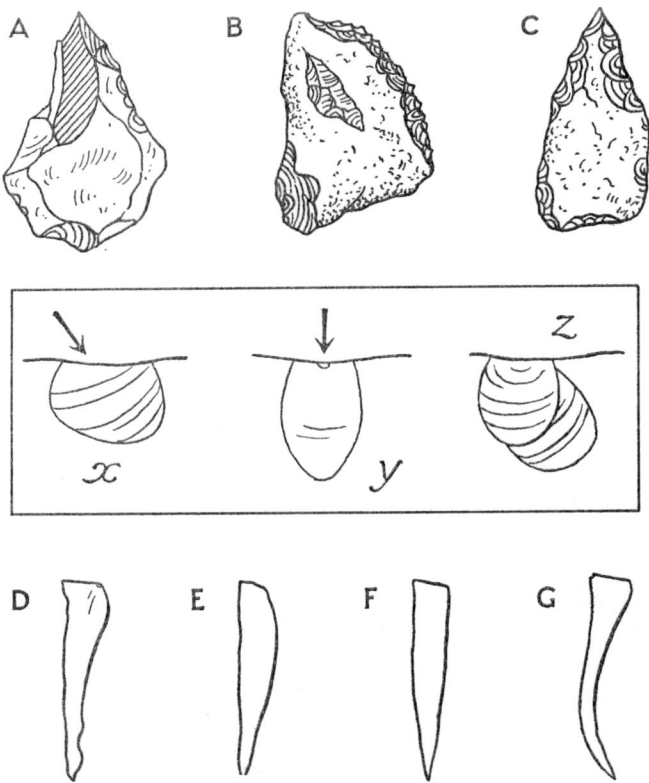

FIG. 39. The natural flaking of flint. A, B, C, Flints accidentally 'trimmed' by subsoil pressure-flaking. *Inset:* Types of flaking, enlarged; see the text. D, side-view of a hand-struck flake for comparison with natural flakes E, F, G.

or the movement of soils in the melt-water following severe frost, the lateral meandering of rivers, the advances of the sea, landslides, cliff-falls, earth tremors, and the slow folding or faulting of the strata.
During such movements the stones get pressed against one another

with sufficient force to cause small flakes to spring off their edges. Prolonged but slow movement may cause an edge to appear to have been deliberately sharpened, as in the examples shown in Fig. 39 at A, B and C. However, though these look as if they had been systematically worked they are purely accidental, and such edge-trimming is never, in itself, significant. Edge-trimming is acceptable as evidence only if other signs of human workmanship are also present.

Simplest of these is the regular arrangement and disposition of the flake-scars, and evidence that the force which detached the flakes was applied at right-angles to the edge. In the inset in Fig. 39, x shows the pattern of ripples left by an oblique application of force, while y shows the effect of force applied at a right-angle. The systematic detachment of flakes is often betrayed by the consistency of the ripple-patterns, as in the edge-trimming of the large side-scraper in Fig. 46. Again, a flake struck off so as to overlap the mark of an older flake is said to 'truncate' it, as in Fig. 39 at z, and it has been observed that while naturally-chipped stones often show a great many truncated flake-scars, these are comparatively rare on artefacts[82].

The signs associated with flakes detached by a violent blow are much more easily recognized. Here, the artificial product differs markedly from the natural because the causative circumstances of the fracture are usually quite different. A stone falling from a cliff usually bounces a few times before reaching the bottom, and the natural blows it suffers are seldom equivalent to more than a fall of, say, 20 feet. But a blow struck by hand may be equivalent to a fall of 120 feet, and this produces unique features*.

The recognizable marks of a hand-struck flake are illustrated in Fig. 40. The point of impact or 'point of percussion', where the blow

* A fall of 20 feet is equivalent to a collision at about 25 m.p.h., but one of 120 feet is equivalent to a collision at 60 m.p.h. This is only two-thirds the speed of a ball leaving the hand of a fast bowler at cricket, which has been measured at 93 m.p.h. (H. Larwood, 1933), but violence is not the only factor affecting the form of the flake detached from a flint by a blow. The manner and the angle of the blow are equally important, and these are even less likely to be matched in a mechanical accident. Flint 'knappers' say that they never use excessive force, so it would seem that the main cause of the differences between artificial fracture and natural fracture is that the first is produced by a swift light blow and the second by a slower heavy one, but there must be many anomalies.

ARTIFICIAL FRACTURE

was struck, is usually recognizable as a minute pimple or bead on the flake struck off, or as a corresponding hollow in the core. It is not always to be found on surviving fragments but may generally be seen on the edge of a 'striking platform' when this is present. The striking platform is a flat surface produced by striking off a knob, or by some other means, as a preliminary to systematic flaking.

Immediately below the point of percussion the flake shows a prominent swelling called the 'bulb (or cone) of percussion', and from some

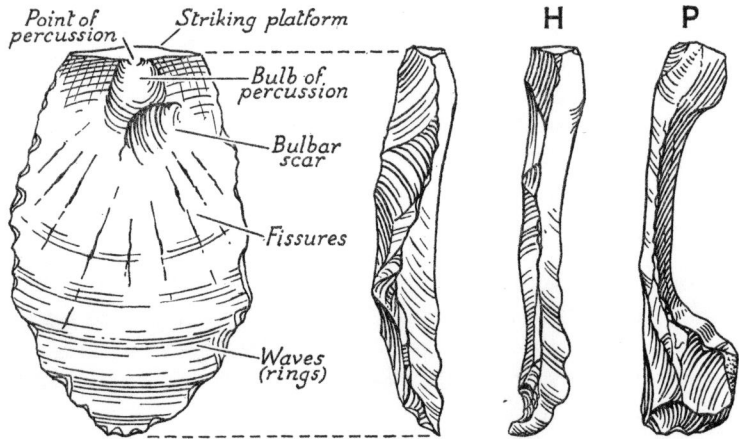

FIG. 40. Artificial fracture of flint. *Left:* The characteristics of a hand-struck flake. H, Hinge fracture. P, Plunging fracture.

part of this a thin scale generally flies off leaving a 'bulbar scar' or *éraillure*. The rest of the flake sweeps away from the bulb, its surface being rippled into waves which are concentric with the point of percussion. Radiating from this point, too, there are usually some fine fractures or 'fissures' which cross the waves at right-angles. A blow of inadequate force may produce the 'hinge' fracture shown at H, and occasionally the 'plunging' fracture shown at P, but the ideal flake tapers to a more or less sharp edge.

These characteristics seldom appear in fractures produced by the slower processes of nature, though some of them may be present in a modified form. For example, side-views of hand-struck flakes are shown in Fig. 40 and at D in Fig. 39, where E, F and G are naturally-produced flakes for comparison. It will be noted that these have no strongly-developed ripples, though in some specimens caricatures of all these features may be imagined.

Fractures produced by sudden pressure may show (fairly flat) bulbs of percussion below the point of application of the pressure, although there has not really been any 'percussion'. When a fracture is caused by natural pressure, the broken stone has suffered by being squeezed between two other stones, neither of which is the more 'important'. The result is that if a bulb of percussion is produced on one side, there is generally also a second bulb on the opposite side. This does not happen with artificial pressure-flaking because none of the methods used provides rigid resistance on the opposite side, though it may occur in true percussion flaking, as we shall see.

There are five principal ways of shaping a flint by percussion, but the first is suitable for only the crudest sort of work. It is simply to bring the stone down sharply on to another, larger stone, controlling the angle of impact so as to split a flake off the workpiece without cracking the 'anvil'. This method was probably often used to reduce very large nodules to a manageable size, or to knock off useless or awkward protuberances. Pebble-tools and the cruder 'choppers' may have been trimmed entirely in this way.

In the second method, the workpiece is placed on the anvil and then struck with a third stone, called the 'hammer-stone'. Since it thus suffers violence between two stones, it is virtually struck upwards by the anvil as well as downwards by the hammer—or rather, the blow it receives is reflected back into the lower end by the anvil with almost equal force. The consequence is often that the detached flake has a bulb at each end and the core a corresponding pair of hollows. Some of the earlier hand-axes bear deep hollows and lumpy protuberances which suggest manufacture by this method. (See Plate XXII.)

A better way of shaping a nodule, and one which detaches flakes with useful sharp edges, is to hold the workpiece in the left hand and strike it with a hammer-stone held in the right. The left hand may be steadied by resting it on the knee, which then becomes a sort of resilient anvil. (See Fig. 41 A.) This method is still used by the

Australian aborigines, who are said to require only a few minutes to knock out a usable implement*[75].

In the fourth method of shaping stones by direct percussion, the hammer-stone is replaced by a baton of bone or very hard wood, as illustrated in Fig. 41 C, but this is used for more accurate shaping

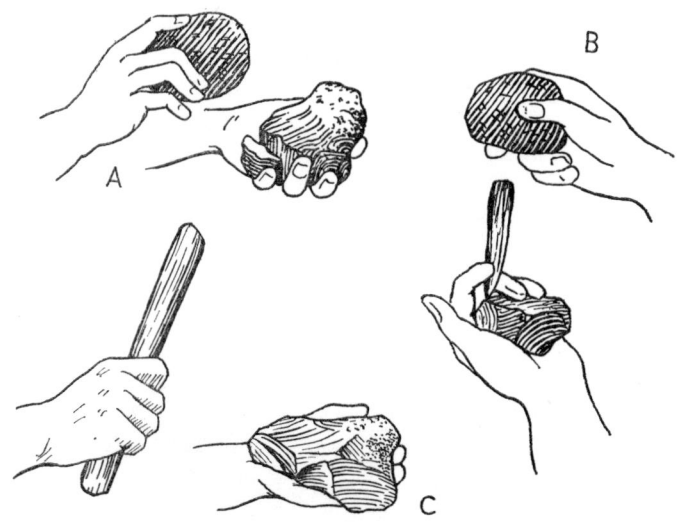

FIG. 41. Artificial fracture of flint: by percussion. See the text. (*After* W. H. Holmes (B), K. P. Oakley (A) and W. Watson (C).)

and for the production of usable flakes. The type of implement made by simply shaping a stone is called a 'core' tool, but there is a whole class of sharp cutting implements made from the slivers struck off the core, and these are called 'flake' tools. The baton was used especially for this more exacting work, which demands considerable skill. It is said that a Queensland aborigine may discard two or three

---

* In the absence of flint, they use obsidan (volcanic glass), chalcedony, chert, jasper, quartzite, igneous rocks such as porphyry, basalt and diorite, and even bottle-glass. However, according to Dr. Jennings (see page 44), there is little doubt that Eocene 'flints' were mined in the Koonalda Cave on the Nullarbor Plain about 15,000 years ago, where they gave rise to a stone industry contemporary with the European Upper Palæolithic.

hundred flakes before producing one suitable for finishing off as a knife.

Finishing an implement is generally done by 'pressure-flaking', to be described in a moment, and sometimes by grinding, but in North America the 'indirect percussion' method is often used. In this, a small pointed stick or piece of bone is held vertically by the fingers of the left hand with its point on the spot it is desired to strike. A hammer-stone is then used on the top of the stick, as in knocking-in

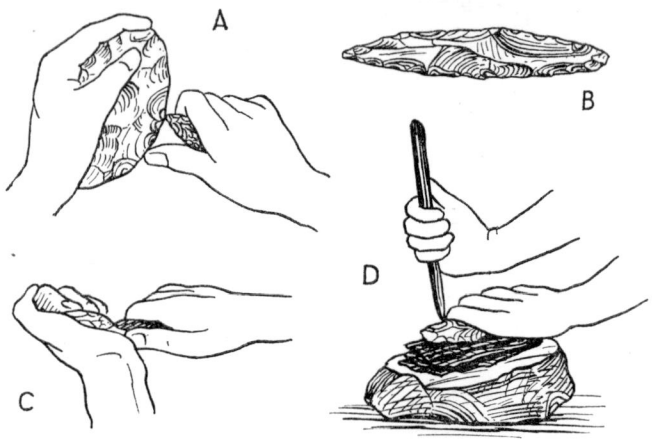

FIG. 42. Artificial fracture of flint: by pressure. See the text. (*After* D. S. Davidson (D), W. H. Holmes (C) and R. A. Smith (A, B).)

a nail. (See Fig. 41 B.) When the blow is delivered, a small flake springs off the under surface of the stone, beneath the point of percussion.

Finishing or dressing an implement by pressure-flaking became common from Middle Palæolithic times onwards, and culminated in the quite perfect work of the Neolithic and Bronze Ages. The remarkably fine 'leaf' and 'ripple' flaking illustrated in Fig. 49, the saws in Fig. 48, and the arrow-heads in Plate XXVI, could not have been achieved in any other way. Were it not for such specimens we should hardly have credited that such control could ever be obtained over so hard and wayward a material as flint.

Four distinct methods of pressure-flaking are known and three of them are illustrated in Fig. 42. Here, the small flint implement shown at B is usually considered to be a pressure-flaking tool and is commonly called a 'fabricator'. Another example is given in Plate XXVI, but some see in the blunted ends of such small flints evidence of their use in striking fire from lumps of iron pyrites. But it hardly seems likely that any one form of implement was consistently and exclusively used for a single narrow purpose throughout the world for, say, 50,000 years!

It is probable that the trimming of hand-axes was done with a stone fabricator in the manner shown at Fig. 42 A, where a twist of the wrist might detach a very small flake. At C, a bone fabricator is being used by pressure against the palm, a method still practised by North American Indians, while at D downward pressure is applied by means of a pointed stick or piece of bone (see Fig. 51 B). Here, the workpiece rests on a few sheets of bark laid on a stone anvil, and these take up the shock when the flint gives way and protect the point of the stick. This method has been observed in use by the aborigines of Western Australia, where, according to Oakley[75], 'a skilful flaker can make a spearhead of bottle-glass in about ten minutes'.

The fourth method of pressure-flaking is that employed by the Aztecs and some North American tribes. This is called 'impulsive flaking' and is done by means of a stick 2 or 3 inches in diameter and from 2 to 4 feet long. The lower end is tipped with bone or hardwood, and a cross-bar is fixed to the upper end. The implement to be trimmed is stuck in the ground, where it is held in position by the feet of the trimmer, who may be either sitting or standing. When the point of the stick has been satisfactorily placed on the workpiece, the trimmer presses suddenly on the cross-bar with his chest. According to a 19th-century report, a Mexican flaker could produce as many as 100 sharp blades by this method in one hour.

Pebble and core tools

The oldest known worked implements are sharpened or trimmed pebbles similar to those illustrated in Fig. 43. They were made by blows directed on to the edge or end, and not away from it, so that the process was more like chopping wood than sharpening a pencil.

It will be noted that the part of the pebble not chipped made a useful and comfortable handle, and the practice of leaving smooth natural handles of this kind became quite common with more elaborate tools, such as the side-scraper in Fig. 45 and the 'pick' in Plate XXVII.

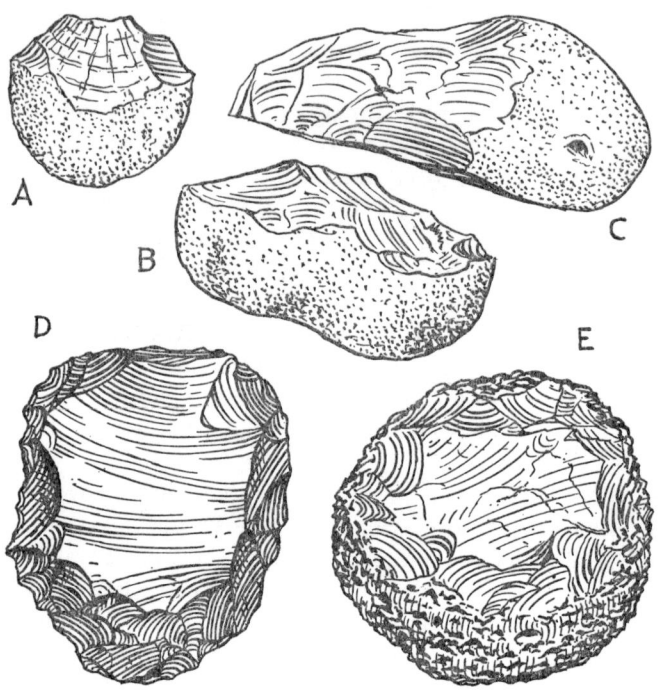

FIG. 43. Core implements. A, Oldowan pebble. B, Kafuan pebble. C, Rostro-carinate 'eolith'. D, Tortoise-core (Levalloisian). E, Hammerstone (Neolithic).

For many kinds of implement, stones with conveniently-shaped handles could not be found, and from Lower Palæolithic times onwards we find a variety of large implements carefully trimmed all over to make shapes which could be held comfortably in the hand. They are generally broad, with two trimmed faces, and are therefore classified as 'bifaces'; but however trimmed, they are most commonly referred to as 'hand-axes' ('*coups-de-poing*' or '*bouchers*').

A typical pointed hand-axe is shown in Fig. 44, where the edge making a sort of reversed-S is characteristic of the Acheulean culture. It seems to be the natural result of right-handed workmanship, though less plausible explanations have been proposed. A flint is trimmed with a hammer-stone by striking it obliquely on one side of its edge, when a flake springs off from the opposite side. We may suppose the implement shown to be held in the left hand and trimmed with the right, the work being done always on the part being held away from the body. Now, the blows applied to the right edge would

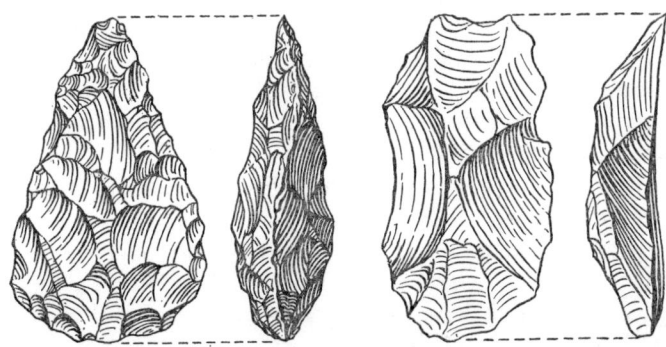

FIG. 44. *Left:* Palæolithic hand-axe (Acheulean). *Right:* A flake implement, probably a scraper (Clactonian).

be much stronger than the more awkward blows applied to the left of the edge, so that larger flakes would spring off the left side than off the right side. The implement would then be turned round for its other end to be trimmed, with a similar result, and the completed edge would have the reversed-S form. However, both earlier and later axe-makers achieved straight-edged implements, some no doubt using different techniques or simply exhibiting greater skill.

Oval-shaped axes, or 'ovates', are usually trimmed to a sharp edge all round. If used as a hand-axe such an implement must have been most uncomfortable to hold, but they may have been throwing-stones. They can be thrown so as to spin horizontally, like a hat being tossed or 'skimmed' on to a peg, and their sharp edges could inflict very severe wounds. On the other hand, they may have been hafted in a cleft stick and used as choppers or knives.

Simple stone-throwing undoubtedly predated all attempts to shape stones, and there must have come a time when suitable round pebbles were purposely collected for ammunition. Whether or not we call these 'implements', we can hardly withhold the term from the pairs of 'bolas' stones found associated with worked implements from very early times[71]. Bolas stones are linked together by a long cord and, when properly thrown, will bring an animal down by winding the cord round its legs.

All the tools mentioned in this section are core tools and they are particularly characteristic of the Lower Palæolithic though by no means exclusively so. Other Palæolithic core tools include the 'cleaver', generally a long stone with a broad chisel-like edge across one end, the 'chopper', a rough blunt tool with a zig-zag edge, sometimes worked on only one face, and rough 'points' of the type illustrated in Fig. 47.

The hammer-stone should also be included among the core tools, and an example is given in Fig. 43 at E. This implement is usually a round-ended or bun-shaped nodule, notched and chipped by use. The fact that it may have struck scores of large flakes from their cores, and yet itself have suffered only as many small chippings, shows how important are both the manner of delivery of the blow and its accurate placing on the workpiece. The possible varieties of blow include the staccato rap, the oblique glance, the double knock, the bounce, and the 'sickening thud', and it may be applied to a small knob, a massive shoulder, a flat face, or the edge of a prepared striking platform.

Another type of core, not primarily intended as a tool but a useful by-product in the manufacture of flake implements, is the 'tortoise-core'. This was undoubtedly trimmed and used on some occasions though it seems often to have been discarded as waste material. It is illustrated in Fig. 43 at D and will be described in the next section.

Towards the end of the Lower Palæolithic, after perhaps 800,000 years of practice but still 200,000 years ago, man had acquired a degree of skill never to be exceeded with core implements. Using the baton, he was able to shape perfectly symmetrical tools with straight sharp edges, and to keep the faces of the cutting-edges flat and free from awkward bulges. He exploited the hinge-fracture in a technique called 'step-flaking' or 'resolved flaking', in which light blows delivered directly on the edge detached a series of minute flakes terminating in 'hinges'. The small, regular steps which resulted averaged to form a steadily tapering edge free from large ridges and hollows.

A later type of core implement, having a broad, transverse edge across one end like an adze, is known by the French name *'tranchet'*. Its edge was produced by a blow from the side, which detached a single, broad, crosswise flake. The resulting tool would have been ideal for such work as hollowing a dugout canoe, and was very likely so used by Neolithic man, though the *tranchet* dates back to Palæolithic times. The Mesolithic peoples made square-tipped arrow-heads and other very small implements by the same method, so that both *grands* and *petits tranchets* are recognized, but the *petits tranchets* were made from blades, not from cores. One is illustrated in Fig. 48, near the letter A.

Flakes, blades and microliths

The flakes struck off a nodule in trimming a core often have razor-sharp edges, and these must have been used as knives from the time they were first noticed. Long before Middle Palæolithic times, and especially in central and eastern Europe, successful attempts had been made to produce cutting implements by striking large flakes. The practice became so common in Middle Palæolithic times that it is generally regarded as a major characteristic of this period, though core tools of all kinds continued to be made.

An early flake implement is shown in Plate XXII, for comparison with a core implement reproduced on the same scale. It shows most of the features detailed in Fig. 40, but the original bulb of percussion has been struck off so that there are two bulbar scars. Flakes of this kind were often prepared in this way, but their reverse sides then demanded very careful trimming to avoid cracking the stone right across.

One method which has been studied is that known as the 'Tachenghit' technique. According to H. Alimen[76], it was used in the Sahara and in southern Africa towards the end of Lower Palæolithic times. Fig. 45, which is adapted from explanatory drawings by C. van Riet Lowe[77], shows how a large flake with a very sloping striking-platform was shaped into a much smaller pointed implement. The sections given below are facing downwards, and the arrows show where the blows were struck to produce the next stage of manufacture.

A more reliable way of producing flake implements was then discovered. This was to trim the back of the implement while it was still part of the core, so that when it was finally struck off the flake came away complete and ready for use. A very early example (Clactonian) is shown in Fig. 44, but the trimming is coarse and the

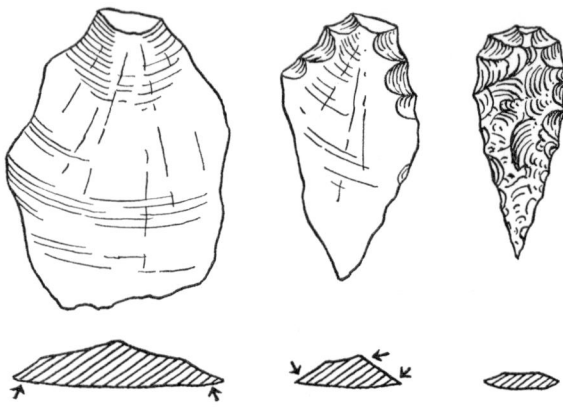

FIG. 45. Successive stages in shaping a biface from a large flake by the Tachenghit technique. (*Adapted from* C. van Riet Lowe.)

implement crude. Improvements followed the realization that the shape of the whole core is just as important as the shape of the flake. To obtain a good flake there must be no disturbing lumps or irregular distributions of mass on the core from which it is struck. The best shape for a core was found to be somewhat like that of a tortoise-shell, so that they have become known as 'tortoise-cores'. In the one illustrated in Fig. 43 the 'tortoise' is lying on its back to show the flat scar left by the detached flake.

Sometimes a tortoise-core shows facets across the edges of the striking platform from which the flake was struck. These are parts of the flake-scars made in the preliminary trimming of the flake-piece, and when they are prominent on the core it may be referred to as a

PLATE XXIII. The two faces of a Paleolithic 'disc-core' about $3\frac{1}{2}$ in. long, possibly used as a throwing-stone.

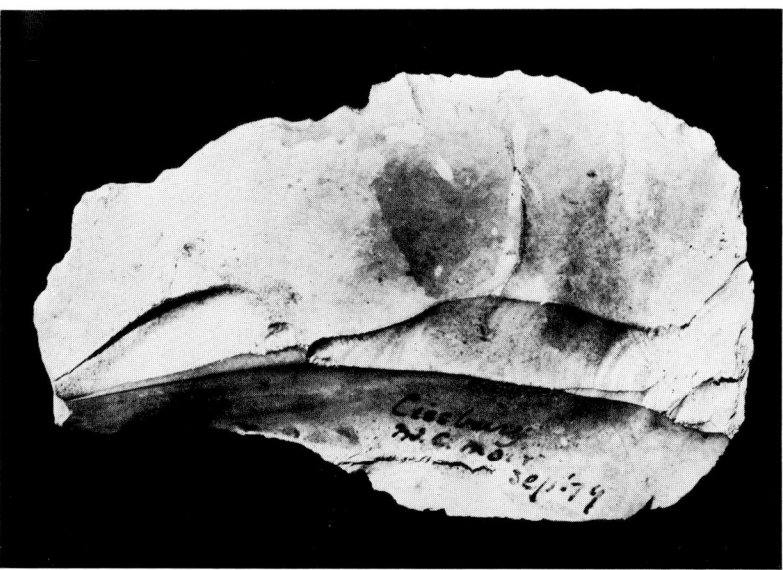

PLATE XXIV. Completely corticated Neolithic blade implements, both about 4 in. long and each based on a single large flake. *Above:* A borer. *Below:* A scraper or knife.

PLATE XXV. Mesolithic and Neolithic implements. *Top* A: halbert-blade scraper and flake. *Centre:* Microliths. *Foot:* 'Leaf-blade' arrow-heads, one showing ripple-flaking.

PLATE XXVI. Neolithic arrow-heads showing delicate workmanship. The two in the centre may be Mesolithic.

'faceted butt'. The core shown in Plate XXIII is similar to a tortoise-core except that its discoid shape suggests that it was intended to serve as an ovate implement or throwing-stone after the desired flake had been detached. It is therefore often called a 'disc-core' or a 'discoid'. The right-hand picture shows the scar left by the flake, and in this some of the ripples and the hollow left by the bulb of percussion (at the bottom) can be seen. The tortoise-core technique is associated chiefly with the Levalloisian and Mousterian cultures*.

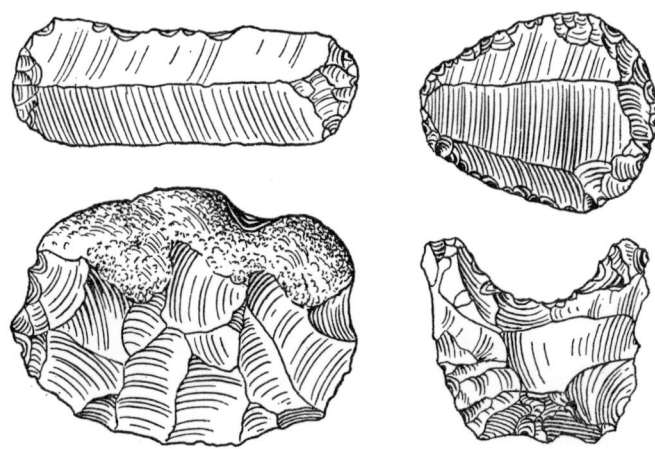

FIG. 46. Types of scrapers. *From left to right, top:* Double-ended scraper, end-scraper (Aurignacian). *Below:* Side-scraper (Mousterian), hollow scraper (Neolithic).

The edges of flake implements are often very sharp but may require 'dressing' at certain places. Plate XXIV shows two flake implements of Neolithic age, the upper one being dressed very slightly near the point to make an awl or borer. In this specimen the point of percussion, the bulb of percussion, the bulbar scar and several ripples are clearly seen. In the lower specimen, the back of the flake faces the camera and a good deal of preliminary trimming was evidently done on it, though not very tidily. But this, perhaps, hardly mattered

* See Appendix VIII. The Mousterian culture was that of Neanderthal Man, either a separate species of man (*Homo neanderthalensis*) or, as is now proposed, a sub-species (*Homo sapiens neanderthalensis*).

because the implement is simply a scraper, used for cleaning out the insides of animal skins. The thin, knife-like character of this flake contrasts strongly with the Lower Palæolithic scraper in Fig. 46, which is a partly-worked core tool probably employed for the same purpose.

Implements of this type are called *'racloirs'* or 'side-scrapers' because the business-edge is along one of the sides. Fig. 46 also shows three other types of scraper, and yet another—the 'halbert'—is illustrated in Plate XXV. The 'end-scraper' was possibly used for scooping marrow out of hollow bones, shredding roots, or other such purpose, and the 'double-ended' scraper may have been a sort of plane for smoothing wood, The 'hollow' scraper was undoubtedly used as a sort of spokeshave for straightening and smoothing spear and arrow shafts, but the peculiar virtues of the halbert scraper remain a mystery.

It will be noted that the double-ended scraper shows two beautifully flat long sides, and if turned over would show its flake-face as equally flat and even. Such long flat surfaces may be obtained only from very carefully prepared cores of good-quality flint. They may be struck by the baton or a hammer, or by impulsive pressure, and, according to Reid Moir[82], ripples can be avoided by applying an absolutely vertical blow or impulse.

An implement made in this way is triangular in section and is the simplest possible form with naturally sharp edges. But it is unnecessarily thick in the centre and a neat way to make it thinner was found by striking another long flake off the ridge forming the apex of the triangle. The result was the form shown in the cross-section in Fig. 47, on the left, and the name 'blade' is generally applied to it. It is particularly characteristic of the Upper Palæolithic (and later periods) and forms the basis of a great many kinds of small and delicate implements, which are made from thin blades by pressure-flaking.

For example, the halbert scraper in Plate XXV was formed from a blade, and so were the three pointed implements in the centre of Fig. 47. These are examples of the 'Helwan' industry, which was developed in Egypt in Mesolithic times according to H. Alimen[76], though J. de Morgan[78] considered it Neolithic. The curious arrowheads are characteristic, the notches forming a Maltese cross being

FLAKES, BLADES AND MICROLITHS

used in binding them to their shafts, and the 'crescent' or 'orange segment' shows another special technique. Its chief feature is the working of the 'back' from both sides to produce one blunt edge, the opposite edge being left sharp. Such an implement had all the advantages of a single-edged razor-blade over one with both edges sharpened.

This knife is only about 4 centimetres (1½ inches) long and affords an example of a 'bladelet', of which a great variety were produced in

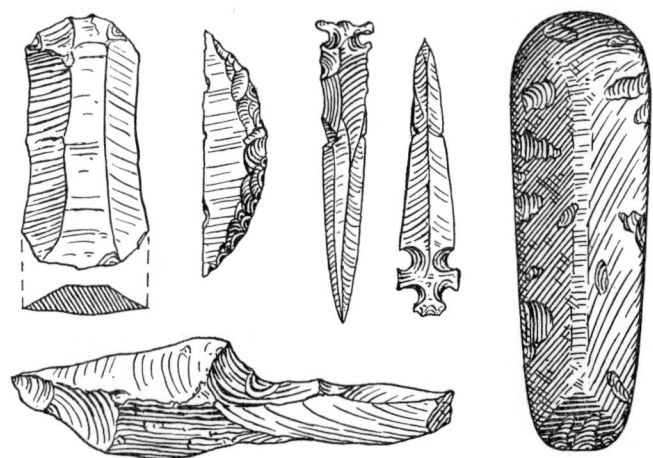

FIG. 47. *Left to right:* Upper Palæolithic blade (Aurignacian), Mesolithic orange-segment blade, Helwan arrow-heads, Neolithic celt. *Below:* Lower Palæolithic point (Clactonian).

Mesolithic times. Other examples are shown in Fig. 48, those at B being so small that they are called 'microliths'. Their uses were legion. Some were undoubtedly used as arrow-heads[79], others as awls for boring the eyes in bone needles, and others again as 'gravers' or 'burins' for scratching designs on wood, bones and antlers, and other such decorative work. (See Fig. 51 A.) However, a vast number of the microliths which have been found (e.g. the two in Plate XXV) are merely the waste-pieces discarded during manufacture, though for a long time their 'uses' puzzled archaeologists.

Burins first appeared in Upper Palæolithic times and examples from the twenty or more types belonging to this period are shown in

Fig. 49. The Mesolithic burins were smaller and more elaborate; they were fabricated on the end of a blade which was afterwards deeply notched so that the unwanted part could be snapped off. The Mesolithic peoples were also adept at making saws, sometimes with teeth so fine that a magnifying-glass is required to see them though they can be felt with the finger-nail. (See Fig. 48 A.)

Small bladelets with saw-teeth were also made for setting into wooden handles for use as sickles, as in the Fig. 48 D, though sometimes larger, untoothed sickle blades, as at C, were used. These sickle

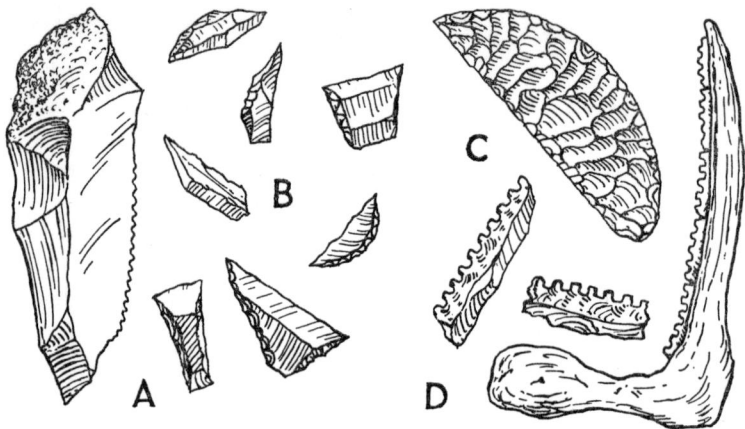

FIG. 48. A, Mesolithic saw. B, Microliths. C, Neolithic sickle-blades. D, small sickle-blades mounted in a bone or wooden handle.

blades and bladelets often show a very fine diffuse polish resulting from friction with the corn or grass stalks, which are rich in silica[81]. The sowing and reaping of corn began in Mesolithic times and sickles showing this 'silica-gloss' have been found in Palestine dating from about 6000 B.C.[75]. But the great adventure in agricultural farming first became a major way of life in Neolithic times, and led to the establishment of fixed settlements, villages and townships. This change from the old nomadic or semi-nomadic life of hunting, fishing and collecting wild fruits and vegetables is called the 'Neolithic Revolution'[79,80].

The finest and most delicate work in flint belongs to the Neolithic and Bronze Ages, when knives and arrow-heads were often made so thin as to be translucent and were correspondingly sharp. Examples of Neolithic ripple-flaking in 'foliates' or leaf-shaped arrow-heads are shown in Fig. 49 and Plates XXV and XXVI. Quite large flint knives were also produced by ripple-flaking, and some have been found with their cutting-edges ground and polished. This was probably intended to straighten and smooth them as much as to sharpen them, for the razor-edge of a newly chipped flake cannot be made any sharper.

In a slightly more elaborate method, used in Egypt (and elsewhere), a flint knife-blade would first be roughly shaped and then

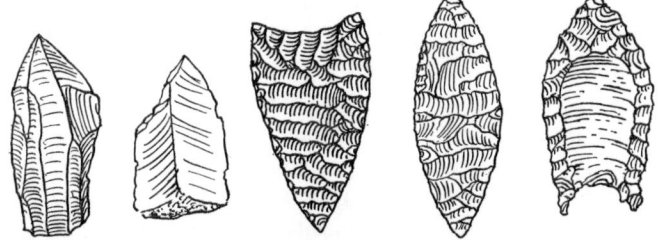

FIG. 49. *From left to right:* Magdalenian graver, Aurignacian graver, ripple-flaking on arrow-head (Neolithic), laurel-leaf point (Solutrean), Folsom point (American Mesolithic).

ground straight and thin by rubbing it on a quartzite or granite grindstone. After a final polishing, the entire surface was then removed by ripple-flaking, pressure being applied to the edge to provide a razor-sharp finish[81]. Some flint knives made in this way and now in the British Museum measure a foot in length and two inches in width. They came from an Egyptian tomb of the 1st Dynasty (*c.* 3000 B.C.[76]) and possibly represent the finest work in flint ever attained.

Celts and hafted tools

The idea of smoothing and sharpening stone tools by grinding them goes back to Mesolithic times[75], when the advantages of smooth-faced axes and adzes for tree-felling and wood-working were realized.

The dugout canoe, invented in Early Neolithic times, may even have owed its existence to this technological advance.

Flint is so hard that only quartz or quartzose rocks make any impression on it, but fortunately sandstones (composed of quartz grains), quartzite, and the massive quartz associated with granite are widely distributed. But with even the best grindstones, it takes a very long time to grind the surfaces of a flint smooth by hand, and longer still to obtain the polish sometimes found on Neolithic axe-heads.

Many stones which cannot be shaped like flint because of their irregular fracture can be made into very good axes by grinding, so that this technique was a very important industrial advance. Axe-heads of all kinds finished by grinding or polishing (or intended to be so) are known as 'celts' (pronounced *selts*), a word which has nothing to do with the race of people called Celts (preferably pronounced—and sometimes spelt—*Kelts*). It is generally agreed[81,83] that the word 'celt' got into our language from a supposed Latin word *celtis*, used only by Jerome in the Vulgate translation of the book of Job*. It is a word without a respectable or even plausible etymology and may therefore be accepted as useful bit of archaeological jargon. It is used to include metal axe-heads of the Bronze and Iron Ages, through which stone implements continued to be made.

A partly ground Neolithic celt is shown in Fig. 47, and one that has been polished but later damaged in Plate XXVII. The finish of this specimen may be compared with the coarse chipping of the pick next to it, for both implements were probably used for shaping wood and the difference in their cutting or splitting powers may be imagined. The pick has a natural 'handle' but the celt was almost certainly hafted. There was, however, nothing new in hafting, for wooden spears were armed with stone in Middle Palæolithic times, and the butts or cores from the flake industries were probably fitted with handles[75] to make clubs or hammers. In Upper Palæolithic times awls, pins and harpoon blades were hafted in bone and antler, and an earlier use of wood for similar purposes must surely be inferred.

---

* Job xix, 24: *Vel celte sculpantur in silice* ('or by a chisel carved in flint'). But since there is no such word as '*celte*' it has been suggested that it was simply miscopied from *certe* ('assuredly'). James Moffatt[84] renders the phrase: 'or lastingly engraved on stone', and it seems that this could hardly be bettered.

Probably the earliest method of providing a tool with a handle was that illustrated at the bottom of Fig. 50. The axe-head or pick would be bound into a cleft stick by gut or hide thongs, or by plant fibres. When smooth-surfaced celts of regular shape were made, handles were pierced by tailor-made holes cut to fit their tool-heads and binding may not have been necessary. The Neolithic example shown at the top of Fig. 50 is of particular interest in this connection and will be referred to again.

But axe-heads fitted in this way, though they seldom worked loose, were liable to split their handles. This snag seems to have been overcome first by the Swiss lake-dwellers[81], who lined the hole in the handle with a sleeve of deer antler. The elasticity of the antler absorbed excessive shocks, and its softness allowed the head to be driven firmly home without splitting the wood.

A better method still, was to make the hole in the stone head instead of in the wooden handle, but a lot of patience was required to bore a large enough hole through a piece of flint. This was, nevertheless, frequently done, the drill-bit being generally a straight, round stick the end of which was constantly fed with a grinding-paste of sand and water. For large holes a hollow stick, like a cane or a piece of elder with the pith pushed out, was often used. This meant that much less stone needed to be ground away. The bit was turned by a bow-drill of a kind not very different from those used until comparatively recently by itinerant menders of broken china for drilling the rivet-holes. Tools intended to be used like a hoe or an adze were sometimes hafted to an angled stick, as illustrated in the centre of Fig. 50, and sometimes tool-blades were let into slots cut in the wood, as in the sickle in Fig. 48.

Mining and trade

It must have been known from very early times that some flints are of much better quality than others, and that flint fresh from its bed in the Chalk is generally better than flint which has been buried in clay or gravel, and far better than flint which has been lying around exposed to the elements. The Neolithic peoples also realized that the flint found in some layers in the Chalk is superior to that found in other layers, and they sunk shafts to a depth of more than 40 feet

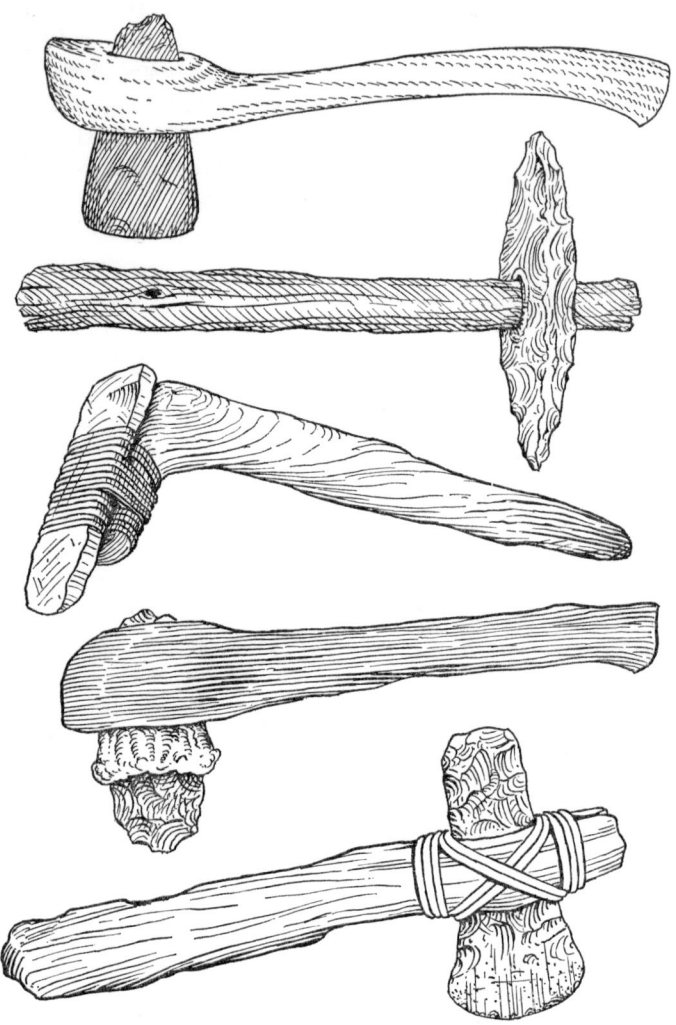

Fig. 50. Methods of hafting flint implements. (See the text.)

MINING AND TRADE

in search of the best quality. Having found a satisfactory seam they mined it by driving tunnels, sinking other shafts at intervals for light, ventilation, and raising the spoils.

Neolithic flint-mines and quarries dating from about 4,000 years ago have been found in many countries, including Britain, France, Belgium, Portugal, Sicily, Sweden, Poland and other regions outside Europe. In England the sites include Grime's Graves in Norfolk, Cissbury Ring, Harrow Hill*, Findon, Blackpatch and Stoke Down in Sussex, Easton Down in Wiltshire, and Peppard in Oxfordshire. (See Fig. 68, Appendix IX.) It is not known whether flint-mining originated independently in England or was introduced from the Continent.

Mining was done with picks and wedges made from deer-antlers, bone levers, and doubtless stone and wooden implements. The antlers with tines are thought to have been used to hook out the flint nodules from their bed, since they would hardly stand up to use as pick-axes. The rubble of waste chalk was cleared out of the way with shovels made from the shoulder-blades of large animals, including oxen, and no doubt the flints were raised to the surface in baskets or skin bags. Some of the uses of bone and antler are illustrated in Fig. 51. Much of the mining was done in the dark but lamps made of carved chalk, probably filled with grease and fitted with a wick, were often used. Not only have the lamp-bowls been found, but sooty patches on the roofs of the tunnels survive to show where the lamps were held.

The shafts and tunnels of these old mines have long since become filled, or partly filled, with rubble and soil, They are recognizable today only by the excessively hummocky and pitted character of the surface of the ground. Many have now been excavated by archaeologists, but they have then been filled in again and turfed over since this is the best way to preserve them. They are re-opened from time to time, and a few shafts are kept permanently open, for the inspection of visitors.

Perhaps the best-known group in England is that comprising Grime's Graves, near the Norfolk-Suffolk border. The origin of the name is unknown, but the lumps and hollows betraying the sites of at least 700 shafts cover 34 acres and might well suggest some sort

* Harrow Hill, 6 miles north-west of Worthing, not Harrow-on-the-Hill in Middlesex, which stands on sand and clay.

of burial-ground. In at least three of the pits human bones have certainly been found, one skeleton being that of a girl about 13 years old, so it is also possible that a family named Grime was once buried here. In 1739 Francis Blomefield expressed the opinion that Grime's Graves was an ancient Danish camp, the large central depression

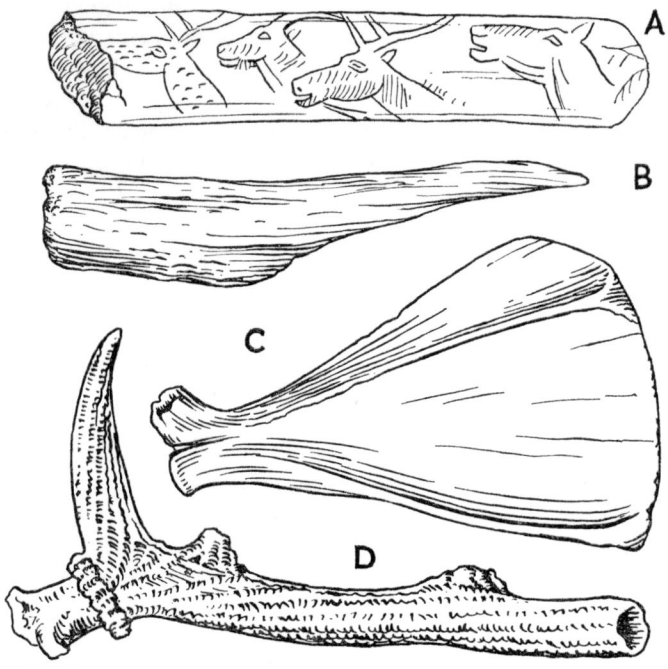

FIG. 51. Uses of bone and antler. A, Magdalenian engraving on bone of deer, goat and horse. B, A bone point used for pressure-flaking. C, Neolithic shovel (an ox's shoulder-blade). D, A deer-antler pick.

marking the site of the commander's tent, and this view was commonly held until 1852, when attempts were made to establish Grime's Graves as an Iron Age village antedating the Roman invasion. However, an end was put to all speculation when W. Greenwell discovered the true nature of the workings by carefully excavating a mine-shaft from 1867 to 1870.

The succession of rocks found at Grime's Graves is shown in Fig. 52, which also suggests how one of the smaller shafts may have been worked. It will be seen that the miners had to dig down through ten feet of sand and clay before finding any chalk, so the question has been raised how or why they expected to find (a) chalk, (b) any flint at all, and (c) first-quality tabular flint 40 feet down. However, the highly valued 'floorstone' forms an almost flat horizontal bed about 5 miles wide running north and south through west Norfolk[86], and they knew it well from surface-exposures elsewhere. Perhaps we

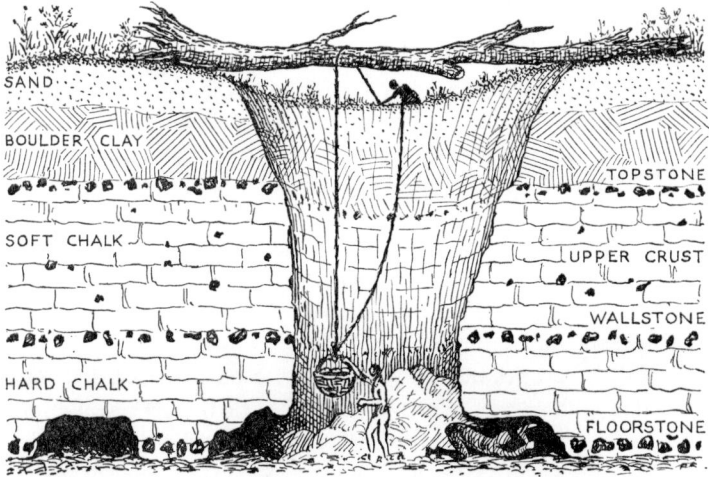

FIG. 52. Section through the shaft of a Neolithic flint-mine, the succession of strata being that at Grime's Graves, Norfolk.

should credit the Neolithic miners with the first practical geological survey!

Experiments have been made to assess the time and labour expended in mining flint with Neolithic tools on this scale, and the figure of six months for working out a galleried pit has been suggested. On this basis, it has been estimated that Grime's Graves were worked through three centuries, probably from about 2200 B.C. to 1900 B.C. The mines could have been extended, but by this time the demand for flint axes was declining in favour of those made from fine-grained igneous rocks and the metal now being introduced by the Bronze Age peoples.

The litter of flint flakes round the mine shows that the heavier stones, at any rate, were flaked into axes on the spot, but some may have been left unfinished for completion elsewhere. The grinding and polishing of celts was undoubtedly the work of specialists, and so was the fashioning of arrow-heads from small flakes and blades. In many regions, and sometimes a long way from the chalk hills, patches of land are found to be littered with thousands of discarded flakes and flint cores, and such places are clearly the sites of major flint implement 'factories'.

When distant from flint-bearing chalk, they were generally situated on or near flint gravels or shingles. Though the stones in such beds are of uncertain quality the larger ones are often usable and, according to W. F. Rankine[57], those found in such deposits as the Chalky Boulder Clay* may be as good as freshly-mined flint. Before Neolithic times flints were obtained from such sources and from chalk cliffs and soils, though many of the implements found in gravel beds may have come from distant places and were contributed to the gravel during the formation of the bed. This is sometimes shown by their water-worn condition.

Neolithic factories occur in many places on the chalk hills, often associated with causeway camps and other earthworks, while Mesolithic and Palæolithic factories generally turn up at lower levels on surfaces from which a covering of soil or recent river deposits has been removed. For example, there is a Middle Palæolithic factory at Crayford, in Kent, conveniently situated at the foot of a flint-bearing chalk cliff which was cut by the Thames about 100,000 years ago, when it was flowing two miles south of its present course. In subsequent floods the river buried the Paloælithic 'floor', as the occupation-level is called, under 36 feet of sand and clay, at the same time interring the bones of woolly rhinoceros, lions, wolves and other animals[81]. This ancient factory remained buried, and was thus well preserved, until it was unearthed by F. C. J. Spurrell in 1880.

On the other hand, there is a Mesolithic floor on the Lower Greensand at Rock, in Sussex, where the fragments and chippings of flint

---

* The Chalky Boulder Clay is a morainic deposit containing many large flints gathered from the Chalk by glaciers during the Pleistocene Ice Age. It covers wide areas of East Anglia, Cambridgeshire, and the counties north of London, attaining a thickness of 180 feet in some places.

once more (or still?) lie on the surface and may be picked up like the Neolithic flakes on the Downs. The quantity of flakes scattered about in such places is remarkable, for people have been picking up arrowheads, scrapers, gravers and other such items for centuries and the supply still seems inexhaustible.

Yet, perhaps it is not so surprising. A North Queensland aborigine making a new knife may strike and throw away as many as 300 flakes before he obtains a suitable blade[75]. These are all left lying about, and in a 'factory' where ten men are constantly working we might expect to find upwards of 10,000 waste flakes at the end of each day. But, to take minimal figures, suppose there are only 1,000 waste flakes per day, scattered over one square mile. Then, after 300 years they would total 100 million flakes, or three in every square foot of that area. If as many as 1,000 of these were picked up every summer by souvenir-hunters, there would still be enough to last 100,000 years!

It is not suggested that flint artefacts exist in such quantities except in favoured localities, but these became more numerous as the population of the country (and the world) increased. It has been estimated that the population of Britain in Palæolithic times seldom exceeded 300, in Mesolithic times 3,000, and in the Bronze Age 30,000[79]. In the Neolithic Age it may have been 20,000[102], or about one person to every 5 square miles, which we may compare in passing with the 3,000 per 5 square miles of today. But when we introduce the time-dimension into our calculations we get a somewhat different picture.

The Palæolithic period lasted at least 500,000 years, so that something like 5 million Palæolithic flint-workers may have left their litter behind. By the same token, the number of Mesolithic and Neolithic workers combined would be about 2 million, and those from the Bronze Age about one million. These figures should be taken as giving no more than a rough comparison derived from various sources, though they may be assumed to be of the right order, but the difference made by the time-scale, which raised the total Palæolithic population above all the others, is certainly worth noting.

Flakes and discarded or lost implements are by no means the only relics to be found on the sites of Stone Age factories. Hammer-stones often turn up, and there are sometimes signs of domestic and even religious activities[87]. Only one of these items concerns us here—the flint 'pot-boiler' illustrated in Plate XVII. The Stone Age method of boiling water was to make stones red-hot in a fire and then drop them into the water-pot, for the available vessels could not safely be stood over the flames*. The flint was thus calcined and then suddenly quenched, the result being a network of surface-cracks as described on page 38.

Also to be found in many districts are excellent smooth-faced axe-heads made from fine-grained igneous rocks, for the Neolithic farmers and forest-clearers preferred them to the rough flint and found they could get them in bigger and heavier sizes than the polished flint celts. They had, however, to get them from other parts of the country and so large axe-grinding industries arose in Cornwall, North Wales and Cumberland. Heavy axes, maces and hammers were traded for sharp flint arrow-heads, knives and sickle-blades, the exchanges being probably made over short distances and spanning the country in several stages. There were similar developments on the Continent and the Neolithic trade in axe-heads is probably the oldest known commercial enterprise.

It received a strong challenge when the first bronze axe-heads appeared, for these were beautifully made, smooth, sharp, not brittle, and easily attached to a haft. Some archaeologists consider that the polishing of the stone celts was really an attempt to copy the bronze in flint, for bronze was scarce and flint was cheap. On the other hand, the early bronze implements seem to have been shaped like the stone axes with which they hoped to compete, and did not acquire their more characteristic forms until Middle Bronze Age times.

There was a fair trade in flint implements with regions where there was no suitable raw flint, and again with places where the flint was of exceptional quality. The Neolithic peoples certainly traded in the honey-coloured flints of Central France[56], and W. F. Rankine[57] has proposed tracing the origins of certain other implements by their colour, or at least showing by this means that they could not have been produced in the regions where they were found.

He suggests three types of explanation to account for the wanderers:

---

* Vessels like sea-shells, gourds and coconuts must have been used from the earliest times, but the Middle Palæolithic vessels seem to have included the skulls of mammoths and other animals, with the openings stopped with clay. Later, rush baskets were probably made waterproof with clay linings, and the origin of pottery has been traced to this practice.

(a) trade, (b) folk-movements, and (c) the exploitation of 'erratics', or stones transported by glaciers or other natural agents far from their places of origin. Among other examples, he cites* non-native brown flints in Surrey, East Anglia, East Yorkshire and South Scotland, and further misplaced red and yellow ones in Scotland. Many implements have been made from the coloured flint erratics in the Boulder Clay of the East Coast, but these were probably brought over from Denmark by glaciers during the earlier stages of the Great Ice Age.

Reconstructions and frauds

Numerous attempts have been made to reconstruct Stone Age habitations, tools and weapons, and to picture the Stone Age way of life at different periods. Such activities have sometimes led to new discoveries, or new interpretations of old ones, and sometimes they have led to mistakes, deliberate deceptions and even downright fraud. There have also been attempts to explain local mysteries by an imaginative reconstruction of circumstances, as in several cases where there are grassed-over piles of rough, untrimmed flints.

When found in the neighbourhood of causeway camps or other signs of occupation they have been 'explained' as stocks of ammunition for hurling at an invader, but as a rule nothing could be more unlikely. When found near a surface-scratching or marl-pit, or at a 'factory', they may be just dumps of waste material. More often they are the remains of piles of stones left handy—perhaps only a few centuries ago—for repairing a nearby road or track.

L. S. Palmer[100] refers of the discovery (in Europe) of 'collected heaps of iron pyrites and flints' which were clearly stores of fire-making materials. Those found at Taubach, in Germany, along with the ashes of hearths, were undoubtedly gathered by Neanderthal Man perhaps 70,000 years ago, but there are others of later date†.

* In a private communication with the author (1950) and probably elsewhere.
† Fire was almost certainly made by this method at least 100,000 years ago and possibly by friction between two pieces of wood by Pekin Man 200,000 years ago. However, the evidence of hearth ashes and charred bones alone shows only that man had learned to *use* fire, not necessarily to make it. He could have obtained it from a natural forest fire, a tree set on fire by lightning, or even by poking a stick into a lava-flow from a volcano.

Very slight undulations or ridges on the ground, marking out squares or rectangles on the chalk downs, are usually buried rows of flints outlining Iron Age or 'Celtic' fields. They are the stones raked off the plots in preparing the ground for cultivation, but the work of earthworms long since buried them so that they are now invisible except in certain lights. They are most easily seen from an aeroplane at sunrise or sunset, when even slight irregularities throw very long shadows.

More mysterious are the flint-filled hollows found by J. B. Calkin[89] in 1952 in the neighbourhood of some Celtic fields and lynchets (cultivation terraces) near Lulworth Cove, in Dorset. They are saucer-shaped depressions 20 or 30 feet across, lined artificially with a red clay and filled with unworked flint nodules, cores and flakes. Fragments of Iron Age pottery were found in one of them. Some very similar hollows have been found in the Isle of Wight, where fifteen occur strung out in a line, and there are probably others elsewhere, but nobody has succeeded in explaining them. They could have been rubbish-pits to receive the flints picked off the fields; but if so, why should they have been lined with clay? They could be small, uncompleted dewponds, filled in with unwanted stones; but why so many in one place?

A reconstruction of a different kind, and a literal one at that, was the restoration of a flint nodule by fitting together all the flakes struck off it 100,000 years ago. This astonishing feat was performed by F. C. J. Spurrell[75] on the site of the Palæolithic factory he discovered at Crayford in 1880 (see page 172). Having found a flint core, it occurred to him that most of the flakes struck off it might still be lying around. By diligence and perseverence Spurrell managed to find most of them and to re-assemble them round the core. Plate XXVIII shows both the core and the reconstructed nodule, which is now at the Natural History Museum, London.

The arrangement of the flakes in Spurrell's specimen reveals the order in which they were detached and how the core was struck. Studies of this and other cores have shown that Neanderthal Man went to work 100,000 years ago in very much the same way as Australian aborigines do today, and some of the early types of flint axe-heads have been very successfully imitated. In the 19th century Edward Simpson, of Whitby, otherwise known as 'Flint Jack', made

PLATE XXVII. *Left:* A late Palæolithic pick with part of the original cortex left for a handle. *Right:* A Neolithic polished celt, probably used as an axe-head.

PLATE XXVIII. *Above:* The Palæolithic core, 4½ in. long, found by H. G. F. Spurrell at Crayford, Kent, in 1879. *Below:* The original nodule, 10 in. long, reconstructed by Spurrell from flakes picked up on the same site and fitted round the core.

a large number of spurious 'Stone Age' implements which he sold to tourists[90]. He was imprisoned for theft in 1867, but there have been other 'flake fakers' since, one operating in the Eastbourne area in the first quarter of the present century.

For the inexpert there may be only one suspicious thing about a fraud of this kind, and that is its harsh splintery appearance. Modern work generally shows a rough or 'matt' surface, even if it is glossy in places, whereas a genuine Stone Age implement is nearly always patinated at least in some degree, and has a waxy lustre and soft feel. (See page 116.) The patination may not be uniform, however, for some genuine flint implements, after becoming patinated with age, have been found by some later Stone Age man and trimmed up for re-use by fresh chipping. The new work has eventually also acquired a patina and the implement now shows two distinct ages of patination. The occurrence of a patina is evidence of age but not in itself of human workmanship, and an expert will also take into consideration all the points raised in the first section of this chapter.

A less common type of fraud, but one which the reader may deem far more heinous, is that evidently practised by Charles Dawson in 1912 and exposed by J. S. Weiner, Kenneth P. Oakley and W. E. Le Gros Clark in 1953[91]. To provide supporting evidence of the authenticity of the Piltdown skull, which he had already planted surreptitiously in the Piltdown gravel, Dawson 'salted' the beds with flint implements faked to look old enough by chemical staining. J. S. Weiner[92] has described the process probably used as dipping in a solution of an iron salt, followed by treatment with a dichromate salt or chromic acid. It is true that the flints were of less importance than the bones, but they were used to support an outrageous fraud and deceived even some experts for forty years.

Another type of deception, but implying ignorance more often than fraud, is the bland assumption that all calcined flints found in fields are Neolithic pot-boilers and exhibiting them as such. Modern specimens may come from beneath a burnt crop or a bonfire, and are often found in the scattered waste from old lime-kilns or pottery works. They generally differ from the genuine pot-boiler by being less cracked on the surface and less shattered as a whole. They have a glassy appearance, almost as if they had been fused, and are generally very white, whereas really old pot-boilers appear stony and are usually stained brown in and around their myriad cracks by iron.

The re-enactment of a Stone Age occupation, undertaken chiefly to test the efficiency of polished stone axe-heads in felling trees, was studied in Denmark in 1953[80,93,94]. A Neolithic celt, made of chert, was fitted to an ash handle copied from a Neolithic haft found preserved in an ancient bog. It was 22 inches long and of the form shown at the top of Fig. 50. It was found that blades fitted too tightly in the handle were liable to break, so a little play was allowed to enable the axe-head to vibrate slightly under shock.

It was also found that the axe was most effective when swung from the elbow to make short sharp cuts, instead of being used in long sweeps from the shoulder as is usual with steel axes. Though the axe-head had not been sharpened for 4,000 years, three men used it in this way to clear 600 square yards of silver birch trees, most of them about one foot in diameter, in four hours!

6

Flint in the Historical Period

THERE IS, of course, no sharp dividing-line between the subject of this chapter and that of the previous one. It has already been mentioned that flint continued to be an important raw material for making tools and weapons through both the Bronze and Iron Ages, and its use in making fire continued into the 19th century. It has also been an important building material, an almost universal road-metal, and a useful element in grinding machinery. Today, it is used on an immense scale for making concrete and in the manufacture of ceramics.

Flint for industrial purposes is obtained chiefly from shingle beaches, but considerable quantities are also dug from gravel-pits and the chalk quarried for lime and cement works may contain nearly 1 per cent of flint. The main British sources are the beaches of Kent, Essex and Sussex, but much is imported from the north coast of France. During 1957 to 1961, the annual consumption of flint by the ceramics industry alone averaged 500,000 tons, and nearly half this was imported[95]. The quantity used annually in making concrete must be very much larger, but since flint is not the only stone included in the 'aggregates' it would be no easy task to discover the exact figure. It may well be of the order of 10 million tons—a very rough guess but a good enough pointer to suggest the present importance of flint to British industry.

Fire and firearms

Going back nearly 2,000 years to pick up the thread of the story, we find a period of perhaps 500 years during which flint had only one special use—the making of fire. The common cognomen for this period—The Dark Ages—would sound ironical were it in the least relevant, but at that time flint provided the normal means of obtaining fire even in civilized Rome. When Virgil wrote

> . . . . *quaerit pars semina flammae*
> *Abstrusa in venis silicis—*

'some seek the seeds of flame hidden in the veins of flint'*, he was describing a common daily task with which every Roman slave was familiar.

Before the Iron Age fire was produced either by striking pyrites (or some similar mineral) with flint, or by knocking together two pieces of pyrites, flint, chert, quartzite or quartz. There was also, of course, the generation of fire by friction between two pieces of dry wood[97]—a method scarcely germane to the story of flint. All these methods have survived into modern times, and though they are practised regularly only by primitive and more or less isolated peoples, they were still being used ceremonially in western Europe in the late 19th century†, and the use of flint and steel for lighting pipes was observed in Estonia as late as 1925[101].

In the Roman Catholic Church the opening part of the Easter Vigil requires the paschal candle to be lit with 'new fire'. Until 1970 this had to be fire 'struck from flint', but since no particular kind of flint was specified it had become acceptable to use a cigarette-lighter because its 'flint' could always be relied on. But this material has nothing to do with true flint‡ and, since a match would produce 'new fire' even more surely, the reference to flint was omitted from the new Missal issued in 1970. Nevertheless, true flint and steel were used for this ceremony throughout Christendom until cigarette-lighters became common.

---

* *Aeneid*, VI, 6–7. In Dryden's translation, 'Some strike from clashing flints their fiery seed'.

† The production of fire from wood by friction was last performed seriously in England in Westmorland in 1848, the firestick being a piece of dry nut-wood. Cattle were then driven through the smoke of the 'need-fire', as it was called, as a charm against disease. Similar fire-rites were being practised in Bavaria in 1875, and in Brittany as late as 1879[96].

‡ Lighter 'flints' are made of Misch-metal, an alloy of cerium and other rare-earth metals with iron.

To yield satisfactory sparks, the flint has to be of good quality. It should be homogeneous in texture and free from fossils or other inclusions, and its fracture-surfaces should be lustreless. The marketed 'strike-a-lights', as they were called, varied in shape according to the fashion of the times. In the 16th century they were oval, but they later became round and finally square. The flint is struck against the steel with a glancing blow, and the sparks produced are white-hot particles torn from the steel by the much harder silica of the flint. As Richard Harvey wrote in 1590, 'When the steele and the flint be

FIG. 53. How sparks are struck from a steel by a piece of flint and made to fall on to the tinder.

knockde togither, a man may light his match by the sparkle'. The 'match' was probably a sulphur match and the action is illustrated in Fig. 53, where the sparks are seen falling on to some pieces of 'tinder'.

Tinder was generally charred cotton or linen cloth (made from old cambric handkerchiefs when such luxuries were available), and a spark alighting on it would often cause it to smoulder. It was then blown upon to brighten it and a 'spill'* of twisted paper or wood—or

* Anglo-Saxon *speld*, a torch, or perhaps Dutch *speld*, a splinter. Wooden spills could be made at home with a special 'spill plane' which, when used on a piece of straight-grained softwood, produced a very thin narrow shaving curled round in a tight spiral to form a long tube.

a sulphur match*—could be ignited from it. Other materials used for tinder included dead leaves, charred birch-bark, sun-dried splinters of resinous softwoods, very dry grass, and plant-down such as 'old-man's-beard' (*Clematis*), dandelion 'clocks' and thistle-down. In the Far East, charred silk floss (the fluffy outer cocoon of the silkworm) was widely used.

Home-made tinder varied greatly in quality and a preparation sold by tobacconists as 'German tinder', but more generally known as 'amadou'† or, in some circles, 'touchwood', was sometimes preferred by those who could afford it. This was made from any of several species of bracket-fungus, the leathery pilei of which grow out horizontally from tree-trunks like semicircular shelves. The favoured genera seem to have been *Polyporus* (found especially on elm), *Boletus* (common on oak and beech), and *Fomes* (chiefly on birch). The pileus was first boiled and dried, then soaked in a solution of saltpetre and finally dried again. It is perhaps remarkable that the use of these fungi for tinder runs back to prehistoric times, long before the discovery of saltpetre. Fragments have been found together with nodules of pyrites and flint on a Mesolithic site at Starr Carr, in Yorkshire, which has been dated at about 7000 B.C.

From classical times, boxes have been specially designed to hold all the fire-making apparatus ready for instant use. They were often elaborately decorated and some were most ingeniously contrived. Known generally as 'tinder-boxes', they range from a simple wooden tray fitted with a handle to elaborate pocket affairs in carved crocodiles' teeth or armadillos' tails, imitation pistols which ignite a match

---

* A splint of wood, often elm, the tip of which had been impregnated with sulphur by dipping it in molten brimstone. It caught fire readily but produced the choking fumes of sulphur dioxide for a few moments. It was in use (when available) from the time of the Romans, who are said to have invented it.

† French, *amadou*, tinder, from *amadouer*, to coax. One of the old '*cris de Paris*' was '*Allumettes! Amadou!*' In London streets the cries of 'Matches!' and 'Card-matches!' were heard, but the pedlar, known to all as the 'tinder-box man' (because he sold flints and tinder, among other things), cried only: 'Buy a mouse-trap or a tormentor for your fleas!' Though the flea-tormentor has not the remotest connection with flint, the reader is offered—'free, *gratis*, and for nothing'— the sad information that nobody is quite sure what this instrument was[103]. It is believed to have been a small wooden frame with a piece of rabbit or other fur stretched across it. Possibly it attracted the fleas away from their human hosts and then tormented them by obstinately refusing to yield any blood.

by sparking-off a pinch of gunpowder, and even an alarm-clock which automatically lights a candle at a pre-set time[97]. A common form of household tinder-box is illustrated in Fig. 54, and an investigation made in 1832 showed that very few housemaids could obtain a flame by such means in less than three minutes and it sometimes took half an hour.

The continuous violent rubbing of flint on steel to produce a large enough shower of sparks to give a light was provided by the 'steel

FIG. 54. A household tinder-box of about 1800, with a candlestick lid. The inner lid, called the 'damper', extinguished the tinder after use and kept it flat in the bottom of the box. On the right are two sulphur matches.

mill' shown in Fig. 55. This was invented about 1760 for the use of coal-miners, the sparks being thought less likely than a lamp-flame to ignite the firedamp (methane) and cause an explosion. The feet of the frame were curved and padded so that the mill could be strapped to a boy's left forearm. His right hand turned the large spur-wheel, which spun the steel fly-wheel five times as fast. With his left hand the boy had to hold the flint firmly on its rest and keep it pressed against the wheel. The steel mill was eventually superseded by Davy's safety-lamp, invented in 1815.

The use of sparks struck from flint for firing small arms dates from the 15th century and was possibly inspired by the automatic spring-powered pocket tinder-boxes imported from Japan by Portuguese traders. However, Spain and Holland have also been suggested as countries of origin, while Leonardo da Vinci illustrated both flintlock and wheel-lock mechanisms in the *Codex Atlanticus*, which has been dated in the 1490's[98,99]. The oldest surviving wheel-locks are German and belong to about 1520, while the oldest 'snaphaunce'* flintlocks are Scandinavian and date from the middle of the 16th century.

The wheel-lock, which German tradition ascribes to a Nuremberg watchmaker in 1515, was perhaps foreshadowed by 'Monk's gun',

FIG. 55. The coal-miners' 'steel mill'.

in which sparks to fire the priming or 'amorce' were produced by pulling a steel file under a piece of flint. The wheel-lock works in a similar way, except that a row of three or four toothed (or smooth) wheels replace the file, and their rapid rotation against the flint or pyrites† is accomplished by means of a strong spring. In Leonardo's design the spring was a long helical spiral, but in the common

* *Snaphaunce* or *snaphance*, from a Dutch word for poultry thief.
† The advantage of using pyrites (which was more difficult to obtain than flint) was that it is softer than the steel instead of harder. Not only were the sparks easier to produce, but they consisted of particles of pyrites instead of particles of steel. This was especially important in the wheel-lock, where the wearing away of the wheels would have required a major repair-job. *Per contra*, a worn hammer in a flintlock could easily be replaced, though it seems seldom to have been necessary.

FIRE AND FIREARMS

wheel-lock a powerful V-spring is usual. The principle of the mechanism is illustrated in Fig. 56, where the position ready for priming is shown at the top, and that for firing in the centre. Note that the wheel (or set of wheels) projects into the bottom of the flashpan through a slot (or slots).

In the second drawing, the spring has already been pulled up by the chain, which is now would round the axle of the wheel. This was done by fitting a key over the square end of the axle and giving it about three-quarters of a turn. The rotation of the wheel also moved the cam (shaded), thus allowing the pan-cover to be slid over the flashpan and protect the gunpowder priming. The 'serpentine', which holds a piece of flint or pyrites in its jaws, has been set so as to press on the pan-cover. The wheel is prevented from rotating by a lever called a 'scear' which is linked to the trigger (neither of which is shown). When the trigger is pulled the spring spins the wheel by means of the chain, the cam knocking the pan-cover back by means of a lever and so letting the flint or pyrites grind against the wheels. The priming then fires the main charge in the barrel through a touch-hole.

In the flintlock, illustrated in the 'cocked' position at the foot of Fig. 56, a similar V-spring (not shown) whirls the serpentine over so as to snap the flint held in its jaws sharply against the 'hammer'. This is a curved piece of steel forming part of the pan-cover, from which it stands up nearly at right-angles*. The blow simultaneously sends a shower of sparks downwards and knocks the hammer back to the position f, automatically raising the pan-cover (c) and exposing the priming in the flashpan. The charge in the barrel is then fired through a touch-hole, as in the wheel-lock.

In some models the blow from the flint caused the pan-cover to slide back in grooves instead of rising on a hinge, and there were many other variations in both mechanism and style, including models with two cocks designed to fire two superimposed charges in succession from the same barrel, double-barrelled pistols and guns, and models with rifled barrels. It took about two minutes to load and prime a firelock, whether pistol or musket, and the flint had to be reset in the jaws of the serpentine from time to time and eventually renewed.

---

* The combined steel and pan-cover was known as a 'battery' or 'frizzen'.

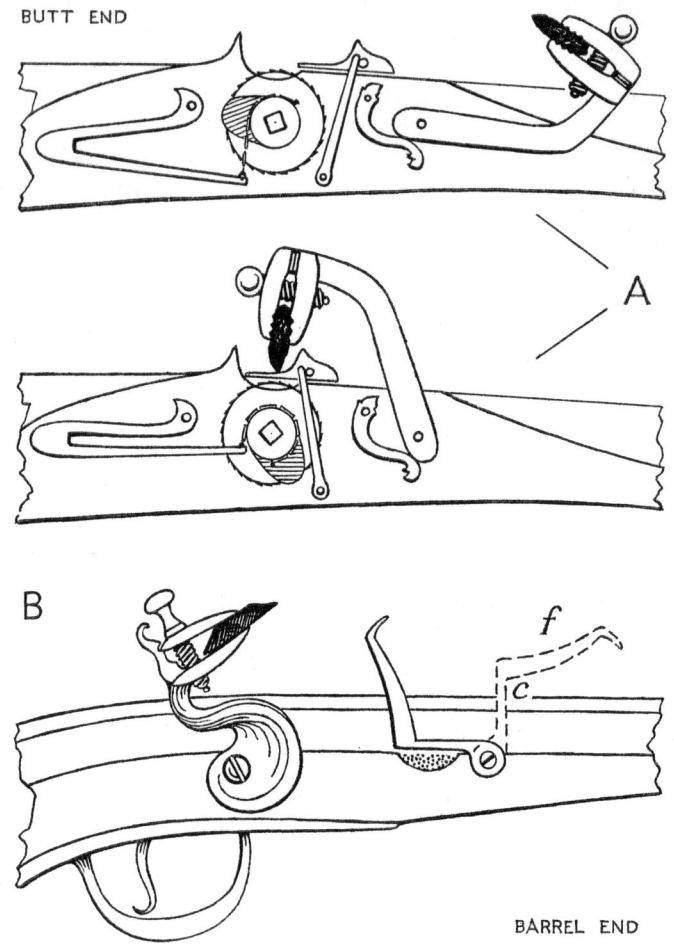

FIG. 56. Flintlock mechanisms. A, The principle of the wheel-lock. B, The snaphaunce flintlock (omitting spring and trigger mechanism).

FLINT KNAPPING

To 'flint' a gun properly required some skill, and it was then said to be 'flinted' or 'well flinted'.

Flint knapping

The constant demand through many centuries for strike-a-lights and gun-flints gave rise to a comparatively large industry with a flourishing export trade. The raw flint was often mined by extending the old Neolithic workings, as at Grime's Graves in Norfolk, but many new quarries and mines were opened up. In a few places a satisfactory quality of 'gunflint chert' was also found and exploited, though no other stone could equal the best black flint.

The shaping and trimming of the flints was called 'knacking' or 'knapping', and the workers were 'knackers' or 'knappers', but the man who roughly shaped the large nodules and made them ready for knapping was formerly called the 'cracker' and more recently the 'quarterer'. 'Knacker' and 'cracker' seem to be the oldest terms, 'knap' and 'knapper' being used in connection with flint for hardly more than a century*.

In England, about 25 of the old flint-knapping sites are known, and some are indicated in Fig. 68. There were some half-a-dozen in East Anglia, about the same number in the Home Counties, upwards of eight in Wiltshire, a few in Hampshire, and at least one—on Beer Head—in Devon. (See Appendix IX.) There were also numerous sites on the Continent, and the French flints made in the departments of Picardy and Champagne were so good that in the 18th century it was forbidden to export them[101]. Good-quality gun-flints were also

---

* The word 'knap' is evidently derived from the Dutch *knappen*, to crack or crush. According to the *Oxford Dictionary*, its first recorded use in England was in 1470, in a reference to the killing of fowls (presumably by snapping their necks). It was used in a slightly different sense in 1535 in Coverdale's Bible: 'He hath knapped the speare in sonder' (Psalm xlv, now xlvi, 9). After that, it was frequently used of breaking spears, snapping thread, and almost anything 'snappy' *except* the breaking of stones—until 1820. In that year, James Cleland, in his report on *Glasgow* (p. 107), referred to 'persons knapping stones for the road'. The first specific reference to flints appears to have been made in 1862, in the *Instructor*, Part I (p. 122), where people are described as 'picking up flints and knapping them, as the method of breaking them is called'. These may not, of course, have been flints *in sensu stricto*, but it is evident that the use of 'knapping' *for the special shaping of flint* is comparatively modern.

made in Loire-et-Cher, notably at Noyers and St. Aignan, and as recently as 1908 French flints were being made for export to Valencia. English gun-flints were renowned all over Europe, and between 1838 and 1848 French gun-flints were being sent to Brandon, in Suffolk, for a final trimming at 1d. each.

Brandon is still celebrated for its gun-flints, which are wanted by collectors and other persons interested in firelocks, and by native tribes which still use old muskets for hunting. The local industry has been in the Edwards family for two or three centuries, the skill being passed on from father to son (and taught to assistants). Herbert Edwards, who recently retired at the age of 75, has recalled* being set to work by his father in 1901, when he was eight, and that when he was thirteen he was paid 1s. 3d. per thousand flints, sometimes making as much as half-a-crown a week.

Gun-flints still go in small numbers to all parts of the world, including countries behind the Iron Curtain such as Czechoslovakia[104], though the trade is affected from time to time by legal regulations. Before they obtained Independence, the peoples of the Gold Coast and other parts of British West Africa were not permitted to carry firearms except flintlocks, and they were allowed to use these only for hunting or defending their homes. Brandon also supplied flints to native tribes in South Africa, but met with difficulties in 1964 when the arms embargo was imposed.

The present output is very small compared with that of the 1850's, when it probably reached its peak. Just before the Crimean War 36 knappers at Brandon were sending 11,000,000 carbine flints annually to Turkey alone. Brandon flints were also used in Abyssinian muskets against Mussolini's troops in 1935, and Brandon was still turning out about 2,000 gun-flints per day (or 700,000 per year) in 1950, chiefly for export to West Africa, Thailand and America.

The Brandon site is less than five miles from the Grime's Graves flint mines described in the previous chapter. In past centuries the Brandon knappers mined the 'floorstone' both at Grime's Graves and at Brandon, but in recent years it has proved more economical to obtain flints from the chalk-pits in the surrounding country. The places supplying flint include Icklingham, Santon, Lingheath, Weeting

* In a private communication with the author, 1950.

FLINT KNAPPING

and Bromehill, and 'Brandon flints' have now become 'Brandon-knapped flints'.

The last Brandon miner, who died in harness at the age of 72, was known as 'Pony' Ashley, and he used to work in tunnels measuring about 2 feet by 3 feet at a depth of 45 feet. He levered out the famous 'Brandon blacks' by candle-light, using a single-tined pick-axe roughly resembling a Neolithic antler-pick. (See Fig. 57 B.) The only other mining tools were a heavy iron hammer, a short crowbar, and a shovel. When the flints had been got to the surface it was found

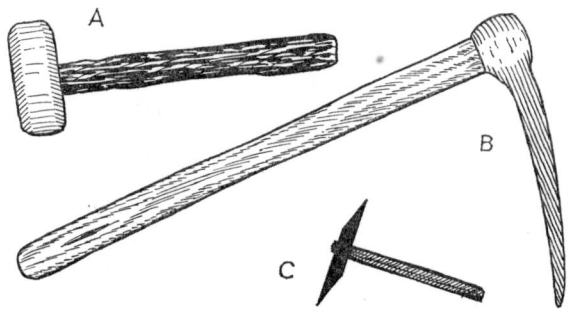

FIG. 57. A, Flint-knapper's heavy hammer. B, Flint-miner's pick. C, A type of small flaking hammer.

advisable to knap them reasonably soon, for some nodules which are quite black while still in the chalk may turn milky (and even crack) after an hour or two's exposure to wind and sun.

The knapper wears a leather apron and works sitting down with a thick leather pad on his left knee. The first process, called 'quartering', consists in roughly dressing the nodule. The quarterer has two hammers, one weighing about 5 pounds, shown in Fig. 57 A, and the other about $3\frac{1}{2}$ pounds. Since a flint nodule generally shows a propensity for splitting easily and evenly in certain particular directions, a preliminary examination is necessary to find the disposition of the 'cleavage', as it is called*. This is done by tapping the flint all round and listening for a satisfactory 'ring'. Then the quarterer knocks the flint into a suitably shaped block with a striking-platform

* There are, of course, no true cleavage-planes in a flint nodule—only directions of minimum toughness.

FLINT IN THE HISTORICAL PERIOD

and straight sides. The hammer-blows are swung from the elbow, which is held close to the hip, and the weight of the hammer is relied on to provide most of the force.

The second process is called 'flaking', and the flaker also has two hammers, one large and one small. The large hammer is shown in use in Fig. 58, and one type of small flaking hammer is illustrated at C in Fig. 57*. At one time a round-nosed or 'English' hammer was used for flaking, but this gradually gave place to the so-called 'French' hammers in the 19th century.

FIG. 58. A flint-knapper using the large flaking hammer. Note the detached flake resting on his knee-pad.

The flaker works his way round the flint block or 'quarter', striking off a succession of long narrow flakes like that shown on the right in Plate XXIX. The example in the centre of Fig. 59 is the back of the same specimen, and is marked by a deep bulbar scar immediately below the striking-platform. For this work the quarter is held on the knee-pad with the striking-platform at an angle of about 45 degrees, and the hammer is never raised more than two or three inches above the elbow. The heavier hammer strikes the longest flakes, which are about 6 inches long by 1 inch wide.

* Both these hammers were traced from photographs reproduced in *Antiquity* to illustrate the article by Rainbird Clarke[101], to whom acknowledgements are here made.

Having worked his way round the quarter once, the flaker continues round a second time, knocking off flakes a little to one side of the first series. He may then go round a third, and perhaps even a fourth time, but it is said that 'the nearer the crust the better the flint' and the core of the quarter is of little use except as building material. The drawing on the left of Fig. 59 shows a complete series of flakes reassembled round the quarter, and that on the right the discarded core, which forms a sort of blunt polygonal cone.

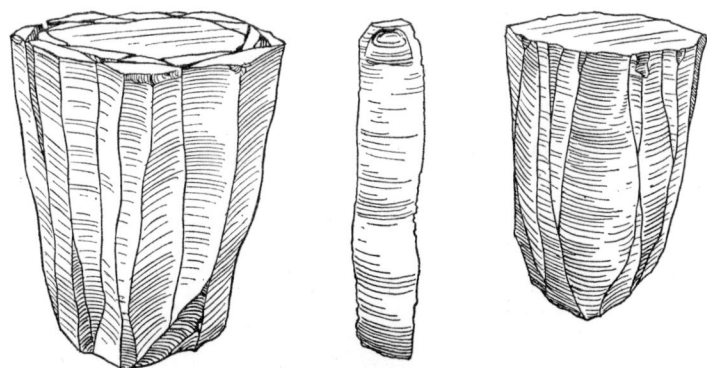

FIG. 59. The method of striking flakes from a block of flint for making gun-flints. On the right is the discarded core.

The last stage is the shaping and trimming of pieces of flint to the sizes required by the several types of flintlock firearm. The long flakes have to be cut into small squares and rectangles, like those shown in Plate XXIX, and this is done with a 'knapping' hammer which, in the Edwards family, consists of an old cast-steel file about 9 inches long and specially tempered. The file is wielded from the wrist only, the work being done on a small anvil. This is made from a rod of soft iron about 6 inches long and 1 inch square, driven into a wooden block at a slight angle and covered with leather. Since the wooden block is often an old oak stump, with the anvil set about 4 inches from its edge, the knapper sits sideways at it and 'clicks off' and trims his squares with astonishing dexterity. In Fig. 60 the parts of a typical gun-flint are named, and it should be noted that the trimming includes slightly undercutting the edge on the face.

FLINT IN THE HISTORICAL PERIOD

Flint-knapping is attended by an occupational hazard—silicosis. This is a malignant form of pneumonoconiosis caused by the inhalation of silica dust and its lodgement in the alveoli of the lungs. The particles penetrate the alveolar walls and may be carried into the lymph nodes, where they form granules. The extensive formation of scar-tissue in the lungs leads to chronic respiratory insufficiency and a predisposition to tuberculosis. The damage, once caused, cannot be repaired and a diligent knapper might not expect to live much beyond forty. Gun-flint knapping was therefore done in the open air whenever possible, but the necessity for a constant output at Brandon demanded the erection of a work-shed. The knappers of fifty years

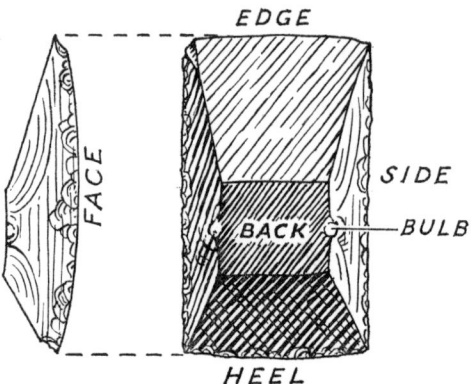

FIG. 60. The parts of a typical gun-flint. Compare with the specimens in Plate XXIX.

ago therefore wore sponges tied under their noses, as air-filters, but vacuum-cleaners were later introduced to draw away the dust as fast as it appeared.

Brandon is possibly the last surviving flint-knapping centre in western Europe but certainly not in the world. The flint-knapping aborigines of Australia have already been mentioned, and there are others in New Guinea, parts of Africa and elsewhere—including Turkey. The Turkish industry remained very obscure until it was investigated by Jaques Bordaz (of Montreal) in 1969[105]. He found a group of knappers in the village of Çakmak who use some 500 tons of the local flint annually in making blades for the 'threshing-sledges'

ODD USES OF FLINT

used by the Turkish farmers. The blades are cut from 5-inch flakes struck in much the same way as the Brandon flakes, which they closely resemble. A Çakmak knapper can produce a straight flake like that in Plate XXIX with each blow of his hammer, and cut it into two 2-inch blades with three more taps. He is said to be able to make about 4,000 sledge-blades per day.

The sledges are used instead of flails to separate the wheat grain from the stalk. A sledge consists of two planks of wood joined together, the under-surface being armed with 600 or 800 flint blades set on edge in specially-cut slots. The driver stands on the sledge, which is pulled by a horse or a yoke of oxen. Threshing is done by spreading the sheaves of corn over a threshing-floor and then driving the sledge round and round so that the flints chop up the straw.

Odd uses of flint

Among the odd uses of flint which are sometimes cited but cannot often be verified is the shaving of hair. In 1634, Thomas Herbert published a *Description of the Persian Monarchy*, later reprinted as *Some Yeares Travels into Divers Parts of Asia and Afrique*, in which he says of certain tribes 'that they shaved their heads with flints and other stones'. These people must have belonged to the 'Late Stone Age' (see Fig. 67), but we have no means of knowing whether prehistoric man ever tried shaving. He probably did, because it is in the nature of man to try things and flint can certainly be sharp enough for a not-too-painful shave.

A story which cannot, however, be credited and yet is sometimes told because it is supposed to have emanated from Brandon itself, is that 'Harley-street brain surgeons have used Brandon flint to scrape human skulls'*. Enquiries about this at the Royal College of Surgeons have failed to turn up any record of either the scraping of skulls with flint, or the scraping of skulls at all—except, perhaps, dead ones being cleaned for anatomical specimens. But flint was certainly used for surgical purposes by Neolithic man about 6,000 years ago, when trepanning† was first practised. It was probably done on sick or mad

---

* From a feature-article in the *Daily Mail*, 7 May, 1949.

† Trepanning, or trephining, is cutting out a circular piece of bone from the skull, thus exposing the brain.

people to let out evil spirits, and flint instruments must have been used because no other material harder than bone was known.

It is perhaps astonishing that the patients sometimes recovered, but this is evident from the growth of new bone round the openings in some of the skulls. Referring to some good examples of this in the *Musée de l'Homme*, Paris, R. Furon[106] has noted some interesting similarities between the technique employed and that used by pre-Columbian American Indians, who also must have used instruments of flint (or a similar stone). Trepanned skulls of Stone Age date have been found in Britain as well as in France and other parts of Europe, and some have turned up in Peru.

Flint has been used for grinding in at least two different ways, but there is no truth in the statement sometimes made* that the French 'burr' (or 'bhur') millstones, used for grinding flour, were constructed of blocks of flint. They were made from blocks of a chalcedonic hornstone (see page 37) of Tertiary age, found in a freshwater limestone at La Ferté sous Jouarre, in the Paris Basin. Flint has been used for grinding corn but only in the early hand-mills or querns, which were sometimes made from the Hertfordshire pudding-stone[54]. The other use of flint for grinding is in the tube-mills and ball-mills described on pages 204 and 206 and illustrated in Fig. 64.

The Hertfordshire pudding-stone has also been ground and polished for use as an ornamental stone in snuff-box lids, small table-tops and so on. The style of decoration it provides can be gathered from Plate XVIII. The polishing of flint pebbles for 'worry stones', and of split pebbles or thin sections for brooches and pendants, is still both a small industry and private hobby. The frontispiece and Plates XVII to XXI should suggest many of the possibilities. The late William Burrough Hill, a well-known Southampton antiquary, had two 'stained-glass windows' made for his study, only the 'stained glass' consisted of slices of stone cut so thin as to be transparent or translucent. The pieces, which were not very large, were set in lead and arranged in festoons among large pieces of clear glass. They included several of the mineral forms of silica—chalcedony, agate and flint being prominent among them.

Other odd uses of flint include the knapping (at Brandon) of small

* For example, in the 'official' guide to the High Salvington windmill (*Durrington Mill*), near Worthing.

pieces for making up patterns in mosaic flooring, and the cutting of thin glass by means of sharp points or edges, as mentioned on page 37. The author has also used flint satisfactorily for scoring fine 'cross-wire' lines on glass discs for setting in telescope eyepieces and other optical devices. They can be made so fine as to be almost invisible to the naked eye, and as even as the spiders' webs that are still sometimes used for this purpose*.

Last of these oddities are the mysterious little flint casts of a small sea-urchin (*Offaster pilula*) found engraved with lines and dots on a Palæolithic site at Kempston, in Bedfordshire. The dots could easily have been punched or chipped out, but the lines (quite deep in the author's specimen) must have taken a long time to cut. These objects were probably used as beads and, like the flint sea-urchins described in Chapter 1, may have had 'magic' or 'lucky' properties. It is just possible that they were a form of tally, or they may be comparable with the later Mesolithic pebbles found at Mas d'Azil in Ariège, southern France. These bear simple graphic marks or 'petroglyphs', painted in oxide of iron, but their significance is not known.

Building and road-work

It is not possible to say when flint was first used as a building material, but in Britain the Romans certainly included it in rubble walls†. The walls of the Roman fort at Pevensey (Anderida), for example, which are twelve feet thick and in places twenty eight feet high, are chiefly of flint, though faced with sandstone and bonded here and there with bricks and slabs of carstone (ironstone). Again, the second Roman city at St. Albans (Verulamium) contained 'houses, shops and temples, all built of flint and brick'[107].

During the Dark Ages there seems to have been little building in

---

* The Vickers Instrument Company, which now employs an electronic engraving process, last used spiders' webs in new instruments about 1959, but states (in a letter to the author) that webs must continue to be used in repair work for many years to come.

† The word rubble is used here of undressed stones or broken pieces of old stones, of all kinds, sizes and shapes, employed for building without any regard to order or arrangement. They may be held in place by any kind of mortar, cob or cement, and this distinguishes 'rubble-work' from 'drystone', though no precise definition seems to be thought necessary.

stone. Wooden-framed houses with wattle-and-daub fillings between the timbers were the general rule, even for kings' residences, and cottages often had walls of 'cob'. This was a mixture of mud or clay, grit and straw, and it often contained flints and other stones to help provide bulk. These walls were about two feet thick and were built in layers, each layer being beaten and trodden flat, and allowed to dry, before the next was added. Cob walls, even when standing alone, were thatched to protect them from rain, and the bottom two feet were often tarred. Cob cottages, thus furnished with 'a good hat and a good pair of shoes', have been known to last more than 300 years.

Another method of building walls was to put up boards of 'shuttering' to enclose the position of the wall, and then pour in a thick mixture of puddled chalk and flints or other stones, with chopped straw. This mixture is called 'pug' in Wiltshire, according to Garry Hogg[115], but elsewhere it is probably 'cob'. Puddled chalk makes a very sticky clay-like substance which Cobbett says is called 'maume, or mame' in eastern Hampshire and is, 'when wet, very much like *grey soap*' (Cobbett's italics)[108]. These walls were afterwards whitewashed and sometimes plastered, and were astonishingly durable.

Buildings chiefly of stone or flint began to appear again before Norman times, and a number of existing flint walls and a few churches have been attributed to the 10th century or even earlier. Much of the parish church of St. Nicholas, Old Shoreham, for example, is dated 'previous to 900'[109], while the high flint walls of the nave of Leatherhead parish church are held to indicate pre-Conquest work (probably about 1060)[110]. Other examples could be given from East Anglia and elsewhere in the Chalk country, though pre-Conquest work is by no means common.

The method of building flint walls was to lay the flints with mortar like bricks, but the mortar had to be stiff to prevent the rounded flints from rolling out of place while it set. A few courses only could be laid at a time for the same reason, and while a very thick wall was easier to keep stable it required a great deal of mortar. This old method may be contrasted with the modern practice of boarding-up the space between the previously erected brick or stone quoins at the ends of the wall, laying the flints in place between the boards, and then pouring in concrete. Two or three courses are done at a time, the concrete being 'sliced' into the small cracks and gaps with a

BUILDING AND ROAD-WORK

trowel, but the work can be continued without waiting for the lower courses to set.

Many of the old flint churches were built of 'clunch' (see page 66) and then faced with a thick outer wall of flint, but the quoins of the building, and the door and window frames, were generally of brick or stone. It was difficult to use flint where sharp angles were required, and it has been suggested that the round flint towers of some village churches were so made to avoid the expense of stone or brick for the corners[111].

A great many flint churches were built in East Anglia and southeast England in the Middle Ages; from that time right through to the present day, cottages, manor houses and even bigger buildings have been built largely of flint. The flint is used in various ways, sometimes forming a rubble to fill up the spaces between timbers, or being inserted as odd nodules between bricks to reduce the total number of bricks required, as in Fig. 61 (*top right*). They may be laid in alternate courses with bricks or stone, or simply used to break up a brick or stone wall with symmetrical patterns, as in Fig. 61 (*bottom left*). In short, their uses range from composing an entire wall (except for the quoins) to forming a mere decorative facing to ordinary brickwork, an example of which is shown at the bottom of Plate XXX*.

The flints used in building are often arranged in distinctive ways which may be called 'bonds' by analogy with brickwork, though actual bonding is scarcely involved. The haphazard or unarranged use of nodules, of which three examples are given in Plate XXX, is inferior to such ordered usages as those shown in Plate XXXI. In both classes of work the flints may be either unworn nodules or 'rolled' flint pebbles (sometimes called 'cobbles'), and the unworn nodules may be untrimmed, partly trimmed, or carefully knapped to form rectangular blocks which may be laid like bricks.

The first example in Plate XXX shows a rough flint wall of untrimmed nodules set in a lime mortar, and might fairly be called rubble-work. Another example is shown at the top of Plate XXXII, which is the fireplace of a New Forest cottage left intact when the

---

* Part of the wall of the Midland Bank at Storrington, Sussex, a modern building.

cottage was demolished to preserve 'Forest Rights' for the owner*. In this picture the difficulty of making square corners in raw flint, without the use of brick or stone, is clearly seen. The specimen at the foot of Plate XXX, already referred to, is also rough work but with the cortices of the flints struck off to expose only the dark cores, which are set in cement. At the top, on the right, is some rubble-work in beach-pebbles, set in mortar and forming part of a garden wall.

At the top of Plate XXXI, on the left, beach-pebbles have again been used, but this time they have been selected for size and colour and arranged carefully in rows. Dark cobbles of this kind are often called 'kidney-flints' and they have been used in the walls of cottages and churches in almost every part of the Chalk country. The 'herring-bone' bond at the foot of Plate XXXI is also common in walls of all kinds. The flints used here are not necessarily oval or sausage-shaped, as might be supposed, but are more often bun-shaped or discoid and set on edge in a mortar containing small flint stones to give it added bulk.

The curved outlines of all unknapped flints cause comparatively large areas of mortar to appear on the surface, even when the flints are actually touching inside the wall. A common way of decorating these areas is to stick chips and small flakes of flint into the mortar between the rows of flints. This is called 'garreting' or 'garneting' and, in Norfolk, 'galleting'[113]. At the top of Fig. 61, on the left, is an example of garreting on a kidney-flint wall, and below it is a similar decoration on a rubble wall of miscellaneous stones.

The finest style of building in flint is undoubtedly that known as 'flush-work', illustrated at the top of Plate XXXI, on the right. This is part of the wall of St. Michael's Church (which also has a round flint tower) in Lewes High Street. The flints have been knapped so accurately that they fit like bricks and need no more than a quarter of an inch of mortar between them. There are many other examples

* In the New Forest the rights to graze ponies, cattle, sheep and pigs at certain seasons in the Forest, and to cut turf, 'are vested, not in individuals, but in property, being attached in each case to a particular holding—a cottage, a manor, or a parcel of land'[112]. If the rights are attached to a dwelling-place a fireplace is sufficient to secure them, for 'where there's a hearth there's a home'. This has nothing special to do with flint, but the reader may have been curious—the picture is an uncommon one.

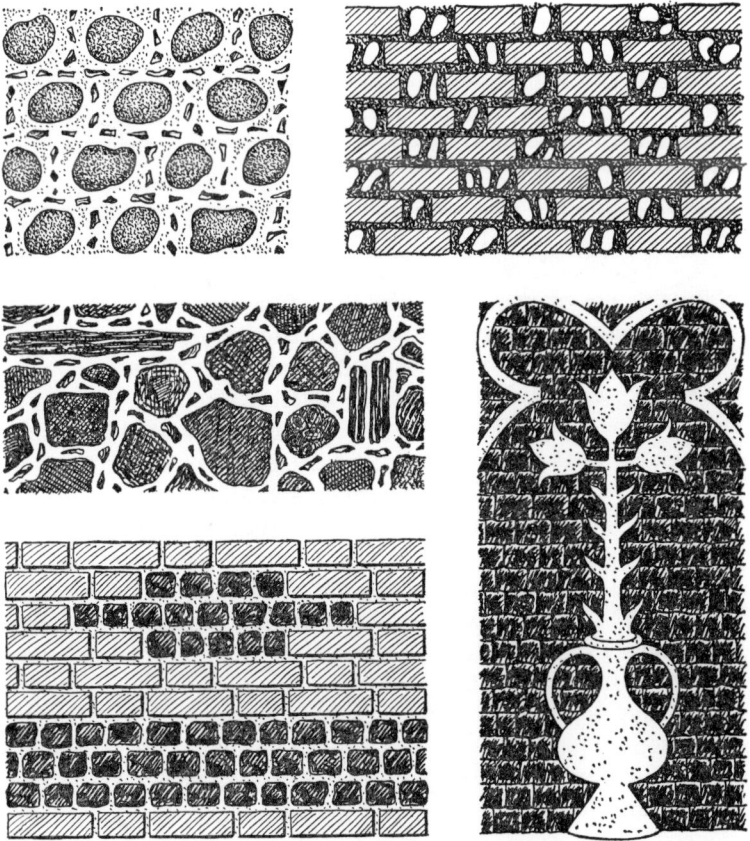

FIG. 61. Ornamental uses of flint in walls.

of this fine flintwork, especially in East Anglia, where the cores discarded by the gun-flint knappers were squared-up for sale to the builders. Larger flints were also knapped for flush-work, and sometimes special shapes had to be produced to enable the flint to be fitted into the irregular spaces of stone tracery. One of the finest examples in the country is the church at Kersey, near Lavenham, Suffolk, where rich and elaborate flint inlay-work covers the entire face of the South Porch. Edmund Vale[114] gives an interesting detail from St. John's Priory, Colchester, here re-drawn on the right of

Fig. 61. He describes it as one of a pair of vases, each holding a large plant of Madonna lilies.

There is also some interesting flush-work in the church of St. John the Evangelist at West Meon, in Hampshire. This is notable not only because the individual flints are remarkably small, measuring little more than two inches square, but because they were all knapped locally by women. Their uniformity and exact squareness is quite astonishing, and since there are several large panels of them, each containing about 2,160 flints—according to Garry Hogg[115]—the skill of these women must have rivalled that of the knappers at Brandon.

Both freestone and brick have been used in alternate squares with black flint to produce a chess-board or 'chequers' pattern. This is called 'diaper work' and one of the oldest examples in England is shown in Plate XXXII, at the foot. Known as 'The Marlipins', this ecclesiastical-looking building (now a museum) stands in the main street of New Shoreham, Sussex, and nobody knows why it was built nor the origin of its name*. The front elevation was erected in 1347 and consists of squares of Caen stone, imported from Normandy, alternating with squares composed of from six to nine black flints. Other parts of the building, including the side-wall of untrimmed flints, date from about 1120.

The only other uses of flint in building seem to be the incorporation of flint gravels in concrete, to be described below, and the use of the Hertfordshire pudding-stone as a durable building-stone. Though it is too hard for ordinary working, rough blocks of this have often been included in rubble-work and flat faces have sometimes been chipped and squared for better-class work. There is an ancient monastic barn at Harmondsworth built almost entirely of it[54].

The earliest use of flints for road-making must have been simply the filling-up of hollows or muddy patches in the ancient trackways with locally-obtained nodules or coarse gravels. Rough-and-ready repairs to roads are still done in this way, and country by-roads and access-lanes are often 'made up' by simply rolling-in large quantities of broken flints, obtained from the chalk-pits and the lime and cement works. But there are also two classes of carefully constructed flint

---

* E. V. Lucas gives an interesting note on these questions in the Sussex volume of the *Highways and Byways* series of county handbooks[116], to which the curious reader is referred.

PLATE XXIX. Gun-flints made at Northfleet in 1851. *Right:* A long flake from which horse-pistol flints were made. *Centre:* A pocket-pistol flint. *Left* (from top): Flints for a fowler, a French pistol, and a horse-pistol.

PLATE XXX. Walls in unarranged and untrimmed or slightly trimmed flint.

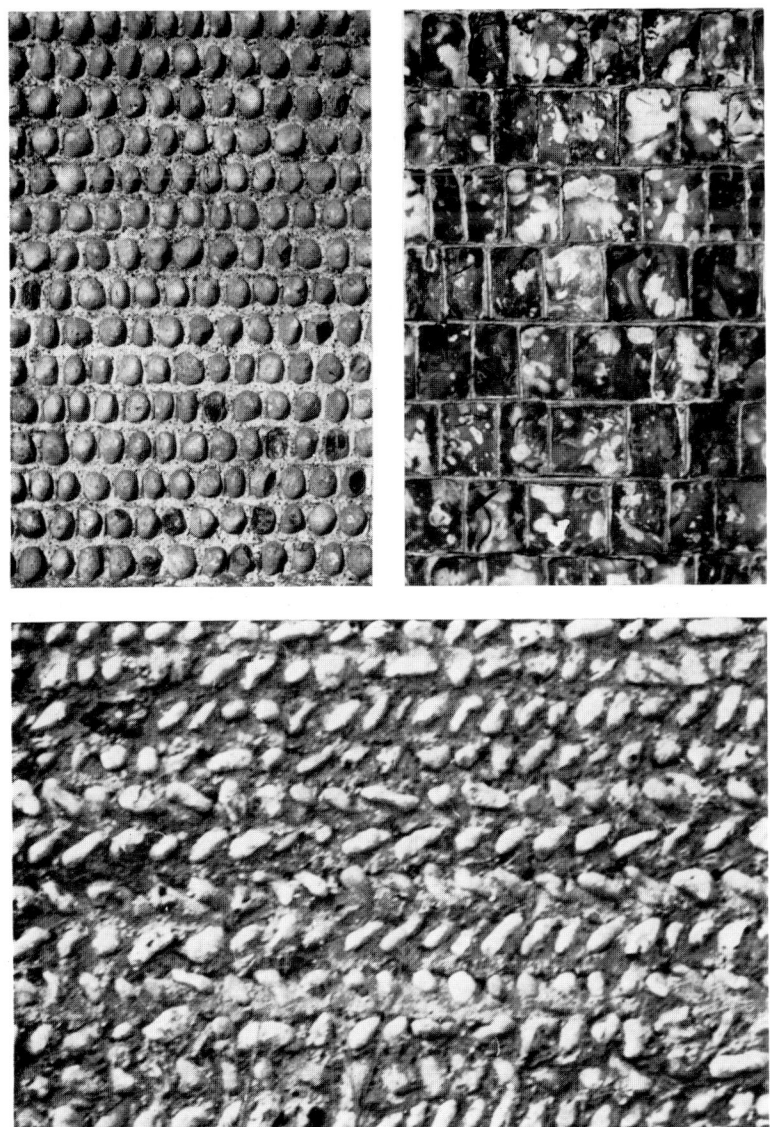

PLATE XXXI. Walls in designed arrangement with both untrimmed (but selected) and knapped flints.

PLATE XXXII. *Above:* A fireplace and chimney saved from a demolished flint cottage at Boldrewood, in the New Forest, to maintain the owner's Forest Rights. *Below:* The 'Marlipins' at Shoreham, Sussex, showing diaper-work in flint and Caen stone.

roads: gravel roads and cobble roads. Both have passed through a history of great usefulness and economic importance, and both have now arrived at a sort of retirement from which they are taken out from time to time by architects, landscapists and town-planners for ornamental use. Concrete roads, though they often contain more than 50 per cent (by volume) of flint gravels, are not here regarded as flint roads.

The Romans used flint and flint gravels, wherever they were available, for making their famous roads and—about 250 years ago—Daniel Defoe described an exposed section of the Fosse Way[117]. He noted 'a laying of clay of a solid binding quality, then flint-stones, then chalk, then upon the chalk rough ballast or gravel'. Modern descriptions[88,111] more or less confirm this and Fig. 62 shows a

FIG. 62. Section across a typical Roman road in southern Britain. The grass verges at V were for horsemen and were bounded on the outside by drainage ditches.

section of a typical Roman road in the east or south of England. A shallow excavation was first lined with large stones or broken chalk. This was covered with a layer of flint nodules and then topped with gravel. The surface was cambered and the ballast held in check by kerb-stones. Beyond these there were often grass verges for horsemen and, finally, V-shaped ditches for drainage. It was only in the north of England that the Roman roads were paved with flagstones.

The Roman roads lasted a long time and very few new roads were made in Britain until the beginning of the 19th century. Repairs to old roads and tracks were made—and compelled to be made by law—from time to time, but chiefly by tipping loose stones of any kind into the deeper ruts and holes. There were other types of road in mountainous, rocky, and marshy places, but our subject is flint and they do not concern us.

The development of the stage-coach and the increasing heavy traffic of fish, vegetables and other provisions into London from the country, eventually demanded properly constructed roads, and about

1750 an efficient and economical way of laying them was suggested by John Metcalf, known also as 'Blind Jack of Knaresborough'. His method was developed and improved, and from about 1815 John Loudon McAdam and Thomas Telford reconstructed on sound lines most of the major roads in the country. The method was to lay a foundation of broken stones on a firm subsoil and then cover them with smaller broken stones, finishing-up with a sharp gravel. This type of road-covering became known as 'macadam', but Telford's roads differed from McAdam's only in having a much heavier stone foundation, and both styles differed very little from the Roman.

In the late 19th century, gravel roads began to appear all over the country; but gravels vary greatly in quality and the best, small, red flint gravels were too expensive for most public works. They were used for topping the drives and footpaths of country estates and the better-class villas and gardens, where their handsome appearance was maintained by diligent weeding and rolling. Some of these displays are kept up even today but they can no longer be considered commonplace.

The best gravels for road-making are subangular or sharp river-gravels, graded by sifting so that the large stones can all be used in the lower layers. The worst gravels to use in a loose state are the coarser shingles of sea-beaches. Their smooth round stones do not hold together but shift about over one another like large marbles. However, very satisfactory roads can be made with them by setting them side by side in a bed of mortar so that they cannot move.

Large stones known as 'cobbles' or 'cobble-stones' are used and the best are egg-shaped. They are set close together and standing on end in a bed of stiff gritty clay, lime mortar, or cement, and are so arranged that their tops all stand at the same level. Cobbles were widely used through many centuries for the main streets of towns, the yards of shops and inns, waterfront and harbour causeways, and any short thoroughfares where traffic was heavy.

A considerable number of old cobbled streets and yards still exist, but travelling over them is both bumpy and noisy, especially with iron-shod wheels, and they never ran for very long distances. It was, however, this type of road that Shakespeare had in mind when he let Friar Laurence say of Juliet*—

* *Romeo and Juliet*, II, 6, line 16.

BUILDING AND ROAD-WORK

> O, so light a foot
> Will ne'er wear out the everlasting flint.

The general appearance of an old cobbled road or pavement is similar to the piece of wall at the top of Plate XXX, on the right, if laid flat on the table. This might be a view of Mermaid Street, Rye, for example—as seen by somebody looking down between his own feet. But when used for purely decorative purposes, cobbles are more often arranged like those at the top of Plate XXXI, on the left. Examples may be seen filling waste strips and squares on the forecourts of modern buildings, on traffic islands, and in other such places. Small pieces of pavement are occasionally made of knapped flints, rather like large cobbles with their top halves knocked off, and sometimes the flints are interspersed with pieces of brick and other rubble. A steep cobbled surface may be seen at Black Rock, Brighton, where its purpose is to protect the foot of the chalk cliffs from the sea, but the flints here are set in concrete, of which they may be considered a part.

Though concrete can be made with pebbles of any kind of hard stone (except those which are slaty or foliated), flint gravels make up the bulk of the 'ballast' used in concrete in this country. In general, concrete is made by mixing Portland cement, sand and ballast, in some such volumetric proportions as 1:2:4, or 2:2:4, with water. The exact proportions, the sizes of the stones in the ballast, the sharpness of the sand, the quantity of water, and the method of mixing, may all be prescribed for concrete required to undergo stresses, for its strength and durability depend largely on them. If a piece of good concrete is broken with a sledge-hammer the flints in it will be cracked across rather than fall out whole.

Flints may enter into the making of the cement, as well as forming part of the concrete. Cement is made by roasting limestone (often chalk) with clay to a very high temperature, when several chemical reactions take place. The roasting is done in a rotary kiln and the product is a white-hot clinker which has to be cooled and ground to a fine powder. This is done in a tube-mill, which consists of a steel cylinder, perhaps thirty feet long and seven feet in diameter. It is divided into compartments containing about 20 tons of iron or steel balls, graded according to size[118].

The tube is charged with the cement clinker and then rotated at about twenty-five revolutions per minute, when the balls tumble about and very efficiently grind the clinker to the fineness of flour. According to W. R. Jones[95], rounded and subrounded flint nodules may be used in the mill instead of steel balls, and when they have themselves become worn too small for further grinding they are sold as silica for use in pottery manufacture.

Pottery and glass

Chalk is quarried for both lime-burning and cement manufacture, and it often contains a lot of flints. These are removed in the 'wash-mills', large concrete tanks filled with water in which the chalk and flints are stirred round and round by means of harrows revolving about eleven times per minute. Most of the chalk breaks up and forms a slurry, the flints settling-down on the bottom. They receive a final cleaning from high-pressure jets of water, and then are screened and sold as 'washmill flints' to the ceramics industry.

According to G. Jackson[119], washmill flints are the most important source of free silica for the manufacture of 'earthenware'*. This term covers all whiteware except bone china and porcelain, and includes tableware, white wall tiles and sanitary ware. Flint was, in fact, first proposed for use in pottery as a whitening agent. A story is told of how John Astbury, a Staffordshire potter, was riding to London when his horse developed an eye complaint. The medicament prescribed was a white powder made by roasting a flint until it was red-hot and then pulverizing it, but it is difficult to believe that this could have done anything but harm to the poor horse's eye! However, Astbury was so much impressed by the whiteness of the powder that in 1720 he began to use calcined flint as a white 'slip' (i.e. a suspension in water) to wash the insides of his buff-coloured wares[121].

Ground calcined flint was then included as an ingredient in the earthenware 'body', as the potter's clay is called, and Daniel Bird is said to have determined the optimum proportion of flint to be about 35 per cent. Among other benefits, the addition of flint to the body is said to check the warping of flat articles like tiles. Flint is also added to some pottery glazes, when Bernard Leach[122] calls it

* P. J. Adams[120] adds flint beach-pebbles to the washmill flints.

'the bone of the glaze' and observes that it helps to prevent peeling and unwanted crazing.

Within a very few years of Astbury's discovery quite a large trade in flint developed, the raw stones being transported from the Chalk country to the Potteries by water, the Trent and Mersey Canal, and the Caldon Canal, providing the chief inland route, and Runcorn the sea-port. The flint was calcined and ground in the neighbourhood of the potteries, but the dry grinding caused silicosis (page 192) in the workers and, in 1726, Thomas Benson took out a patent to grind the flints under water.

The raw flints are first calcined because this riddles them with fine cracks and enables them to be crushed easily. Calcination is done in 'flint kilns', which are wide brick shafts much like lime kilns. A kiln is charged with alternate layers of coal and flint, the proportion by weight being about one of coal to thirteen of flint, the total charge ranging from ten to thirty tons. In the 'batch' process, the kiln is fired for three or four days at about 900°C., to ensure the thorough dehydration and cracking of the flints, and then emptied. In the 'continuous' process, the kiln is repeatedly charged with coal and flint at the top, the calcined flints and coal-ash being removed at the same rate from the bottom. In some modern kilns liquid or gaseous fuels are used instead of coal and there is no ash.

During calcination the flint loses water and therefore density. There is not much change until a temperature of about 250°C. is reached, but then the water is rapidly driven out and dehydration is virtually complete at about 450°C. At this stage the specific gravity of the flint stands at about 2·5, having dropped from about 2·62, so that the water-loss represents a loss in weight of about 4·2 per cent. These relations are shown in Fig. 63, where it will be seen that there is only a very slight loss if the temperature is still further increased until about 1,100°C. is reached. At this temperature there is a catastrophic drop in density denoting radical changes in the structure of the silica, the quartz being probably first converted to tridymite and then to cristobalite, which has a specific gravity of about 2·27. These changes are not desired by the potter, who regards a specific gravity of 2·5 as indicating correct calcination, and fortunately this value is easily achieved since it is maintained over a very wide range of temperatures.

After calcination, the flints are first sieved to remove the coal-ash and then undergo a preliminary crushing, either between steel jaws or in a gyratory crusher. They are then ready for grinding, and in the early days this was often done by water-power, old flour-mills being converted to stamp-mills for this purpose. In the old flint-mill at Cheddleton, Staffordshire, grinding was done in a large 'pan-mill'. The main part of this is a shallow iron pan the bottom of which

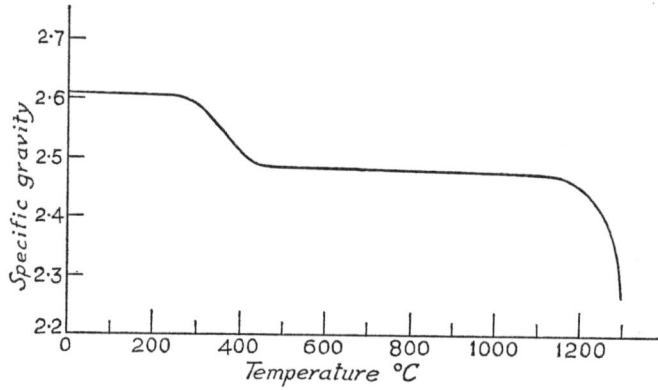

FIG. 63. Curve showing the loss in weight of flint during calcination. (*After* G. Jackson[119].)

is paved with blocks of chert. The pan was partly filled with water and then charged with calcined flints. These were ground by heavy blocks of chert called 'runners', which were pushed round and round over the 'pavers' by cast-iron arms.

Today, grinding is generally done in a 'ball-mill' which is similar to the tube-mills described on page 203, except that it consists of a single drum instead of a long cylinder divided into compartments. The grinding is done in water and iron-staining is avoided by using large round beach-pebble flints, or special ceramic balls, instead of steel balls. The grinding has to be carefully watched because the quantity of flint to be added to the pottery clay depends partly on its particle-size. Flint required for use with glazes may require additional grinding. Some of the machinery for dealing with calcined flints is shown in Fig. 64.

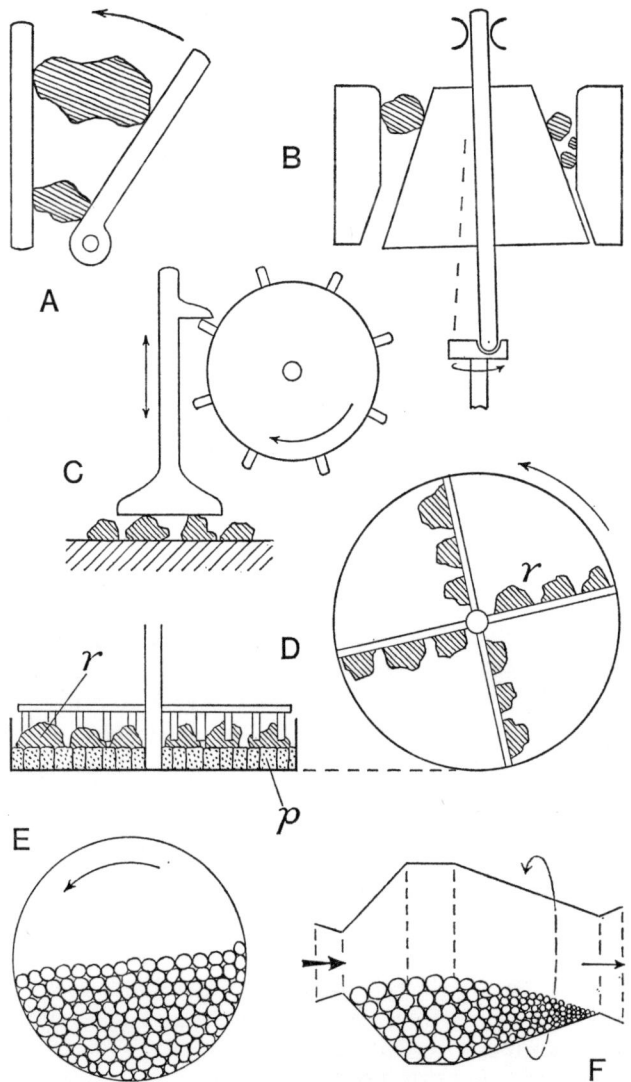

FIG. 64. The principles of some common types of flint crushing and grinding machinery. A, Jaw crusher. B, Gyratory crusher; the cone gyrates but does not rotate. C, Stamp-mill. D, Pan-mill in section and plan; *r*, runners; *p*, pavers. E, Batch ball-mill. F, Continuous grinding ball-mill, so shaped that the balls maintain their grading and grind the flint finer and finer as it passes through from left to right.

FLINT IN THE HISTORICAL PERIOD

Since the grinding is done with water, the ground flint powder runs off in suspension with the water emptied from the mill. It is now called 'slop flint' and is allowed to settle in a tank known as the 'settling ark'. It is finally pumped from this to a 'slip drying kiln', from which it emerges ready for the potter.

Though flint is an important ingredient in many kinds of pottery in this country, it is used much less in America where other forms of silica are readier to hand. Nevertheless, though flint is never used in American stoneware, the familiar American name for stoneware is 'flintware'. We are just as careless in England with our names for glass, for though the silica in the original 'flint' glass was indeed crushed flint, flint has not been used in it for more than a century[123].

Glass is made by heating silica with an alkali (soda or potash) and an alkaline earth (lime or magnesia), *plus* various additives (generally metallic oxides) to improve the quality. It is a non-crystalline complex of the silicates of all the metals present. It was probably discovered by accident about 4000 B.C. in Egypt and was used for such things as beads long before the art of blowing bottles was discovered.

Window-glass was being made by the Romans in the 1st century A.D., and in England it was certainly in use in the 13th century, because Henry III (1216–1272) had glass in the windows of his palace at Westminster. Up to the 17th century the glassmakers of northern Europe used sand for silica, and wood or plant ashes as a source of potash. Their chief product was window-glass and the method of making it—by blowing a glass globe and then spinning it till it formed a disc—was called the 'crown' process.

In southern Europe silica was obtained from crushed flint and soda from the ashes of marine plants[124], and the main production here was of glass vessels. Venetian glassware became deservedly famous and in 1673 the Worshipful Company of Glass Sellers of London commissioned George Ravenscroft to produce an English rival to the sparkling Venetian '*cristallo*'.

Ravenscroft first switched from sand to flint as his source of silica, and produced a silica-potash glass more or less comparable with the silica-soda Mediterranean flint glass, but he found it necessary to use an excessive quantity of potash, and this caused a network of fine cracks, called 'crizzelling'*, to develop in the glass. He then replaced

* The potters' 'crazing' or 'crackle'.

some of the potash with lead oxide and produced the excellent, soft, sparkling glass still known as 'English crystal'—and in Italy as *cristallo inglese* or *vetro di rocca*. This was the first silica-lead-potash glass to be produced in England* though not the first flint glass, which—according to G. R. Porter[125]—appeared in 1557.

Glass was certainly being made in large quantities at about that time in the Weald, where both flint and sand are abundantly available. Chiddingfold and Wisborough Green were noted centres, and at Wisborough Green a single firm is recorded as having burnt 400,000 billets of wood annually for the production of potash. This wholesale destruction of wood so alarmed James I that he forbade it by Royal Proclamation in 1615 and the glassmakers began to use coal instead, but the quality of the glass suffered.

Silica-lead-potash glass is still called 'flint' glass although the potash is now obtained from minerals and the source of silica has been switched back from flint to sand†. Nevertheless, if the supply of clear quartz ran out, crushed calcined flint would come into its own again, for such a glass is stated by W. E. S. Turner[126] to compare favourably with silica-lead-potash glass made from Dutch sand. Further, the use of flint in glass is not confined to the material ordinarily called 'glass'. Its inclusion in pottery glazes has already been mentioned, and it is also used in enamel ware[127,128], but both glazes and enamels are basically glasses.

Man has thus never 'grown out of' using flint. As knife and potboiler, it formed his first kitchen equipment, and it is still in his kitchen—as china basin and enamel saucepan. It owes this extraordinary record mainly to its hardness and abundance. But perhaps some distant inhabitant of the universe could have hazarded a guess that silica must be the principal raw material on a planet whose crust consists of nearly 30 per cent silica—though, of course, much of it

---

* It was not the first silica-lead-potash glass ever to be made, for—according to a cuneiform tablet from Tall-'Umar—the glaze used on Assyrian pottery in the 17th century B.C. had much the same composition as modern 'flint' or lead glass[124].

† Common window-glass is a silica-lime-soda glass and, although it is no longer made by the crown process, it is still often called 'crown' glass. So do the old names tend to persist. In optics, the components of an achromatic lens are also said to consist of 'crown' and 'flint' glass, respectively, but here the distinction lies in their different refractive indices rather than in their chemical composition.

is not in the form of free silica. Of that which is available, flint has the advantages of being widely distributed, remarkably pure, and occurring in large nodules instead of tiny grains (like sand).

How this came about is the main problem surveyed in this book, and the reader will have gathered that there is probably no single answer to it. He may well suspect that the name 'flint' denotes the common result of several quite different but converging processes. What is 'common' is the microscopic size of the quartz crystals and their bulk occurrence in a 'matted' state. Anything which will produce this end-result may be considered a 'cause' of flint.

Similar causes, however, may also produce chert, and it would seem that the distinctive properties of flint are due mainly to its environment, upon which the quantity and state of the water in its pores may partly depend. Cherts formed in hard limestones often differ more widely from cherts formed in sandstones than they do from cherts formed in very pure soft limestones, for some of these are almost indistinguishable from flint—and others, perhaps, *are* flint! The distinction between chert and flint should certainly be considered a minor one. It turns on qualities which happen to be easily seen and have commercial value, but are of no great mineralogical significance.

Considered together, flint and chert simply represent the natural end-state of all random drifts of soluble silica in the earth's crust. There is nothing 'special' about them, though they show considerable variety in outward form. It is the other forms of silica—rock crystal, agate, opal—which are extraordinary. But if flint has this undistinguished status in the mineral kingdom, its importance to the animal kingdom can hardly be exaggerated. This is, perhaps, the secret of the vast mass of literature which has been devoted to it—and to which this book must now be added.

APPENDIX I

The Solubility of Silica

THE RESULTS OBTAINED by different investigators are somewhat at variance, the solubility of quartz, for example, being given as anything between 0·0007 per cent to 0·002 per cent. The solubility of colloidal silica is also uncertain, reports ranging from 0·013 per cent to 0·04 per cent. It was suggested more than fifty years ago by V. Lenher and H. B. Merrill[136] that the solubility of all forms of silica is definite and the same, but that colloidal or opaline silica dissolves so much more rapidly than quartz that its apparent solubility is greater. C. W. Correns[137] found that it took eight months to dissolve 0·01 gramme of quartz in a litre of water, which is 0·001 per cent or one ounce in 624 gallons.

G. Millot[129] accepts the general solubility of amorphous (colloidal) silica as between 0·01 and 0·014 per cent at 25°C., but considers the solubility of quartz to range from about 0·0007 to 0·0014 per cent. He also gives a range of from 0·001 to 0·002 per cent as a sort of 'average' for quartz, chalcedony and opal. It has long been considered that the solubility of quartz varies in the presence of acids or alkalis, and may be increased especially by the acids of humus, but this is contradicted by recent analyses of soil-water (see Appendix II).

All dissolved silica was once believed to become eventually colloidal, when the strength of the solution would be influenced by its pH value (acidity), the presence of dissolved salts (electrolytes), the variability of the water-content if the source is a gel, and both the temperature and pressure. However, investigations made in 1954 by G. B. Alexander *et al.*[135], in 1957 by G. Okamoto *et al.*[130], and in 1959 by K. B. Krauskopf[138], have shown that this is much too simple. There is general agreement that below pH 9 (that is, with increasing

APPENDIX I

acidity) nearly all dissolved silica forms simple molecules of monosilicic (orthosilicic) acid, $Si(OH)_4$, with a very low solubility, but that above pH 9 the acid dissociates and the solubility rises sharply and considerably.

According to Sherwood Taylor[139] the molecules of monosilicic acid may become highly polymerized to form the colloidal $(H_4SiO_4)_n$, but G. Millot asserts that this occurs only in solutions of more than 0·012 per cent strength and of pH value less than 9. If such a solution is afterwards diluted, the acid depolymerizes only very slowly, but reverts finally to a true solution.

The lowering of the temperature of a solution of colloidal silica (silica-sol), or an increase in the electrolytes present, causes coagulation or flocculation, and the precipitated silica-gel holds a very large quantity of water in combination. Once precipitated, it does not readily redissolve even if the temperature is again raised or the electrolytes removed. Precipitation seems to be inhibited by the presence of organic colloids, so that the concentration of a silica-sol may in this way be raised somewhat above the limit imposed by the other conditions.

APPENDIX II
Silica in Natural Water

THE AVERAGE PERCENTAGE of silica dissolved in oceanic water is 0·00015, but the bottom water contains noticeably more silica, at least in the Pacific Ocean, and the percentage may be locally as high as 0·002. The average percentage of silica dissolved in river water is 0·0013, which is about one ounce in 500 gallons[140].

The silica in natural water was formerly thought to be wholly in the colloidal state, but G. Millot[129] showed in 1960 that the reverse of this is true and that in ordinary concentrations it assumes the form of monosilicic acid in true (crystalline) solution. The normal mineral precipitation of silica cannot therefore be explained by a variation in pH value or by the presence of ions in any ordinary circumstances. In particular, the silica in fresh-water could not be precipitated by the ions in sea-water (or only rarely).

However, Millot notes that Okamoto, Okura and Goto[130] found that aluminium ions could reduce the solubility of amorphous silica from 0·013 to 0·0015 per cent, which is about the maximum solubility of quartz. He remarks '*ceci est considerable*', but since the normal content of silica in sea-water is only about 0·00015 per cent the influence of aluminium ions can be only rarely felt. It could presumably be effective in natural water containing 0·002, 0·004 or 0·006 per cent of silica, as occasionally happens, but precipitation could then be explained without invoking aluminium ions.

Millot points out that such concentrations indicate either dilute solutions of amorphous silica or supersaturated solutions of crystalline silica. Such solutions, he says, if augmented by silica from the hydrolysis of silicates (or by other means) will behave like super-saturated solutions of quartz. Crystalline silica will then be precipitated and, though the reactions are slow, the growth of quartz minerals would be assured and direct.

Silica in solution in soils is almost entirely present as monosilicic acid, the concentration commonly ranging from 0·003 to 0·004 per cent. The solubility is independent of the pH value between 2 and 9, but increases sharply above pH 9 as described in Appendix I. However, the presence of free sesquioxides (chiefly iron) may reduce the solubility by adsorption to only 0·0007 per cent, while in black clay free of sesquioxides it may rise to more than 0·0067 per cent[141,142]. The adsorption is at a maximum when the pH value is about 9·5, but decreases above or below this value[43].

The supply of oceanic silica

The rivers and other land drainage contribute about 400 million tons of silica to the oceans annually. To this, submarine vulcanism probably adds another 200 million tons, making a total supply of about 600 million tons[140]. The silica-secreting organisms—chiefly diatoms, *Radiolaria* and sponges—use up the whole of this, but there is always a reserve in the oceans of about two million million tons, or a permanent stock sufficient for 3,000 years if the regular supplies failed.

The deep oceanic (pelagic) sediments, as a whole, contain about 7·5 per cent of silica. Taking the average thickness of the sediments as about 1,000 feet, this is equivalent to 30,000 million million tons of silica.

APPENDIX III

The Fossils in Fig. 18

THE FOSSILS HAVE been placed by levels in the Chalk in which they may be found, though some have much wider ranges. The Chalk strata are correctly ordered but are not drawn to scale for the sake of the smaller formations, which would otherwise have been crowded out. Their thicknesses also differ widely in different regions so that no definitive scale would be possible. Reading from the top downwards the fossils are as follows:

On the left:

Liostrea lunata (syn. *Ostrea lunata*), an oyster.
Belemnitella mucronata, a belemnite guard.
Glomerula gordialis, a coral.
Micraster coranguinum, a sea-urchin.
Inoceramus labiatus, a bivalve mollusc.
Orbirhynchia cuvieri (syn. *Rhynchonella cuvieri*), a brachiopod (lamp-shell).
Actinocamax plenus, a belemnite guard, from which the Plenus Marls are named.
Schloenbachia varians, an ammonite.

On the right (sponges):

Laosciadia planus (syn. *Seliscothon planus*).
Ventriculites infundibuliformis.
Siphonia koenigi.
Doryderma ramosum.
Stauronema carteri.

APPENDIX IV

Effects of Folding on the Water-Table

IN REGIONS WHERE strongly folded strata are permeable to a considerable depth, the general form of the water-table can be partly accounted for without invoking drying-out by surface evaporation or loss by springs. When rocks which are not absolutely dense are folded sufficiently gently they will bend without cracking or showing shearing movements between successive layers. It follows that if the rock is porous the spaces between its particles must be reduced towards the centre of curvature, where they are under compression, but widened towards the periphery, where they are under tension. Fig. 65 shows what must happen in an anticlinal and a synclinal fold, and in both cases the rocks at a would be expected to be more compressed than the rocks at b.

That is to say, the pores in the rocks must be rather smaller in the regions marked a than in those marked b, and we can calculate how much smaller they will be for a hypothetical but wholly reasonable formation. We may postulate an anticline with a radius of curvature of 300 metres, or (say) 1,000 feet, and compare the size of the pores in the rock at the surface with that of those at a depth of 90 metres, or 300 feet, where the radius of curvature will by $300 - 90 = 210$ metres.

If the anticline is roughly cylindrical, all linear measurements horizontally at right-angles to the axis of the fold are reduced in proportion to the radius of curvature, the other measurements remaining unchanged. That is to say, the pores will be reduced in volume by 210/300, or 7/10. Since all fissures and cracks will be similarly reduced, this alone means that the water at this depth is already hindered from draining away from the core of the anticline, both by

APPENDIX IV

the reduction in the capacity of the channels and by increase in friction. The reverse conditions hold towards the flanks of the anticline and water arriving here disperses more rapidly.

But there must be a further hindrance to the central drainage owing to the water permanently held in the rock by capillary attraction. The formulae for the rise of water by capillarity are: (*a*) for

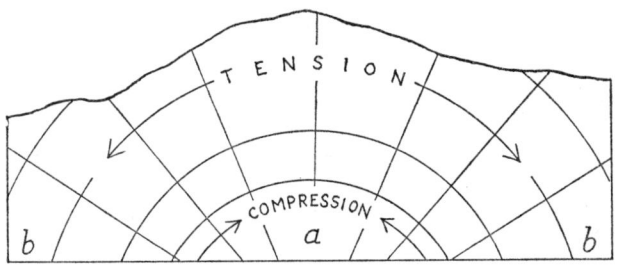

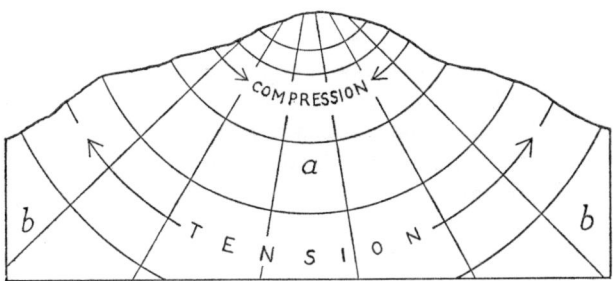

FIG. 65. The stresses in folded strata at different levels.

tubes, $h = \dfrac{4t}{gd}$, and (*b*) for parallel plates, $h = \dfrac{2t}{gd}$, where $h =$ the rise of the water, $t =$ the surface tension, and $d =$ the diameter of the tubes or the distance between the plates. In both cases, h varies inversely as d, so that whatever the capillary rise in the surface rocks, we may expect a similar change in the deeper rocks whether a simple anticline or a geanticline is involved. And in both cases the result in the above example would be an increase in height by a factor of 10/7.

APPENDIX IV

The effect of capillary attraction on the form of the water-table is to hinder diffusion downwards by establishing impermeability. Thus, the level of water-saturation in the anticline takes the form shown in Fig. 66. Reference to Fig. 65 will show that a virtually similar result would occur in a synclinal hill, for the rocks at the summit are exposed to erosion and may be assumed to admit water in spite of

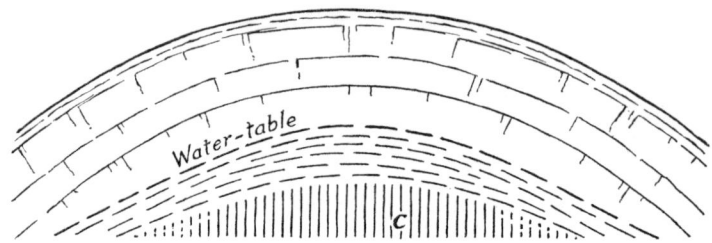

FIG. 66. The expected form of the water-table in an anticline. C, rock rendered comparatively impermeable through holding water by capillary attraction.

their state of compression, but the effect would probably be less marked.

It should be added that this is a purely theoretical excursion. No systematic data comparing the densities of rocks in different parts of the same formation in a fold appear to be available. Nevertheless, effects of the type described have been noted by water engineers, and R. C. S. Walters[39] writes: 'These anticlines not only loosen the Chalk, but cause more of the flinty Middle Chalk to be exposed at the surface and so facilitate the rapid transit of water underground. . . . Elsewhere, between the anticlines, the Chalk is in synclinal form and the yields are not spectacular like those in the anticlines.'

APPENDIX V
Silica and Vegetation

A GREAT MANY plants take up silica from the soil and deposit it in both their stems and tops, and those which absorb appreciable quantities are called 'silica accumulators'. Chief among them are the horsetails (Equisetaceae) and grasses (Gramineae), the grasses containing from ten to twenty times the concentrations of silica found in other (dicotyledonous) herbs. E. J. Russell[143] gives the following interesting analyses*. A crop of wheat covering one acre yields 97 pounds of silica. One acre of meadow-hay, weighing 1½ tons, yields about 200 pounds of ash containing 58 pounds of silica. Dead forest leaves contain up to 107 pounds of silica per acre. Rye contains about 2·41 per cent of silica, dry weight, and, according to P. Halais and D. H. Parish[144], the leaf-sheaths of sugar-cane grown on siliceous gravelly soil contain 5 per cent. T. S. Lovering[42] estimates that grasses and horsetails in a tropical climate may remove about 750 pounds of silica per acre of soil per year, while 100 pounds per acre may be dissolved by the ground-water.

Silica obtained from the ashes of plants is used by potters and, according to a list given by Michael Cardew[145], the highest yield of silica comes from the Australian turpentine (a hardwood tree). His figures, obtained from such authorities as the Forestry Commission of New South Wales, seem very high compared with those given by E. J. Russell, the 77 per cent for a Nigerian thatching-grass, for example, being nearly three times as great as Russell's 29 per cent for meadow-hay. He cites nearly 90 per cent for the turpentine tree,

---

* Russell gives the figures for silicon (the element), but here they have been converted to the corresponding quantities of silica (the oxide), the form in which it is deposited.

APPENDIX V

86 per cent for a bamboo, 82 per cent for rice straw, 66 per cent for wheat straw, and 52 per cent for Australian white mahogany. However, the ashes used in ceramics appear to have been calcined at very high temperatures (900°C. is mentioned), and then washed before analysis, and this must have removed most of the volatile and soluble constituents. Bamboos certainly take a great deal of silica from the soil, for a single plant of the commercial madake (*Phyllostachys bambusoides*) may produce nine tons of roots, forming a shallow underground network ten miles in total length, and send up two or three tons of stems every year to a height of sixty feet[146]. A single plant of this size might well hold a ton of silica in its tissues.

T. S. Lovering[42] describes experiments with the rough horsetail or Dutch rush (*Equisetum hyemale*), the tropical giant reed (*Arundo donax*), and such common grasses as cocksfoot or orchard grass (*Dactylis glomerata*), putting beyond doubt that many silica accumulator plants take their silica directly from felspars and other mineral silicates in contact with their roots. They also utilize dissolved silica but are dependent neither on this nor on the presence of humus. It is not known if they require the assistance of micro-organisms.

According to W. Heinen[147], L. Holzapfel found that the roots extract the silica in the form of esters of carbohydrates and silicic acid, while W. Engel identified a silicon-galactose compound in rye straw. The silica taken up in solution has been found in the form of monosilicic acid in the xylem sap of oats in concentrations similar to that of the external solution (K. A. Handreck and L. H. P. Jones[148]), but in other plants the concentration is less. In all plants, the silica is finally deposited as 'plant opal' or 'tabashir', chiefly in the stems, and it is finally made available for redistribution in the soil when the plant dies. It is further considered that the opaline silica in normal soils is supplied entirely by the vegetation.

In permanent grassland there is never any more silica held above ground than one crop can contain, yet the chemical attack on the soil-rock goes on continuously and much of the opal returned to the soil is leached out by drainage water. T. S. Lovering[149] has estimated that 'a forest of silica accumulator plants might extract about 2,000 tons of silica per acre in 5,000 years, which would be equivalent to the silica in one acre foot of basalt'. His data were obtained from laboratory experiments, but this does not necessarily imply that the quantities involved in natural growth are notably less.

APPENDIX VI
Silicates in the Chalk

THE COMMON SILICATES found in the Chalk are the green-staining glauconite (a hydrous silicate of iron and potassium, often with aluminium, magnesium and calcium) and the hydrous aluminium silicate of the clay in the marly bands. A non-crystalline form of this silicate, known as 'allophane', also forms encrustations lining cavities and cracks, particularly in the Upper Chalk. The rarer occurrence of felspars, formed chemically within the Chalk and not contributed to it from extraneous sources, is of greater interest. Felspars are double silicates of aluminium and potassium, sodium or calcium, and are best-known as major constituents of igneous rocks. They have been found in chalk at a few sites on the Continent, but long searches by the author, following suggestions made by the late Professor P. G. H. Boswell, failed to discover any in the English Chalk.

Reports of authigenic felspars in the Continental Chalk go back at least to 1888, when A. Lacroix[150] reported crystals of albite in the yellow Chalk of the Pyrenees. In 1895 L. Cayeux[151] found numerous crystals of orthoclase in the Chalk of the Paris Basin, and since then felspars have been found in the Chalk near Kiev by V. N. Chirvinsky[152], and by P. A. Zemyatchensky[153] in a compact chalk at Liski in the government of Voronezh (U.S.S.R.) and again at Knubr in the government of Orel. These last included orthoclase, soda-orthoclase, anorthoclase, and (more rarely) albite. Felspars were also found in the Upper Chalk of the Pyrenees by J. de Lapparent[154], and there have been numerous reports of authigenic felspars in other limestones. The pioneer discoveries were collated and ably summarized by Edmondson Spencer[155] nearly fifty years ago, and no great discoveries have been made since.

APPENDIX VI

Several writers give good reasons for believing that authigenic felspars in limestones (including the Chalk) were formed in the calcareous mud on the sea-floor during deposition, and de Lapparent attributed the growth of the albite crystals in the Pyrenees to the action of Algae. According to F. Grandjean[156], the felspar crystals cease to grow once they are buried, which implies that none can even start to form within the rock itself. This is, however, open to question in the light of the experiments by P. S. Roller and G. Ervin described below.

It is also possible that sub-microscopic particles of felspar are present in the Chalk much more extensively than the visible crystals might suggest. Examination likely to detect small scattered groups of molecules has seldom been made, but it seems probable that the visible crystals grew from nuclei of molecular dimensions and it would be odd if these were the only ones ever to exist. The hydrous aluminium silicate occurs in traces of this kind but in detectable quantities through the Chalk, though seldom forming more than 0·1 per cent of the rock (except in the marly bands). Silicates should certainly be looked for in all analyses of the kind referred to on page 103, where a contrary result might have required a complete re-assessment of the chemical theories of the segregation of flint.

There can be no doubt that the various ions in the percolating water wander into all sorts of associations and form stray molecules of many different compounds. In strong solutions such aberrant associations are quite negligible, but in very weak solutions they may form a significant proportion of the solute. Further, the minuteness of the quantities involved, and the transient nature of some of the compounds formed, do not preclude their producing substantial effects through some tens of millions of years. Some of the possibilities have been tentatively studied as plausible agents in the deposition of silica.

For example, in the surface chalk, where it underlies the soil, molecules of both hydrous calcium silicate and calcium hydroxide (lime water) are certainly likely to occur, for the silica in solution in the ground-water is in the form of monosilicic acid (Appendices I and II). It has been shown by P. S. Roller and G. Ervin[157] that calcium silicate and calcium hydroxide form definite compounds of calcium oxide and silica 'in the solid, and not just solid solutions'. The probable

APPENDIX VI

formulae given are $CaO \cdot SiO_2$ and $3CaO \cdot 4SiO_2$, in either of which the removal of the CaO would precipitate the silica. Deposition by this process would leave no evidence by which it could be traced, though clues might exist in buried chalk surfaces receiving acid soil-water.

The possible occurrence of calcium silicate in the Chalk, referred to in Chapter 3 (page 103), turns on similar associations of ions. The author's original suggestion was that the following reactions might take place in the extremely dilute solutions involved (calcium silicate being represented by $CaO \cdot SiO_2$):

1. $CaCO_3 + H_4SiO_4 = CaO \cdot SiO_2 + CO_2 + 2H_2O$
2. $CaO \cdot SiO_2 + 2CO_2 + H_2O = SiO_2 + Ca(HCO_3)_2 + H_2O$

These various groups of atoms would be all drifting about at the same time and coming into all possible associations, but on the whole it would be a one-way process. This is because the given materials are a comparatively insoluble calcium compound and a soluble silicon compound, but among the products are a comparatively insoluble silicon compound and a soluble calcium compound. The silica, once deposited, may be considered *hors de combat*, and it does not matter how often or how seldom the ions necessary to cause this happen to drift together.

The net result is the exchange of chalk for flint, molecule for molecule, the silica arriving in solution and the calcium leaving in solution (as the soluble bicarbonate). Quite a number of other temporary reactions can also be imagined as happening, including the formation of lime-water, and they probably all do, but there is no need to elaborate the scheme. The unlikelihood of finding any of the calcium silicate ($= CaSiO_3 = CaO \cdot SiO_2$ in the equations) is evident because it is formed only to be destroyed, but it must be present in the intervals, however short. The conjuror's saying, 'Now you see it, now you don't!' should describe the situation, but so far only the second half of it is true.

The more sophisticated equations worked out by Buurman and Plas[132] are as follows:

1. $2CaCO_3 + H_4SiO_4 + 2H^+ = CaSiO_3 + Ca^{++} + 2CO_2 + 3H_2O$
2. $CaSiO_3 + 2H^+ = Ca^{++} + SiO_2 + H_2O$

APPENDIX VI

These changes are imagined as taking place on an interface between siliceous and calcareous matter, the interface shifting through the calcareous mass until it is all replaced by silica. The interface is pictured as an extremely thin film with carbonate on one side and silica on the other: 'In the film we have to assume the formation of phases of silica and calcium ions and water. Transport of ions has to be possible in this film, because in the end calcium and CO_2 have to be removed and SiO_2 deposited.'

This description may explain how a flint grows but hardly how it started. The idea of a carbonate surface in wet contact with a silica surface assumes the silicification well advanced at the outset. The authors observed both surfaces and measured the distance between them, inferring that the interface was in process of migrating through the carbonate and leaving more silica in its wake. One wants to know where this extra silica is supposed to have come from, and how the original silica-face came into being.

If we try to clarify this by substituting the surface of a percolating solution of silica for the silica-face, we run into difficulties, for the thickness of the so-called 'interface' could not then have been measured accurately. We may accept that Van der Waals forces are simultaneously at work throughout a *volume* of chalk saturated with silica-solution through vast ages. There seems to be no reason why the changes should start in one place rather than another, and so it seems grotesque to say that an interface migrates through the solid*.

It may be that we are merely objecting to the terms used, for the supposed 'interface' rapidly becomes a three-dimensional chaos. The authors state that the replacement of calcite by silica sometimes follows the outline of a fossil shell but sometimes cuts across it, eating away some calcite crystals here, sparing others elsewhere. And again, silicification was far from complete in one of the flints examined, several isolated calcite crystals being found in it. These observations, interesting though they are, do not help to clarify the confused picture given by the description, and the reactions might have been better presented as occurring simply in the surface-films of weak solutions. This would allow for the initiation of the calcium-silica exchange in the wetting-film over the grains of chalk, and would

---

* An 'interface' is a statistical construct; the term cannot be rationally used of encounters between free atoms, ions or molecules.

APPENDIX VI

have been preferable to any account requiring support from such expressions as, 'we have to assume', 'has to be possible', 'have to be removed' and 'have to be deposited'.

Other agents which have been suggested as able to exchange silica for calcium in the Chalk (in more or less roundabout ways) include the sodium carbonate frequently present in ground-water, and the sodium chloride frequently retained in sedimentary rocks after emergence from the sea. Both occur in traces in some chalk-water but both are rare, though they may have been more abundantly supplied from overlying rocks in past ages. The Thanet Sand, for example, which overlies the Chalk in some areas, retains a considerable amount of salt (0·77 per cent), and so do many of the older limestones—such as the Forest Marble and the Great Oolite[39]. Near the coast (e.g. at Eastbourne) wells sunk into the Chalk often contain saline water by infiltration from the sea, and *all* the Chalk has at some time either formed part of a coast or lain directly beneath one.

R. Liesegang and William Hill are among those who have thought the draining-out of the sea-water from the Chalk to be significant, and the possible chemical reactions suggest one of the sodium silicates as an intermediary substance. It would have only momentary existence in extremely dilute solution so that its solubility need not be taken into account. Possible equations are as follows, the second one accounting for the occasional trace of sodium carbonate in chalk-water. The calcium-chloride is presumed lost by solution, but it would be very hard to detect in the presence of all the other ions involved. The intermediate substance is sodium metasilicate:

1. $CaCO_3 + 2NaCl + H_4SiO_4 = Na_2SiO_3 + CaCl_2 + CO_2 + H_2O$
2. $Na_2SiO_3 + CO_2 = SiO_2 + Na_2CO_3$

If sodium silicate is considered a not very probable intermediary, another pair of equations involving a sodium calcium silicate of the same composition as the secondary mineral pectolite has been proposed:

1. $5CaCO_3 + 2NaCl + 6H_4SiO_4$
   $= 2HNaCa_2(SiO_3)_3 + CaCl_2 + 5CO_2 + 11H_2O$
2. $2HNaCa_2(SiO_3)_3 + 6CO_2$
   $= 6SiO_2 + Na_2CO_3 + 3CaCO_3 + Ca(HCO_3)_2$

APPENDIX VI

Here again, sodium carbonate appears among the final products, which also include both the carbonates of calcium. However, five molecules of normal calcium carbonate were removed and only three are returned (the bicarbonate going into solution with the sodium carbonate). These three would very likely be deposited as calcite crystals, the appearance of which in the Chalk is not accounted for in any other sets of equations.

In the absence of positive evidence of the presence of sodium silicates in the Chalk, the devising of these equations must be regarded as little more than a game. They have never been very seriously entertained and, in the author's view, have not played any significant part in the segregation of flint. It may be pointed out, however, that if the reactions described ever did occur, they are most likely to have taken place while the Chalk was still beneath the sea. Liesegang's and Hill's (and Van Tuyl's) idea of the process of the 'draining-out of the sea-water' is an out-of-scale piece of imagination. The rate of emergence was so slow that, at all times, all the chalk that was not submerged was already free of salt. There was never any more 'draining' than occurs today round the coast, where the salt waves and rain or ground-water alternately wash the chalk cliffs. But even if the Chalk retained as much salt as the Thanet Sand now holds, all the possible reactions involving salt would probably have been completed long before its emergence.

APPENDIX VII
Water on a Molecular Scale

WE SHOULD NOT assume that the behaviour of water in channels and cavities as small as the pores in flint is normal. Flint is wetted by water, which would adhere to the walls of a channel and (on so small a scale) reduce or eliminate shear stresses and inhibit flow. The water would then be in the state it exhibits in a Berthelot tube and have a tensile strength of perhaps 300 pounds per square inch. This must surely have some effect on the fracture of flint, and might even be responsible for its conchoidal character, for this disappears with no other change than a loss of water by cortication or calcination.

Another effect might well occur in any continuous microscopic channel. The movement of a few molecules at one end of the channel would pull all the rest along like a piece of string. Ordinary diffusion, such as occurs in absorbents with pores a hundred or a thousand times larger, would be replaced by new phenomena and hydration transferred from one flint to another would be more likely to produce discrete spots than graded areas (see page 134).

This is not as fantastic as it may sound. The principle has already been invoked to explain the raising of sap in tall trees, for the old theory that transpiration from the leaves draws up the sap by suction cannot be true of plants more than 34 feet high, above which a Torricellian vacuum would form. That the tensile strength of water is utilized in even smaller plants has been demonstrated in America where desert shrubs have been found to draw up water from the parched soil by exerting a measured pull of up to 1,200 pounds per square inch (80 atmospheres). A. T. J. Hayward[158] has described a mechanical pump which will raise water through 54 feet by similar means.

APPENDIX VII

Yet another possible complication is the formation of 'polywater' or 'cyclimetric water' by condensation in the pores of flint. Known also as 'superdense water', or 'water II', this strangely viscous liquid is formed from ordinary water when it condenses in ultra-fine glass or quartz capillary tubes[159]. It was discovered in Russia in 1967 by Boris V. Derjaguin and co-workers, and has since been under investigation at the Port Sunlight laboratory and in several centres in America. It has been shown to form naturally in the spaces between particles of powdered quartz and, when mixed with normal water, it moves spontaneously towards a point where evaporation is taking place[160].

Anomalous water exhibits properties which may well play a part in the formation of banded flints and other such phenomena, and possibly in the opalization or chalcedonization of fossil inclusions. At the moment, nothing is known of its mineralogical significance, but in the light of the recent discoveries it would certainly be rash to assume a normal diffusion of water in flint.

APPENDIX VIII
Stone Age Cultures and Industries

FIG. 67 SHOWS in broad outline the distribution of the chief types of workmanship in flint and similar stones in the Old World. The 'Late Stone Age', in Africa, refers to tribes which still fabricate tools and weapons from stones, and this sector could be extended to include the aborigines of Australia, who have never ceased to follow their own quasi-Palæolithic traditions.

The time covered by the diagram is so enormous that an effort should be made to convey the true time-scale. Supposing the section above, and including, the Mesolithic to be correctly represented and denoted by the letter 'D' (for *datum*). Then the part below the Mesolithic down to the middle of the Mousterian should measure about 10 D, and that from the Mousterian to the middle Acheulean about 20 D. The remainder of the diagram, though drawn only about one-third of its total depth, should measure something in the neighbourhood of 50 D. Giving arbitrary measurements, if D is only 2 inches deep, then the whole diagram should measure about $4\frac{1}{2}$ yards from top to bottom.

Rough dates marking the transition between the cultures have been given in Fig. 37 in Chapter 5 (page 147), but the interested reader should consult books on archaeology or prehistoric anthropology for more detailed and precise information. As an inexpensive introduction to the subject, Kenneth Oakley's *Man the Tool-maker*[75] may be strongly recommended. This little work contains a list of books for further reading in special aspects of the subject.

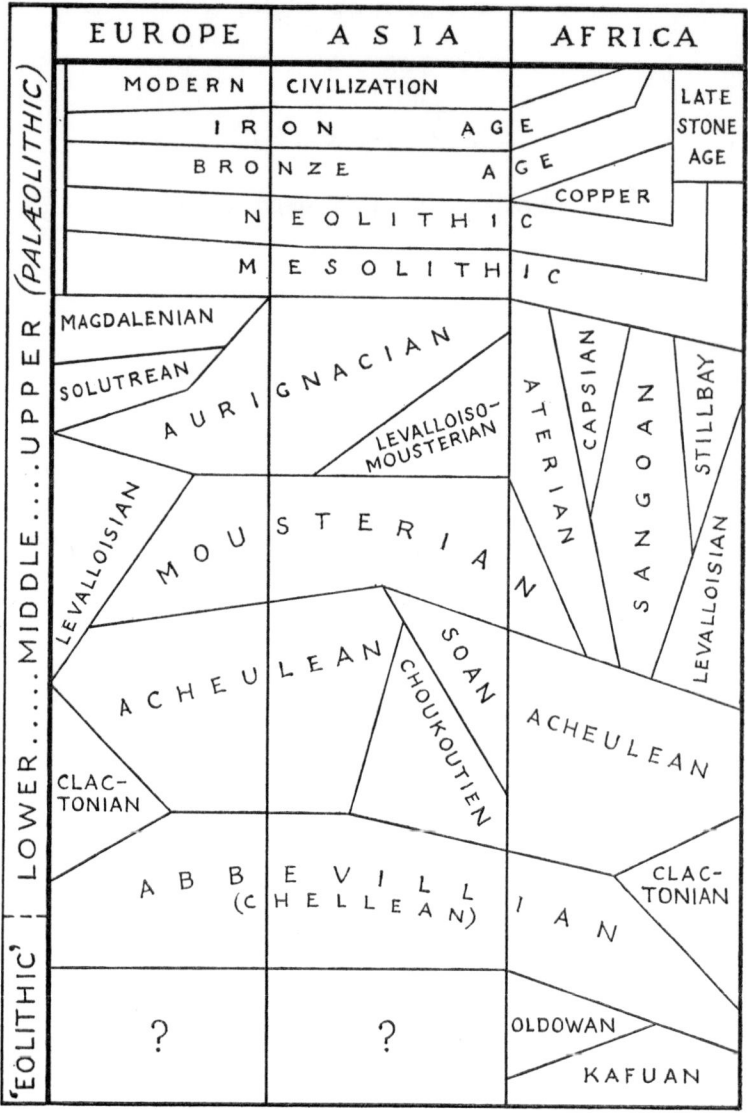

Fig. 67. The chief Stone Age cultures or main styles of workmanship. Any marked local activity or distinctive style may be called an 'industry' and is usually named after its region, but there is a great deal of overlapping resulting from the interchange of ideas, long distance trading, capture in skirmishes—and coincidental discovery of the obvious.

APPENDIX IX

Later English Flint Workings

THE MAP GIVEN in Fig. 68 shows almost the whole of the exposed Chalk in England south of the Wash. Most of the important Downland sites which have yielded Neolithic flint implements are indicated, but the object of the map is largely to show how the Neolithic flint-mines cluster chiefly about the hills of west Sussex, while most of the historic gun-flint factories are crowded round the mouth of the Thames.

The flint-mines at Grime's Graves and the gun-flint works at Brandon appear fairly isolated from the grand centres of these industries, though flints required for the Brandon factory were fetched from as far off as Whitlingham, to the north-west of Norwich, and there is another cluster of gun-flint works round Salisbury.

If a ruler (or strip of paper) is laid across the map parallel with the top edge, and then drawn slowly down to the foot, the places not already named on the map will be uncovered in the order given below, the names linked by brackets being dealt with in groups. (NOTE: The 'Seven Barrows' named for No. 22 is the site near Basingstoke, not its namesake near Wantage.)

APPENDIX IX

1. West Rudham

2. Whitlingham

{ 3. Grime's Graves
{ 4. Weeting
5. Stanton
6. Icklingham

{ 7. Therfield Heath
{ 8. Royston Cave

{ 9. Purfleet
10. Gray's Thurrocks
11. Crayford
12. Lewisham
13. Greenhithe
14. Northfleet
15. Chislehurst
16. Eynsford

{ 17. Windmill Hill
{ 18. Avebury
{ 19. Knap Hill

{ 20. Combe Gibbet
{ 21. Ladle Hill
{ 22. Seven Barrows

{ 23. Stonehenge
{ 24. Winterbourne Stoke
25. Danebury Down
{ 26. Figsbury Ring
{ 27. Laverstock Down
{ 28. Broad Chalke
{ 29. Clarendon
{ 30. Dean Hill

31. Easton Down

32. Butser Hill

{ 33. Bow Hill
{ 34. Stoke Down

{ 35. Harrow Hill
{ 36. Blackpatch
{ 37. Findon
{ 38. Cissbury Ring

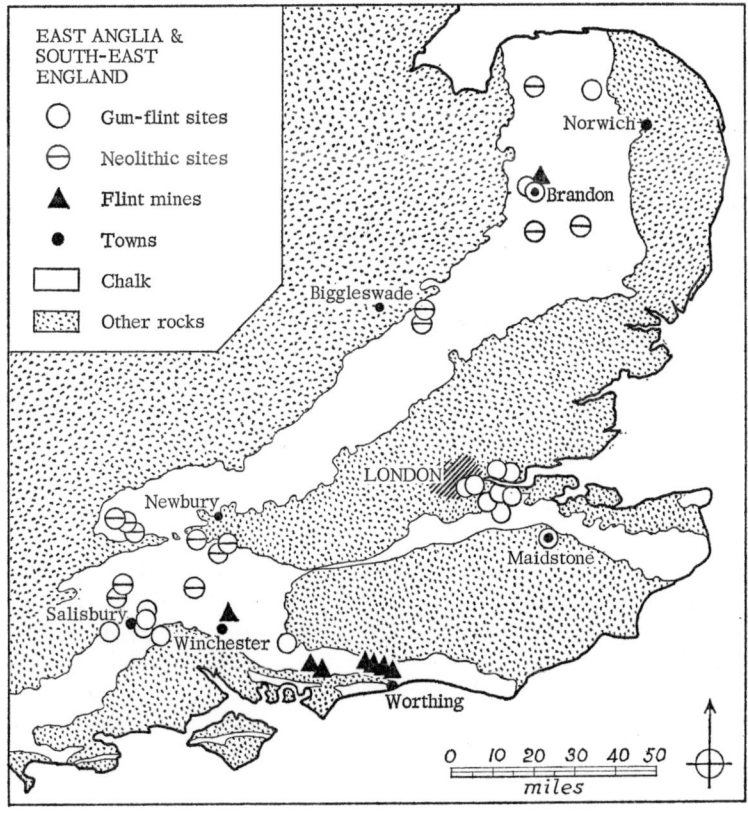

FIG. 68. Some of the localities in the English Chalk country notable for their associations with Neolithic and later flint. The names of all the sites marked are given in the list opposite, and instructions on page 231 show how they may be identified.

APPENDIX X

'Flint' in Many Tongues

TO SATISFY A possible curiosity in the reader, the word for flint is given below in twenty-eight living languages, taken at random from all parts of the world. The people who use these words also have at least some expressions similar to our 'hard as flint', 'flinty eye', 'skinflint', and so on. For many, the word applies to some local stone which takes the place of flint in their economy, whether it be chert, hornstone, obsidian, or some other rock. Others use a word which simply means the stone for making fire, but in all cases the word used denotes what 'flint' denotes for us: a hard, spark-producing stone used for many vital—and fatal—purposes from time immemorial.

Afrikaans:	Vuurklip	*Irish:*	Cloch thine
Albanian:	Stërrall	*Italian:*	Silice
Armenian:	Khijabagi	*Norwegian:*	Flint
Bulgarian:	Krem'k	*Persian:*	Sang í chákmák
Chinese:	Huo shih	*Polish:*	Krzemień
Danish:	Flint	*Rumanian:*	Cremene
Dutch:	Vuursteen	*Russian:*	Kremen
Eskimo:	Kukiksaut	*Spanish:*	Pedernal
French:	Silex	*Swahili:*	Gumu sana
German:	Feuerstein	*Swedish:*	Flinta
Greek:	Pyrites	*Turkish:*	Çakmak taşi
Hebrew:	Challamish	*Welsh:*	Callestr
Hindustani:	Chaqmaq pathrí	*Yoruba:*	Okúta ibọn
Hungarian:	Kova	*Zulu:*	Ityelomlilo

References

1. CHATWIN, C. P., 1948. East Anglia and adjoining areas. *Brit. Reg. Geol.*, H.M.S.O., London; pp. 35, 68.
2. ROSE, C. B., 1859. On the Cretaceous group in Norfolk. *Proc. Geol. Assoc.*, **1**, p. 230.
3. REID, CLEMENT, 1882. The geology of the country around Cromer. *Mem. Geol. Surv.*, H.M.S.O., London; p. 4.
4. HILL, WILLIAM, 1911. Flint and chert. *Proc. Geol. Assoc.*, **22**, pp. 61–94.
5. CAYEUX, L. Études des gîtes minéraux de la France: less phosphates de chaux sédimentaires de France. *Mém. Serv. Carte. géol. dét. Fr.*, **3**, 1950.
6. BROMLEY, R. G., 1967. Some observations on burrows of thalassinidean Crustacea in chalk hardgrounds. *Quart. Journ. Geol. Soc.*, **123**, 157–182.
7. MIERS, H. A., 1902. *Mineralogy*, 2nd ed. rev. BOWMAN, H. L., 1929. Macmillan, London; p. 433.
8. FOLK, R. L., and WEAVER, C. E., 1952. A study of the texture and composition of chert. *Amer. Journ. Sci.*, **250**, pp. 498–510.
9. WEYMOUTH, J. H., and WILLIAMSON, W. O., 1951. Some physical properties of raw and calcined flint. *Min. Mag.*, **29**, pp. 573–593.
10. WHITE, J. F., and CORWIN, J. F., 1961. Synthesis and origin of chalcedony. *Amer. Mineral.*, **46**, pp. 112–119.
11. MIDGLEY, H. G., 1951. Chalcedony and flint. *Geol. Mag.*, **88**, pp. 179–184.
12. JENSEN, A. T., WOHLK, C. J., DRENCK, K., and ANDERSEN, E. K., 1957. Classification of Danish flints . . . based on

REFERENCES

X-ray diffractometry. *Dan. Nat. Inst. Build. Res., Acad. Tech. Sci.* Progress Report DI, Copenhagen.

13. MELDAU, R., and ROBERTSON, R. H. S., 1952. Morphologische Einflusse auf technische Staubeigenschaften. *Ber. deut. keram. Ges.*, **29**, p. 27.
14. WHITE, H. J. OSBORNE, 1912. The geology of the country around Winchester and Stockbridge. *Mem. Geol. Surv.*, H.M.S.O., London; pp. 20–39.
15. CARUS-WILSON, C. Reported in *Proc. Lin. Soc. of London*, 1909–1910: 4th Nov., 1909.
16. DAVID, T. W. EDGEWORTH, and BROWNE, W. R., 1950. *The Geology of the Commonwealth of Australia.* Edward Arnold, London.
17. DUNSTAN, B., 1913. Queensland Mineral Index and Guide. *Queens. Geol. Surv.*
18. REID, CLEMENT, 1898. The geology of the country around Eastbourne. *Mem. Geol. Surv.*, H.M.S.O., London; p. 15.
19. SORBY, H. C., 1879. Anniversary Address. *Proc. Geol. Soc. of London.*
20. SHERLOCK, R. L., 1935. London and the Thames Valley. *Brit. Reg. Geol.*, H.M.S.O., London; pp. 24, 50–52.
21. EARLAND, A., 1939. Chalk: its riddles and some possible solutions. *Trans. Herts. Nat. Hist. Soc. and Field Club*, **21**, Pt. 1.
22. DREW, G. H., 1913. On the precipitation of calcium carbonate in the sea by marine bacteria . . . *Mar. Biol. Assoc. Journ.*
23. BLACK, MAURICE, 1953. The constitution of chalk. *Proc. Geol. Soc. of London*, **1499**.
24. BLACK, MAURICE, and BARNES, BARBARA, 1959. The structure of coccoliths from the English Chalk. *Geol. Mag.*, **96** (5), pp. 321–328.
25. MACGINITIE, G. E. and NETTIE, 1949. *Natural History of Marine Animals.* McGraw-Hill, New York; p. 112.
26. DAVIES, A. MORLEY, 1925. *An Introduction to Palaeontology*, 3rd ed. rev. STUBBLEFIELD, C. J., 1961. Murby (Allen and Unwin), London; pp. 231–232.
27. OAKLEY, KENNETH P., 1939. The nature and origin of flint. *Sci. Prog.*, **34**, No. 134; pp. 277–286.

REFERENCES

28. TARR, W. A., 1917. Origin of the chert in the Burlington Limestone. *Amer. Journ. Sci., Ser.* IV, **44** (264), p. 428.
29. TARR, W. A., 1926. The origin of chert and flint. *Univ. Missouri Studies*, **1**, No. 2; 54 pp.
30. ILLIES, HENNING, 1949. Zur Diagenese der südbaltischen Schreibkreide. *Geol. Fören Förhandl.*, **71**, H.1; pp. 41–50.
31. BRYDONE, R. M., 1920. The origin of flint. *Geol. Mag.*, pp. 401–404.
32. DEAN, R. S., 1918. The formation of Missouri cherts. *Amer. Journ. Sci.*, Ser. IV, **45** (269), pp. 411–415.
33. TUYL, F. M. VAN, 1918. The origin of chert. *Amer. Journ. Sci.*, Ser. IV, **45** (270), pp. 449–456.
34. JUKES-BROWNE, A. J., and HILL, W., 1889. The occurrence of colloid silica in the Lower Chalk of Berkshire and Wiltshire. *Quart. Journ. Geol. Soc.*, **45**, pp. 403–421.
35. DEWEY, H., BROMEHEAD, C. E. N., CHATWIN, C. P., and DINES, H. G., 1924. The geology of the country around Dartford. *Mem. Geol. Surv.*, H.M.S.O., London; pp. 16, 23–32, 86–87, 100.
36. SOLLAS, W. J., 1905. The origin and formation of flints, in *The Age of the Earth and Other Geological Studies* (Ch. VI). T. Fisher Unwin, London; pp. 133–165.
37. CLARK, AILSA M., 1962. Starfishes and their relations. *Brit. Mus. (Nat. Hist.)*, H.M.S.O., London; pp. 8–9, 83.
38. NICOL, J. A. COLIN, 1960. *The Biology of Marine Animals*. Pitman and Sons, London; pp. 632–633.
39. WALTERS, R. C. S., 1936. *The Nation's Water Supply*. Ivor Nicholson and Watson, London; pp. 40–42, 60–61.
40. RICHARDSON, W. A., 1919. The origin of Cretaceous flint. *Geol. Mag.*, **56**, pp. 535–547.
41. NORDMANN, V., (Ed.) 1928. Summary of the geology of Denmark. *Den. Geol. Surv. pubn.* C. A. Reitzel, Copenhagen; pp. 51–65.
42. LOVERING, T. S., 1967. Translocation of silica from rock into *Equisetum* and three grasses. *U.S. Geol. Surv. Bull.*, B14–B16.
43. JONES, L. H. P., and HANDRECK, K. A., 1967. Silica in soils, plants, and animals. *Advances in Agronomy*, **19**, pp. 108–114, 125–127, 144.

REFERENCES

44. LIESEGANG, R., 1913. *Geologische Diffusionen*. Dresden and Leipzig, p. 126.
45. LIESEGANG, R., 1914. *Jahrb. Min. Geol. Pal.*, **39**, p. 268
46. COLE, G. A. J., 1917. The rhythmic deposition of flint. *Geol. Mag.*, **54**, pp. 64–68.
47. STANSFIELD, J., 1917. Retarded diffusion and rhythmic precipitation. *Amer. Journ. Sci.*, Ser. IV, **43**, pp. 1–26.
48. HEDGES, E. S., 1932. *Liesegang Rings and Other Periodic Structures*. Chapman and Hall, London.
49. WROOST, VOLKMAR, 1936. Vorgänge der Kieselung an Beispiel des Feuersteins der Kreide. *Abh. Senckenb. naturf. Ges.*, **432**, pp. 1–68.
50. HOLMES, ARTHUR, 1965. *Principles of Physical Geology*, rev. ed. Nelson, London and Edinburgh; pp. 393–394.
51. CHATWIN, C. P., 1948. The Hampshire Basin and adjoining areas. *Brit. Reg. Geol.*, H.M.S.O., London; p. 56.
52. REID, CLEMENT, 1902. The geology of the country around Ringwood. *Mem. Geol. Surv.*, H.M.S.O., London; p. 6.
53. CAYEUX, L., 1897. *Contribution à l'étude micrographique des terrains sédimentaires*. Lille; p. 362.
54. WOODWARD, H. B., 1909, 2nd ed. rev. BROMEHEAD, C. E. N., 1922. The Geology of the London District, *Mem. Geol. Surv.*, H.M.S.O., London; pp. 18, 87, 90.
55. GEHRKE, E., 1935. Die Patina von norddeutschem Flint. *Z. Geschiebeforsch.*, **2**, pp. 107–114.
56. WATSON, WILLIAM, 1956. *Flint Implements*, 2nd ed. *Brit. Mus. pubn.*, H.M.S.O., London; 80 pp.
57. RANKINE, W. F., 1952. Implements of coloured flint in Britain. *Archaeol. News Letter*, **4**, No. 10, pp. 145–149.
58. WOODWARD, S. P., 1864. Banded flints. *Geol. Mag.*, **1**, p. 145.
59. TISELIUS, ARNE, 1934. Diffusion of water in a zeolite crystal. *Nature*, **133**, (3354), pp. 212–213.
60. HEDGES, E. S., and HENLEY, R. V., 1928. *Journ. Chem. Soc.* (2714).
61. MUKHERJEE, L. N., and CHATTERJI, A. C., 1930. *Kolloid-Z.*, **50**, 147.
62. PARKINSON, JAMES, 1804–1811. *Organic remains of a former world*. Sherwood, Neely, and Jones, London.

REFERENCES

63. THOMAS, H. DIGHTON, 1935. Spiral concretions: a possible solution. *Nat. Hist. Mag.*, **5**, No. 35, pp. 129–132.
64. HATSCHEK, E., 1920. *Kolloid-Z.*, **27**, 225.
65. WILLIAMS, W. W., 1960. *Coastal Changes*. Routledge & Kegan Paul, London; pp. 49–50, 71.
66. CALMAN, W. T., 1919. Marine boring animals. *Brit. Mus. (Nat. Hist.)*, Econ. Ser. No. 10. H.M.S.O., London; p. 28.
67. STEP, EDWARD, 1927; rev. WELLS, LAURENCE, 1945. *Shell Life: an Introduction to the British Mollusca*. Frederick Warne, London; pp. 162–163.
68. TEBBLE, NORMAN, 1966. British bivalve shells. *Brit. Mus. (Nat. Hist.)*. H.M.S.O., London; pp. 180, 182.
69. STEERS, J. A., 1953. *The Sea Coast*. Collins, London; pp. 156–159.
70. MCLINTOCK, W. F. P., 1912, rev. SABINE, P. A., 1951. *A Guide to the Collection of Gemstones in the Geological Museum*. H.M.S.O., London; p. 65.
71. DAY, MICHAEL H., 1965. *Guide to Fossil Man*. Cassell, London; pp. 13, 154, 168 ff., 211.
72. CORNWALL, I. W., 1964. *The World of Ancient Man*. Phoenix House (J. M. Dent and Sons), London; pp. 238 ff.
73. ZEUNER, F. E., 1950. *Dating the Past*. Methuen and Co., London; pp. 110 ff.
74. ZEUNER, F. E., 1959. *The Pleistocene Period*. Hutchinson, London; pp. 208–219.
75. OAKLEY, KENNETH P., 1949, 3rd ed. 1956. *Man the Tool-maker*. *Brit. Mus.*, H.M.S.O., London; 98 pp.
76. ALIMEN, H., 1957. *The Prehistory of Africa*. Hutchinson, London; pp. 92, 103, 283 ff.
77. LOWE, C. VAN RIET, 1952. The development of the hand-axe culture in South Africa. *Proc. 1st Pan-Afr. Cong. on Prehist.*, 1947.
78. MORGAN, J. and H., DE, 1926. *Préhistoire orientale:* Vol. II, *Egypt and N. Africa*. Geuthner, Paris.
79. CLARK, GRAHAME, and PIGGOT, STUART, 1970. *Prehistoric Societies*. Pelican (Penguin), Harmondsworth; p. 134.
80. COLE, SONIA, 1959. The Neolithic Revolution. *Brit. Mus.*, H.M.S.O., London; 60 pp.

REFERENCES

81. SMITH, REGINALD, 1926, based on earlier editions (2nd ed. 1911). A guide to antiquities of the Stone Age. *Brit. Mus.*, H.M.S.O., London; pp. 5–6, 35, 94, 188–189.
82. MOIR, J. REID, 1916. Flint fracture and flint implements. *Sc. Prog.*, **XI**, 37–50.
83. DALE, W., 1900. Neolithic implements from the neighbourhood of Southampton. *Papers and Proc. Hants. Field Club and Archaeol. Soc.*, p. 184.
84. MOFFATT, JAMES, 1924, rev. ed. 1935. *A New Translation of the Bible.* Hodder and Stoughton, London.
85. SHORE, T. W., 1900. The physical geology and early archaeological associations of the neighbourhood of Cheriton. *Papers and Proc. Hants Field Club and Archaeol. Soc.*, p. 138.
86. CLARKE, R. RAINBIRD, 1963. Grime's Graves, Norfolk. *Min. of Pub. Build. and Works*, H.M.S.O., London; 32 pp.
87. HAWKES, JACQUETTA and CHRISTOPHER, 1949. *Prehistoric Britain.* Chatto and Windus, London; pp. 39–40.
88. WOOD, ERIC S., 1963. *Field Guide to Archaeology.* Collins, London; pp. 128, 130–131, 135.
89. CALKIN, J. BERNARD, 1952. Flint-filled hollows in Celtic fields. *Archaeol. News Letter*, **4**, No. 10; pp. 150–151.
90. LATHAM, EDWARD, 1904. *A Dictionary of Names, Nicknames and Surnames of Persons, Places and Things.* George Routledge, London; E. P. Dutton, New York; p. 111.
91. WEINER, J. S., OAKLEY, KENNETH, P., and CLARK, W. E. LE GROS, 1953. The solution of the Piltdown problem. *Bull. Brit. Mus. (Nat. Hist.)*, **2**, No. 3, H.M.S.O., London; pp. 141–146.
92. WEINER, J. S., 1955. *The Piltdown Forgery.* Oxford Univ. Press, London; pp. 58–59, 154 ff.
93. INVERSEN, J., 1956. Forest clearance in the Stone Age. *Sci. Amer.*, **194**, No. 3, pp. 36–41.
94. JØRGENSEN, S., 1953. Forest clearance with flint axes. *Fra Nationalmuseets Arbejdsmark*, pp. 36–43, 109–110.
95. JONES, W. R., 1963. *Minerals in Industry.* Pelican (Penguin), Harmondsworth; pp. 101, 102.
96. DEXTER, T. F. G., 1931. *Fire Worship in Britain.* Watts & Co., London; §§ 6, 7 and 8.

REFERENCES

97. O'DEA, W. T., 1964. Making fire. *Sci. Mus.*, H.M.S.O., London; 20 pp.
98. CALDER, RITCHIE, 1970. *Leonardo and the Age of the Eye.* Heinemann, London; pp. 94, 195.
99. HAYWARD, J. F., 1969. European firearms. *Victoria and Albert Mus.*, London; pp. 5, 9.
100. PALMER, L. S., 1957. *Man's Journey Through Time.* Hutchinson, London; pp. 4, 79, 83, 158.
101. CLARKE, R. RAINBIRD, 1935. The flint-knapping industry at Brandon. *Antiquity*, IX, No. 33, pp. 38–56.
102. CLARK, GRAHAME, 1939. *Archaeology and Society.* Methuen, London.
103. NELSON, RAPHAEL, 1941. *Cries and Criers of Old London.* Collins, London, p. 50 (No. 24).
104. *Antiquity*, XLII, 165, 1968. Editorial, p. 2.
105. *Scientific American*, 220, No. 4, April, 1969. 'Science for the Citizen', p. 51.
106. FURON, R., 1957, in *Histoire Générale des Sciences*, ed. by TATON, RÉNÉ, I, *Préface*, p. 10. Presses Universitaires de France, Paris.
107. VERULAM, the EARL OF, ed., 1949. *St. Albans.* The St. Albans City Council; p. 40.
108. COBBETT, WILLIAM, 1822. *Rural Rides.* Everyman ed., 1, p. 139. J. M. Dent and Sons, London.
109. SIMPSON, F. S. W., 1958. *The Churches of St. Nicholas, Old Shoreham, and St. Mary de Haura, New Shoreham, Sussex.* Brit. Pub. Co., Gloucester; p. 25.
110. SMITH, G. H. (work not dated). *The Church of St. Mary and St. Nicholas with All Saints, Leatherhead.* Brit. Pub. Co., Gloucester; p. 9.
111. FLEURE, H. J., and DAVIES, M., 1971. *A Natural History of Man in Britain*, rev. ed. Fontana New Naturalist series, Collins, London; pp. 272, 283.
112. MOORE, JOHN C., 1934. *The New Forest.* Chapman and Hall, London; p. 13.
113. BATSFORD, HARRY, and FRY, CHARLES, 1944. *The English Cottage.* Batsford, London; pp. 63–64; plates 70–74.

REFERENCES

114. VALE, EDMUND, 1937. *How to see England*. Methuen, London; p. 66.
115. HOGG, GARRY, 1971. *Exploring Britain*. John Baker, London; pp. 274–275, 303.
116. LUCAS, E. V., 1904. *Highways and Byways in Sussex*, 2nd ed. 1935 (reprinted 1950). Macmillan, London; pp. 451–455.
117. DEFOE, DANIEL, c. 1725. *Tour through the Whole Island of Great Britain*, **2**, Appendix. Everyman ed. *A Tour through England and Wales*, **2**. J. M. Dent and Sons, London; p. 119.
118. PANNELL, J. P. M., 1957. *Materials of Civil Engineering*. Hutchinson, London; pp. 198–199.
119. JACKSON, GEORGE, 1969. *Introduction to Whitewares*. Maclaren and Sons, London; pp. 20–21, 40–46.
120. ADAMS, P. J., 1961. Geology and Ceramics. *Geol. Mus.*, H.M.S.O., London; p. 7.
121. *Run of the Mill*, 1969. An illustrated and authenticated leaflet issued by the Cheddleton Flint Mill Preservation Trust, Briton House, Tittensor, Stoke-on-Trent; 6 pp.
122. LEACH, BERNARD, 1940, 2nd ed. 1945. *A Potter's Book*. Faber and Faber, London; pp. 99, 134, 165, 176.
123. BOSWELL, P. G. H., 1918. Memoirs on British resources of sand and crushed rocks used in glass making. *Ministry of Munitions and Imp. Coll. Sci. and Technol.* Longmans, Green & Co., London.
124. JANSON, S. E., 1969. Glass technology. *Sci. Mus.*, H.M.S.O., London; pp. 3, 7, 9.
125. PORTER, G. R., 1832. *Porcelain and Glass*. London; p. 138.
126. TURNER, W. E. S., 1940. Notes on British sources of sands for making colourless glass. *Journ. Soc. Glass Tech.*, **24**, p. 206.
127. JOHNSTONE, MARGERY G., 1961. *Minerals for the Chemical and Allied Industries*. Chapman & Hall, London; p. 508.
128. *Kingzett's Chemical Encyclopedia*, 9th ed., 1966. Baillière, Tindall and Cassell, London; p. 346.
129. MILLOT, G., 1960. Silice, silex, silicifications et croissance des cristaux. *Bull. du Serv. de la Carte Géologique d'Alsace et de Lorraine*, **13**, Pt. 4. Univ. of Strasbourg; pp. 129–146.
130. OKAMOTO, G., OKURA, T., and GOTO, R., 1957. Properties of silica in water. *Geoch. et Cosmoch. Acta*, **12**, pp. 123–132.

REFERENCES

131. BARGHOORN, ELSO S., 1971. The oldest fossils. *Sci. Amer.*, **224**, No. 5, pp. 34–39.
132. BUURMAN, P., and PLAS, L. VAN DER, 1971. Chalk of the Netherlands and Belgium. *Geol. en Mijnbouw*, **50**, No. 1, p. 9.
133. DONNAY, J. D. H., 1936. La biréfringence de forme dans la calcédoine. *Ann. Soc. géol. Belgique*, LIX, pp. 289–302.
134. CORRENS, C. W., and NAGELSCHMIDT, G., 1933. Über Faserbau und optische Eigenschaften von Chalzedon. *Zeitschr. für Kristall.*, **85**, pp. 199–213.
135. ALEXANDER, G. B., HESTON, W. M., and ILER, H. K., 1954. The solubility of amorphous silica in water. *Journ. Phys. Chem.*, **58**, pp. 453–455.
136. LENHER, V., and MERRILL, H. B., 1917. The solubility of silica. *Journ. Amer. Chem. Soc.*, **39**, p. 2630.
137. CORRENS, C. W., 1940. Ueber die Löslichkeit von Kieselsäure in schwach sauren und alkalischen Lösungen. In *Chemie der Erde* (ed.), Jena; pp. 92–98.
138. KRAUSKOPF, K. B., 1959. *Soc. Econ. Pal. Min. Spec. Pubn.*, **7**, pp. 4–19.
139. TAYLOR, F. SHERWOOD, 1948. *Inorganic and Theoretical Chemistry*. Heinemann, London; p. 461.
140. GREGOR, BRYAN, 1968. Silica balance in the ocean. *Nature*, **219**, (5152), pp. 360–361.
141. JONES, L. H. P., and HANDRECK, K. A., 1963. *Nature*, **198**, pp. 852–853.
142. JONES, L. H. P., and HANDRECK, K. A., 1965. *Plant Soil*, **23**, pp. 79–96.
143. RUSSELL, E. J., 1950. *Soil Conditions and Plant Growth*, 8th ed. Longmans, Green and Co., London and New York; pp. 29, 483, 510.
144. HALAIS, P., and PARISH, D. H., 1963. *Mauritius Sugar Ind. Res. Inst. Ann. Rept.*, pp. 74–76.
145. CARDEW, MICHAEL, 1969. *Pioneer Pottery*. Longmans, Green & Co., London and New York; p. 42.
146. AUSTIN, ROBERT, and UEDA, KOICHIRO, 1970. *Bamboo*. Walker and Co., New York.
147. HEINEN, W., 1963. Silicum verbindungen, in PAECH, K., and

REFERENCES

TRACEY, M. V., *Moderne Methoden der Pflanzenanalyse*, **6**. Springer, Verlag, Berlin and Heidelberg; pp. 3–20.

148. HANDRECK, K. A., and JONES, L. H. P., 1967. *Austral. Journ. Biol. Sci.*, **2**, pp. 483–485.
149. LOVERING, T. S., 1959. Significance of accumulator plants in rock weathering. *Geol. Soc. Amer. Bull.*, **70** (6), pp. 781–800.
150. LACROIX, A., 1888. Notes sur quelques minéraux français. 1, Albite de Pouzac (Hautes-Pyrénées). *Bull. Soc. Franc. Min.*, **11**, pp. 70–71.
151. CAYEUX, L. 1895. Existence de nombreux cristaux de feldspath orthose dans la craie du bassin de Paris. Preuves de leur genèse *in situ*. *Compt. Rend. Acad. Sci.*, Paris, **120**, pp. 1068–1071.
152. CHIRVINSKY, V. N., 1916. Felsparization of chalk from Kiev. *Min. Abstr.*, **2**, from the (Russian) *Geol. Messenger* (Petrograd), **3**, pp. 132–133.
153. ZEMYATCHENSKY, P. A., 1916. *Bull. Acad. Imp. Sci.* (Petrograd), Ser. 6, **10**, Pt. 1, pp. 99–122.
154. LAPPARENT, J. DE, 1918. Sur les cristaux du feldspaths développés dans les calcaires du Crétacé supérieur pyrénéen. *Min. Abstr.* **1**, 276, from *Compt. Rend. Acad. Sci.*, Paris, **167**, pp. 784–786.
155. SPENCER, EDMONDSON, 1925. Albite and other authigenic minerals in limestone from Bengal. *Min. Mag.*, **20** (110), pp. 374–376.
156. GRANDJEAN, F. 1909, 1910. Le feldspath néogène des terrains sédimentaires non metamorphiques. *Bull. Soc. Franç. Min.*, **32**, 103–133, and **33**, pp. 92–97.
157. ROLLER, P. S., and ERVIN, G., 1940. *Journ. Amer. Chem. Soc.*, **62**, pp. 461–471.
158. HAYWARD, A. T. J., 1970. New law for liquids. *New Scientist*, **45** (686), pp. 196–199.
159. 'MONITOR', *New Scientist*, 1969; **42** (651), 456; **43** (657), 55. 1970: **45** (694), p. 599.
160. DERJAGUIN, BORIS V., 1970. Superdense Water. *Sci. Amer.* **223**, No. 5, pp. 52–71.

Index

Aborigines, 153–154, 173, 176, 229
Abyssinia, 188
Accidental flints, 24 ff.
Acheulean, 157, 229, 230
Actinocamax plenus, 65
   quadratus, 82, 85
Africa, 19, 40, 71, 145, 146, 159, 188, 192, 229, 230
Agate, 31, 88, 89, 105, 124, 127, 194
   moss, 25*n*.
Albertus Magnus, 26
Alexander, G. B., 211
Algae, 46, 71, 73, 112, 122, 222
Alimen, H., 116, 159, 162
Allophane, 221
Aluminium, 45, 84, 213, 221, 222
Amadou, 182
Amberley, 103, 104*n*.
America, American, 19, 36, 40, 42, 59, 130, 155, 165, 188, 194, 208, 228
Amethyst, 30
Ammonia, 69, 93
Ammonite, 65, 66
Anaxagoras, 'plurist' theory of, 26
Anaximander, 26*n*.
Anderida, 195
Andros Island, 48
Antler, 163, 166 ff.
Aragonite, 50
Ariège, 195
Aristotle (mentioned), 26
Arrow-heads, 159, 162–163, 165, 174
Arundo donax, 220
Ashley, 'Pony', 189
Asia, 19, 40, 145, 230
Astbury, John, 204

Atlantic Ocean, 47, 51, 59, 70*n*.
Atlantis, 60, 61, 62
Aurignacian, 161, 163, 165, 230
Australia, Australian, 19, 31, 36, 40, 44–45, 61, 219–220, 229. *See also* Aborigines
Australopithecines, 146
Avebury, Lord, 146*n*.
Avicenna, 26
Aztecs, 155

Bacteria, 48–49, 71, 100, 123
Bacterium calcis, 48
Bahamas, The, 48
Ballard Cliff, 83
Ballast, 201, 203
Ball-mill, 206, 207
Bamboo, 220
Bands, flint, *see under* Flint
   diffusion, *see* Zones
Barghoorn, Elso S., 71
Barnea parva, 141
Barnes, Barbara, 51
Basingstoke, 231
Battery, 185*n*.
Bavaria, 180*n*.
Beaches, beach pebbles, 129–130, 134, 136 ff., 179, 198, 202, 206
   grading of, 142–144
Beads, 195
Bedfordshire, 195
Beer Head, 187
Belemnite, 27, 65, 67
Belemnitella mucronata, 65, 82, 85
Belgium, 63
Benson, Thomas, 205

INDEX

Berkshire, 86, 102
Bible (quoted), 17–18, 166n.
　Coverdale's, 187n.
Biface, 156, 160
Bird, Daniel, 204
Black, Maurice, 50–51
Black Rock, 203
Blackheath Beds, 134
Blackpatch, 169, 232–233
Blade, 162 ff.
Bleaching, 109, 119
Blind Jack of Knaresborough, 202
Blomefield, F., 170
Bolas, 158
Bone, 153 ff., 162 ff., 166, 170
Bordaz, Jaques, 192
Borer, 161
Boswell, P. G. H., 221
Boucher, 156
Boulder Clay, 133, 175
　Chalky, 44, 172
Brachiopod, 27, 51, 66, 67, 70, 71, 73
Brandon, 188 ff., 231, 233
Brighton, 139, 203
Britain, 19, 40, 62, 147, 169, 194, 195, 201
　population (Stone Age), 173
British Isles, *see* Britain
British Museum, 25, 116, 128, 129
Brittany, 180n.
Bromehill, 189
Bromley, R. G., 29, 50, 78
Bronze Age, 147, 166, 171, 173, 174, 179, 230
Brown, J. Allen, 145
Brydone, R. M., 71–72, 80–81, 86n., 100
Bryzoa, 27, 28
Building, 66–67, 195 ff.
Bulb of percussion, 151, 159, 192
Bulbar scar, 151, 159, 190
Bull Head Bed, 87, 105, 114, 127
Burin, 163–164
Burr (bhur), 194
Burrows, crustacean, 28, 29, 78
Buurmann, P., 35n., 36, 103–104, 223–224

Cairngorm, 30
Çakmak, 192–193
Calcination, 205–206

Calcispongiae (Calcarea), 55–57
Calcite, 24, 27, 42, 48, 50, 57, 79, 97, 109–110, 224 ff.
　solubility of, 110
Calcium bicarbonate, 97 ff.
　carbonate, 45, 46, 48, 52, 55, 58, 77, 88, 97 ff., 112, 223 ff.
　chloride, 225
　hydroxide, 222–223
　phosphate, 45, 52, 58–59, 66n., 129
　silicate, 103, 104, 221, 222 ff.
Caldon Canal, 205
Calkin, J. B., 176
Callianassa, 29
Callopegma, 138
Cambridgeshire, 44, 133, 172n.
Canada, 71
Carbon dioxide, 88, 97, 100–101, 223 ff.
Cardew, Michael, 219
Carnelian, 31
Carus-Wilson, C., 44n.
Casey, R., 59, 70n.
Catworth, 133
Cayeux, L., 29, 105, 221
Celt, 163, 166–167, 174, 178
Cement, 203–204
Cenomanian transgression, 40
Ceramics, 179. *See* Pottery
Cerithium Limestone, 87
Chalcedony, 25, 31 ff., 35, 89, 106–107, 194, 211
Chalk, distribution, 41, 44, 60 ff., 85–87
　experiments with, 92 ff.
　fossils in, 42, 52. *See also* Sponges *and under* Flint
　hardgrounds, 59, 78
　nature of, 20, 42 ff.
　silicified, 78, 102, 104–105
　solubility of, 101–102
Chalk, The, 40, 58 ff., 100, 113, 132–133
　bedding 20, 74, 77, 87
　English 64 ff., 80–81, 85–87, 91, 233
　faults in, 74
　folds in, 60 ff., 74, 87
　Gingin, 44n.
　Kansas, 42
　Lower, 64–66, 80
　Middle, 62, 65–67, 80, 100, 102, 105
　Red, *see* Red Rock

INDEX

Chalk, The (*contd.*)—
  thickness of, 43, 61, 64
  Upper, 62, 65, 67, 80, 86, 94, 100, 102, 112, 114, 221
Chalk Marl, 65, 66
Chalk Rock, 65, 67
Chalk Sea, The, 41 ff., 50 ff., 57 ff., 64, 68 ff., 75 ff., 111
  depth of, 43, 76
Champagne, 187
Chanctonbury Ring, 112
Chattering, 115, 136, 138
Chatterji, A. C., 125
Cheddleton, 206
Cherhill Down, 112
Chert, 30, 35–36, 44, 77, 97, 178, 180, 187, 206, 210, 234
  Fig Tree, 71, 74
  Gunflint, 71, 74
  Radiolarian, 36*n*.
  Rhaxella, 36
Chiddingfold, 209
Chiltern Hills, 63, 114
Chirvinsky, V. N., 221
Chiselhurst Caves, 25*n*.
Chlorella, 46
'Chloritic' Marl, 65
Chondrites, 79
Chopper, 158
Choristida, 55
Churches, 196–197
Cissbury Ring, 169, 232–233
Citrine, 30
Clactonian, 157, 160, 163, 230
Clark, W. E. Le Gros, 177
Clarke, Rainbird, 190*n*.
Clay, 70, 112, 203, 221. *See* Boulder Clay, Marls
  potter's, 204
Clay-with-flints, 112 ff.
Cleaver, 158
Cleland, James, 187*n*.
Cliona, 57
'Clunch', 66*n*., 197
Cob, 196
Cobbett, William, 196
Cobbles, 197, 198, 202–203
'Coccolith Chalk', 87
Coccoliths, 46, 50–51
Coccospheres, 46, 49, 106
Codex Atlanticus, 184

Colchester, 199
Cole, G. A. J., 90, 91
Concrete, 179, 203
Conglomerate, 135
'Continent', *see* Europe
Continental drift, 59*n*., 61
Copper, 124, 136
  sulphate, 91, 92 ff.
Corals, 65, 77
Core, *see under* Flint
  tools, implements, 155 ff., 176
Cornwall, 174
Cornwall, I. W., 146
Correns, C. W., 32, 211
Cortex, cortication, 22 ff., 33, 34, 81 ff., 104–105, 109 ff., 115 ff., 122
  'soft', 102–105
Corwin, J. F., 33
Coup-de-poing, 156
Crayford, 172, 176, 232–233
Cretaceous, 40, 57, 61
Crimean War, 188
Cristobalite, 33, 35
Crizelling, 208
Crushing, 206, 207
Crustaceans, 28 ff., 50, 52, 78
Cumberland, 174
Czechoslovakia, 188

Dactylis glomerata, 220
Damper, 183
Dark Ages, 147, 180, 195
Davy, Humphry, 183
Dawson, Charles, 177
Day, M. H., 146
Dean, R. S., 76, 97–98
Defoe, Daniel, 201
Denmark, Danish, 34–35, 61, 63, 175, 178
Derjaguin, Boris V., 228
Devonshire, 85, 187
Dewey, H., 114
Diaper work, 200
Diatoms, 36, 214
Disc-core, 161
Donnay, J. D. H., 32
Dorsetshire, 83, 85–87, 105, 128, 176
Doryderma, 57, 65
Downs, N. and S., 62–64, 112, 128, 145, 173, 231–233
Dreikanter, 122

INDEX

Drew, G. H., 48
Drewite, 48, 50
Drilling, 167
Dryden, John (quoted), 180*n*.
Dumfriesshire, 88
Dutch, *see* Holland
Dyer, John (quoted), 17

Earland, A., 48, 49
East Anglia, 133, 145–146, 172*n*., 175
  187, 197, 199
Eastbourne, 225
Easton Down, 169, 232–233
Echinocorys, 72
Echinoderm, 52, 84. *See* Sea-urchin
Edge-trimming, 150, 165
Edwards, Herbert, 188
Egypt, 162, 208
Enamel, 209
Engel, W., 220
England, 60, 63 ff., 112, 133, 139, 145, 169, 180*n*., 187, 197, 208, 209, 231–233. *See also* Downs *and* towns and counties
Enoploclytia leachi, 29
Eocene, 44, 63, 64, 87, 112, 136
Eolith, 146, 156
'Eolithic', 145–146, 147, 230
Epigenetic theories, 80 ff.
  chemical, 97 ff.
  physical, 88 ff.
Equisetaceae, *see* Horsetails
Éraillure, 151
Ervin, G., 222
Essex, 179
Estonia, 180
Europe, the 'Continent', 19, 40, 59, 61, 87, 145, 169, 175, 180, 194, 208, 221, 230
Evans, Caleb, 21

Fabricator, 155
Faceted butt, 161
Farnham, 107
Felspar, 83, 220, 221–222
Findon, 169, 232–233
Fire, 37, 38, 175, 179 ff.
Firearms, 183 ff.
Flakes, 159 ff., 173
  gun-flint, 190–192
  hand-struck, 150 ff.

Flakes (*contd.*)—
  natural, 149
  truncated, 150
Flaking, 150 ff., 190 ff.
  resolved, 158–159
  ripple, 154, 165
  step, *see* resolved
  subsoil pressure, 148 ff.
Flashpan, 185
Flask Shell, 141
Flea-tormentor, 182*n*.
'Flint' (connotations), 18, 36
  in idiom, 17
  lighter, 19, 180
  linguistics, 18, 29, 37, 234
Flint, accidental, *see* Accidental flints
  agate-rinded, 84, 105
  appearance, 20–24, 83–84, 105–107.
    See also Gravel, Shingle
  banded, 124 ff.
  bands, belts, layers (in Chalk), 20, 73–75, 77, 82, 86–88, 91, 100, 114
  calcined, 34, 38, 123, 174, 204 ff.
  colours of, 22–24, 84, 105, 107, 114–115, 118–119, 122–124
  composition of, 29, 32 ff.
  core, 22–23, 34, 82, 84, 117, 122, 191
  cortex, *see* Cortex
  derived, 108 ff.
  desilicified, 104, 109 ff.
  distribution of, 19, 65–67, 129 ff., 136 ff., 231–233
  fossils, 24 ff., 109, 195
  fracture of, *see* Fracture
  furrowed, 128
  gloss, *see* Gloss
  grey, 24, 25, 34, 106
  growth of, 26, 82 ff., 97, 111, 105–107
  hardness, 37, 128, 130, 140
  hollow, 21, 53, 81, 83, 106–107
  implements, 150 ff., 231
  inclusions in, 24, 25, 82, 124
  kidney, 198
  knapping, *see* Knapping
  'marbled', 114, 127*n*.
  mine, *see* Mining
  nodule, nodular, 20–22, 24 ff., 57–58, 72–73, 76, 78, 130, 136
  occurrence of, 20, 22, 68–69, 73–74, 77–79, 80–81, 108, 171

INDEX

Flint (contd.)—
  origin of, 68 ff., 210, 222 ff.
  patination, see Patination
  pebbles, see Beaches, Cobbles, Gravel, Shingle
  physical properties, 37 ff.
  rings, see Rings
  rolled, 197
  rotted, see desilicified
  secondary, 83, 84, 105
  slop, 208
  soil, 108 ff., 115–116, 119, 128
  sources (economic), 179, 208–209, 233
  specific gravity, 37, 117, 205–206
  spiral, 25, 128–129
  sponges in, see Sponges
  staining of, see Staining
  structure of, 23, 32 ff., 108
  sub-angular, 130
  tabular, 20, 67, 105, 115, 171
  washmill, 204
  water in, 33, 36, 106, 122, 123, 124 ff., 227–228
'Flint Jack', 176–177
Flint meal, 21, 81
Flint-mill, 206–208
Flintlock, 184 ff.
'Flintstone', 24n., 201
'Flintware', 208
Floorstone, 171, 188
Flush-work, 198
Foliates, 165
Folk, R. L., 32
Folkestone Sands, 107
Foraminifera, 46, 47, 50, 109
Fosse Way, 201
Fossils, see under Chalk, Flint
Fracture, artificial, 148 ff.
  columnar, 39
  hinge, 151, 158
  natural, 37–39, 111, 124, 137
  plunging, 151
  pot-lid, 39
  starch, 39
France, French, 60, 169, 174, 187, 190, 194, 195
Frizzen, 185n.
Frost-pitting, 39
Fungi, 182
Furon, R., 194

Garetting, galleting, garneting, 198
Gastrochaena dubia, 141
Gastropoda, 27, 42, 129
Gault, 63, 64
Gehrke, E., 116
Germany, German, 70, 175, 184
Glacial period, 147. See Ice Age, Great
Glass, 208 ff.
  cutting, 37, 195
Glauconite, 42, 67, 221
Glauconitic Marl, 65
Glaze, 204–205, 206, 209
Globigerina, 46, 47
Glomerula gordialis, 65
Gloss, 116
  evaporation, 120, 121
  fracture, 120
  friction, 120–121
  silica, 164
  solution, 118, 121
Gonioteuthis quadrata, 85
Goodhew, P. J., 103
Goto, R., 213
Gramineae, see Grasses
Grandjean, F., 222
Grasses, 87, 110, 135–136, 219–220
Gravel, 124, 129 ff., 201, 202
  plateau, 114, 133, 144, 179
Graver, 163
Greensand, Lower, 129
  Upper, 64
Greenwell, W., 170
Greywether, 112, 136
Grime's Graves, 169 ff., 187, 188, 231–233
Grinding, 165, 166, 167, 179, 194, 204 ff.
Groynes, 142–143
Guildford, 112
Gun-flint, 187 ff., 231
  sites, 233

Hafting, 166–167, 168
Hag-stone, 21
Halais, P., 219
Hammer, flint-knapper's, 189 ff.
Hammer-stone, 156, 158, 173
Hampshire, 26n., 114, 187, 196, 200
  Basin, 63, 64
Hand-axe, 155, 157
Handreck, K. A., 220

INDEX

Harmondsworth, 200
Harrison, Benjamin, 145
Harrow Hill, 169, 232–233
Harvey, Richard, 181
Hatschek, E., 129
Hayward, A. T. J., 227
Head, 133–134
Hedges, F. S., 125, 129
Heinen, W., 220
Helwan, 162–163
Henley, R. V., 125, 129
Henry III, 208
Herbert, Thomas, 193
Herodotus, 26n.
Hertfordshire, 135–136, 194, 200
Hexactinellida, 55, 57
Hiatella (Saxicava) rugosa, 141
High Salvington, 194n.
Hill, William, 77–78, 83, 225, 226
Hill, William Burrough, 194
Hogg, Garry, 196, 200
Holland, Dutch, 103, 181n., 184, 187n., 209
Holmes, Arthur, 101n., 146
Holzapfel, L., 220
Hornstone, 37, 194, 234
Horsetails, 87, 110, 111, 219–220
Humus, 110, 112, 119, 220. See also Soil
Hunstanton, 64
Huntingdonshire, 133
Huxley, T. H., 47

Ice Age, Great 64, 133, 144, 172n.
Icklingham, 188, 232–233
Illies, Henning, 70
Implement, *see under* Flint factories, 172 ff.
Indian Ocean, 47
'Industry', 230
 Helwan, 162
Inoceramus, 66, 79, 80
 labiatus, 65, 105
 platinus, 42
Ions, 74, 97 ff., 122, 222–224
Iron, 37, 49–50, 88, 89, 107, 112, 119, 122–124, 127–128, 135, 136
 oxide, 45, 50, 57, 84, 129
 silicate, 114, 221
Iron Age, 147, 166, 170, 176, 179, 180, 230

Jackson, G., 204
James I, 209
Japan, 36n.
Jennings, J. N., 44–45, 153n.
Jensen, A. T., 34–35
JOIDES, 36n.
Jones, L. H. P., 87n., 220
Jones, W. R., 204
Jukes-Browne, A. J., 77–78

Kafuan, 146, 156, 230
Kansas, 42
Kempston, 195
Kent, 25, 50, 85, 105, 114, 134, 172
Kersey, 199
Keston, 105
Kidney-flints, 198
Kiev, 221
Kiln, cement, 203
 flint, 205
 rotary, 203
 slip drying, 208
Knapping, 187 ff.
Koonalda Cave, 153n.
Kranskopf, K. B., 211

Lacroix, A., 221
La Ferté sous Jouarre, 194
Lamp-shell, *see* Brachiopod
Laosciadia planus, 65
Lapparent, J. de, 221, 222
Late Stone Age, 193, 229, 230
Lavenham, 199
Leach, Arthur, 116n.
Leach, Bernard, 204
Leatherhead, 196
Lenher, V., 211
Leptothrix, 123
Leucosolenia blanca, 54n.
Levalloisian, 156, 161, 230
Lewes, 198
Liesegang, R., 77, 89 ff., 124–125, 225, 226
Limonite, 50, 107, 112, 135
Lingheath, 188
Liostrea lunata, 65, 85
Lithistida, 55
Loire-et-Cher, 188
London, 66, 101, 113, 132
 Basin, 63, 64
 Clay, 63

INDEX

Lovering, T. S., 219, 220
Lowe, C. van Riet, 159–160
Lubbock, John, 146*n*.
Lucas, E. V., 200*n*.
'Lucky stone', 21
Lulworth Cove, 176

Magdalenian, 165, 170, 230
Manganese, 112, 122, 124, 136
Marcasite, 37, 49–50, 66. *See also* Pyrites
Marlipins, The, 200
Marls, 44, 59, 65, 66, 70, 112
  Plenus, 65, 215
Marsupites testudinarius, 82
Martyn, John, 36
Mas d'Azil, 195
Match, 180, 182, 183
'Maume', 196
McAdam, J. L., 202
Melbourn Rock, 65, 66
Meldau, R., 34, 110*n*., 111
Merrill, H. B., 211
Mesolithic, 147, 159, 162 ff., 173, 182, 195, 229, 230
Mesozoic, 40
Micraster cor-anguinum, 65, 67, 82
  cortestudinarium, 82
Microlith, 163, 164
Middle Ages, 197
Midgley, H. G., 33
Miers, H. A., 31, 32
Mill, ball, 206, 207
  Cheddleton, 206
  Durrington, 194*n*.
  flint, 205, 206–208
  High Salvington, 194*n*.
  pan, 206–207
  stamp, 206, 207
  steel, 183, 184
  tube, 203–204
  wash, 204
  wind, 194*n*.
Millot, G., 74, 103–104, 211, 212, 213
Mining, mines, 167 ff., 189, 233
Miocene, 87, 136
Misch-metal, 180*n*.
Mocha stone, 25
Moffatt, James, 18, 166
Moir, J. Reid, 162

Molluscs, 51, 52
  marine boring, 140–141
Monaxonida, 55, 57
'Monk's gun', 184
Monoraphis, 55
Monosilicic (orthosilicic) acid, 212, 213–214, 220, 223 ff.
Moore, Henry, 24*n*.
Morgan, J. de, 162
Mortillet, Gabriel de, 145
Mousterian, 161, 229, 230
Mukherjee, L. N., 125
Musée de l'Homme, 194

Nagelschmidt, G., 32, 111
Natural History Museum, 25, 176
Neanderthal Man, 161*n*., 175, 176
Neolithic, 146*n*., 147, 156, 159–174 (*passim*), 178, 187, 193–194, 230, 231–233
Neolithic Revolution, 164
New Forest, 197–198
New Guinea, 192
Newhaven, 45
Nodule, nodular, *see under* Chalk, Flint, Marcasite, Pyrites, Phosphatic
Norfolk, 21–22, 64, 67, 81, 85, 86, 169, 187
Normandy, 200
Northfleet, 232–233
Norway, 133
Norwich, 231, 233
Noyers, 188
Nullarbor Plain, 44, 153*n*.

Oakley, Kenneth, 83, 177, 229
Offaster pilula, 195
Okamoto, G., 211, 213
Okura, T., 213
Oldowan, 146, 156, 230
Oligocene, 136
Ontario, 71
Onyx, 31, 88, 124
Ooze (oceanic), 42–43, 45, 51–52, 214
  bacterial, 48–49, 50
  Chalk, 47 ff., 58 ff., 69 ff., 74, 75 ff.
  Coccolith, 50–51
  deposition (rate of), 47, 51
  Foraminiferal, 36*n*., 47
  Globigerina, 46, 47
  Radiolarian, 76*n*.

INDEX

Opal, 30 ff., 35, 77, 126n., 211
  plant, 87, 220
Orbirhynchia cuvieri, 65
Orel, 221
Ostrea lunata, 65, 85
Ovate, 157
Owen, Richard, 68–69
Oxfordshire, 169

Pacific Ocean, 36n., 47, 213
Palaeolithic, 19, 146, 147, 154–173 (*passim*), 174n., 195, 230
Palestine, 164
Palmer, L. S., 175
Pan-mill, 206, 207
Paramoudra, 21, 22, 89
Paris Basin, 63, 83n., 105, 194, 221
Parish, D. H., 219
Parkinson, James, 128
'Patina', 115–116
Patination, 115 ff., 123, 124, 177
  artificial, 118
  basket, 119
  graphic, 118
  spider's web, 120
  toad-belly, 119
Pebble tools, implements, 155–156
Pebble-beds, 41, 63, 129
Pebbles, 36, 134 ff., 197, 198
  wave-battered, 136–137, 138
  See also Beaches, Cobbles, Gravel, Shingle
Pectolite, 225
Pekin Man, 175n.
Penecontemporaneous theories, 75 ff.
Pennine Chain, 61
Penrhyn slates, 88
Peppard, 169
Peru, 194
Petroglyph, 195
Pevensey, 195
Pholas parva, 141
Phosphatic nodule, 66, 67. *See also* Calcium phosphate
Phyllostachys bambusoides, 220
Phytolith, 87
Picardy, 187
Pick, 156, 166, 167
  flint miner's, 189
Piddock, Little, 141
Piltdown, 177

Pipes, 98–99
Pistol, *see* Firearms
Plas, L. Van Der, 35n., 36, 103–104, 223–224
Plasma, 31
'Plastic virtue', 25–26
Pleistocene, 133. *See* Ice Age, Great
Plenus Marls, 65, 215
Plocoscyphia, 57
Plot, Robert, 26
Point, 158, 163
  Folsom, 165
  leaf, 154, 165
Polesden Lacy, 99
Polychaete worms, 138, 139–140
Polydora, 139–140
Porosphaera, 57
Porter, G. R., 209
Potamilla, 139–140
Potassium permanganate, 91, 94 ff.
Pot-boiler, 173–174, 177–178
'Pot-lid', 39
'Potstone', 22
Potteries, The, 205
Pottery, 174n., 176, 204 ff.
  Assyrian (glaze used on), 209n.
Prestwich, J., 145
Protococcus, 112
Protozoa, 28, 46
Pseudowollastonite, 103
Pteridophytes, 87, 135. *See also* Horsetails
'Pudding-stone', 135–136, 194, 200
Pug, 196
Purley, 94
Pyrenees, 221
Pyrites, 37–38, 49, 175, 180, 182, 184n., 234
  'spear', 50

Quarter, quarterer, quartering, 187, 189 ff.
Quartz, 19, 30 ff., 105, 106, 107, 110, 166, 180
  melting-point, 121
  powdered, 126, 228
  solubility of, 211, 213
Quartzite, 136, 165, 180

Racloir, 162
Radiolaria, 36, 76n., 214

INDEX

Rain-water, 44, 77, 80, 116
Rankine, W. F., 172, 174–175
Raphidonema, 57
Rattle-stone, 21
Ravenscroft, G., 208
Red Chalk, *see* Red Rock
Red Nose, 141
Red Rock, 64
Reduction patch, 119, 135
Residual deposits, 108 ff.
Rhynchonella cuvieri, 65
Richardson, W. A., 70*n*., 80–81, 86–87, 91, 97, 116
Riddlesdown, 21, 106
Rings, flint, 21, 22
   Liesegang, 89 ff.
   in slate, 88
Roads, 179, 195, 200 ff.
Robertson, R. H. S., 34, 110*n*., 111
Rock (Sussex), 172–173
Rock crystal, 30
Roller, P. S., 222
Romans, 147, 180, 182*n*., 195, 201, 208
Rose, C. B., 22
Rostro-carinate, 146, 156
Rubble, rubble-work, 195, 197, 200
Runcorn, 205
Ruskin, John (quoted), 18
Russell, E. J., 219
'Rust balls', 50
Rye, 203

St. Aignan, 188
St. Albans, 195
St. Catherine's Hill, 112
Salisbury, 231, 233
Santon, 188
Sarsen, *see* Greywether
Scear, 185
Schloenbachia varians, 65, 85
Schopf, J. W., 71
Scotland, Scottish, 60, 62, 175
Scraper, 156, 157, 161–162
Sea, force of, 136–137
Sea-floor, *see* Chalk Sea, Ooze
   pressure on, 58, 76
Seaford, 106
Sea-urchin, 51, 72–73, 84, 195
   fossil, 27–28, 67
   speed of, 73
Sea-water, 52, 77, 80, 225–226

Seaweed, 119, 144
Seliscothon planus, 65
Serpentine, 185
Settling ark, 208
Shakespeare (quoted), 203
Shaving, 193
'Shepherd's Crown', 27
Shingle, 129–130, 136 ff., 179
Shore, T. W., 26*n*.
Shoreham, 196, 200
Sickle-blade, 164
Silica, 29 ff., 45, 52, 55 ff., 68 ff., 80 ff., 109 ff., 208 ff., 222 ff.
   colloidal, 69–70, 74 ff., 98–100
   cycle, 87
   in natural water, 71, 74, 99, 103, 135, 213–214
   secondary, 105–107, 114. See also *under* Flint
   solubility of, 69, 110, 211–212
   sources (economic), 179, 208–209
Silica accumulators, 110–111, 219
Silica-gloss, 164
Silicates, 103–104, 135, 221 ff.
Silicispongiae (Silicea), 55
Silicosis, 192, 205
Silver dichromate, 89, 90, 92, 125
Simpson, Edward, 176
Siphonia, 57, 65
Sloane, Hans, 25
Snaphaunce, 184
Sodium carbonate, 225, 226
   chloride, 225–226
   silicate, 221, 225, 226
Soil, 87, 100–101, 107, 108 ff., 119
Sollas, W. J., 80, 114
Solution-holes, 98–99
Solutrean, 165, 230
Sorby, H. C., 46
Southampton, 25, 194
Spall, 39
Spencer, Edmondson, 221
Spider's webs, 195
Spill, 181
Spit, 142
Sponges, anatomy, 53–55
   classification, 55 ff.
   fossil, 27, 35, 65, 139
   as sources of silica, 68 ff., 84, 214
   spicules of, 23, 36, 46, 54 ff., 69–70, 73, 76, 77, 80 ff., 109

INDEX

Spurrell, F. C. J., 172, 176
Staffordshire, 206
Staining, 24, 57, 114, 119, 122 ff., 138
  artificial, 88*n*., 177
Stamp-mill, 206–207
Stansfield, J., 90, 91, 92, 124
Starr Carr, 182
Stauronema carteri, 65
Steel, 180, 181, 183 ff., 206
Steel mill, 183, 184
Stoke Down, 169, 232–233
Stone Ages, 145, 147, 229–230. *See* Mesolithic, Neolithic, Late, Palaeolithic
Storrington, 197*n*.
Strabo, 26
'Strike-a-light', 181
Striking platform, 151, 159, 190
Suffolk, 119, 169, 188, 199
Sulphur, 49, 50, 52, 182, 183
Sulphuretted hydrogen, 48, 49, 50
Surgery, 193–194
Surrey, 94, 99, 114, 134, 175. *See also* Farnham, Riddlesdown.
Sussex, 45, 85, 103, 112, 169, 172, 179, 197*n*., 200
Swallow-holes, 99
Syngenetic theories, 68 ff.

Tabashir, 220
Tachenghit technique, 159–160
Taplow Terrace, 132
Tarr, W. A., 70, 74
Taubach, 175
Taylor, F. Sherwood, 212
Telford, Thomas, 202
Tertiary, 79, 87. *See also* Eocene, Miocene, Oligocene
Tetraxonida, 55, 57
Textularia, 46
Thailand, 188
Thames, 132, 133, 172, 231
Thanet Sand, 114, 225–226
Theophrastus, 26
Thomas, H. Dighton, 128–129
Tinder, tinder-box, 181 ff.
Tiselius, Arne, 125
Topstone, 171
Tortoise-core, 156, 160–161
Totternhoe Stone, 65, 66
Touch-hole, 185

Touchwood, 182
Trade, 174–175, 187, 188, 205
Tranchet, 159
Transvaal, 71
Trees, felling, 178
  silica content of, 219–220
Trent and Mersey Canal, 205
Trepanning, trephining, 193–194
Tridymite, 33, 35
Tube-mill, 203–204
Tudor House Museum, 25
Turkey, 188, 192–193
Turner, W. E. S., 209
Tuyl, F. M. Van, 77, 226

U.S.A., *see* America
U.S.S.R., 221

Vale, Edmund, 199
Valencia, 188
Vallée du Cher, 105
Ventifact, 122
Ventriculites, 57, 65
Verruculina, 57
Verulamium, 195
Vinci, Leonardo da, 184
Virgil (quoted), 180
Voronezh, 221
Vulcanism, submarine, 52, 59, 70, 214

Wageningen, 103
Wales, N., 174
Walls, *see* Building
Wallstone, 171
Walters, R. C. S., 218
Washmill, 204
Water, acidity of natural, 101–102
  cyclimetric, 228
  in flint, *see under* Flint
  sea, *see* Sea-water
  superdense, 228
  tensile strength of, 227
Water-concentration, zones of, 125 ff.
Water-table, 85–87, 100, 216–218
Weald, The, 63–64, 209
Weaver, C. E., 32
Weeting, 188
Weiner, J. S., 177
West Meon, 200
Westmorland, 180*n*.
Weymouth, J. H., 33

INDEX

Wheel-lock, 184 ff.
Whitby, 176
White, J. F., 33
White, H. J. Osborne, 114
Whitlingham, 231–233
Wight, Isle of, 67, 102, 114, 176
Williamson, W. O., 33
Wilson's Bluff, 44
Wiltshire, 86, 102, 112, 169, 187
Winchester, 112, 233
Wisborough Green, 209
Wood, flint in, 43, 44*n*.
    fossil, 43
Woodward, S. P., 124, 127
Wroost, V., 99–100, 102

Xenophanes, 26*n*.

Yorkshire, 85, 175, 182

Zeolites, 125, 126–127
Zemyatchensky, P. A., 221
Zeuner, F. E., 146
Zones, zoning, 31, 82 ff., 88 ff., 106, 114, 124 ff.